HOLY MOLÉ

Joy in the heart, is a state of grace!

2018

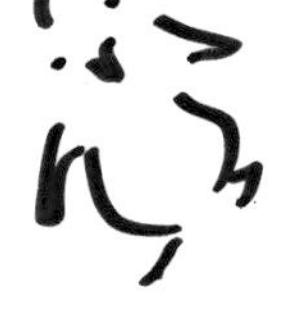

Published by Willow Creek Press, Inc.
P.O. Box 147, Minocqua, Wisconsin 54548

Printed in the United States

HOLY MOLÉ

LIFE IS WHAT YOU MAKE IT

by Rick Hotton

WILLOW CREEK PRESS®

From the Cartoonist

In 2007 an odd thing happened. Born perhaps from what I perceived as a world that had become cold and overly materialistic, I began drawing small vignettes on scrap sheets of paper. In these small stories, I attempted to reach back to what my spirit seemed to long for—a return to a kinder, more organic way of living. I could have picked up a guitar and written songs, but I have no musical talent, nor do I own a guitar.

But I have always had a knack for drawing.

As I wrote and drew these small stories, I felt oddly connected to the cave painters of primal cultures. The stories were simple and by default distilled down to the most essential message. In a strange way, I had discovered the art of cartooning—or perhaps it discovered me! Sometimes the drawings were funny, sometimes thoughtful and sometimes I'm not exactly sure what they were, but I drew them anyway. In a way, I simply surrendered my pen to the paper and let whatever pass through to occur. That act alone is what I now feel is life at its essence—not a journey outward into the material world, but a spontaneous connection to the creative force which we cannot see.

Thank you for looking over my humble attempt at this process. I hope it brings you joy.

Rick Hotton

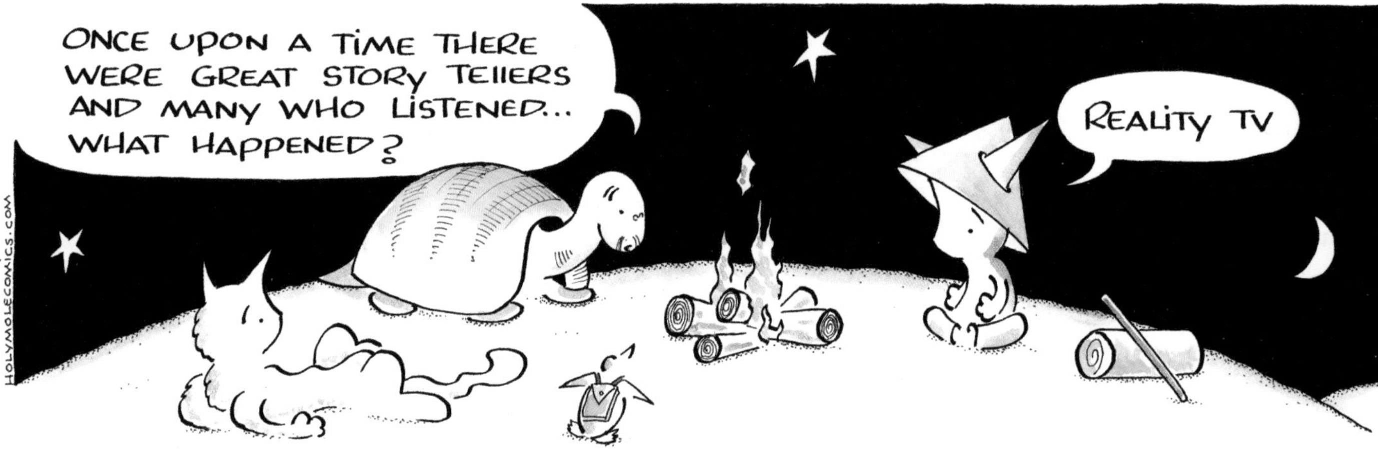
ONCE UPON A TIME THERE WERE GREAT STORY TELLERS AND MANY WHO LISTENED... WHAT HAPPENED?
REALITY TV
HOLYMOLECOMICS.COM
COPYRIGHT ©

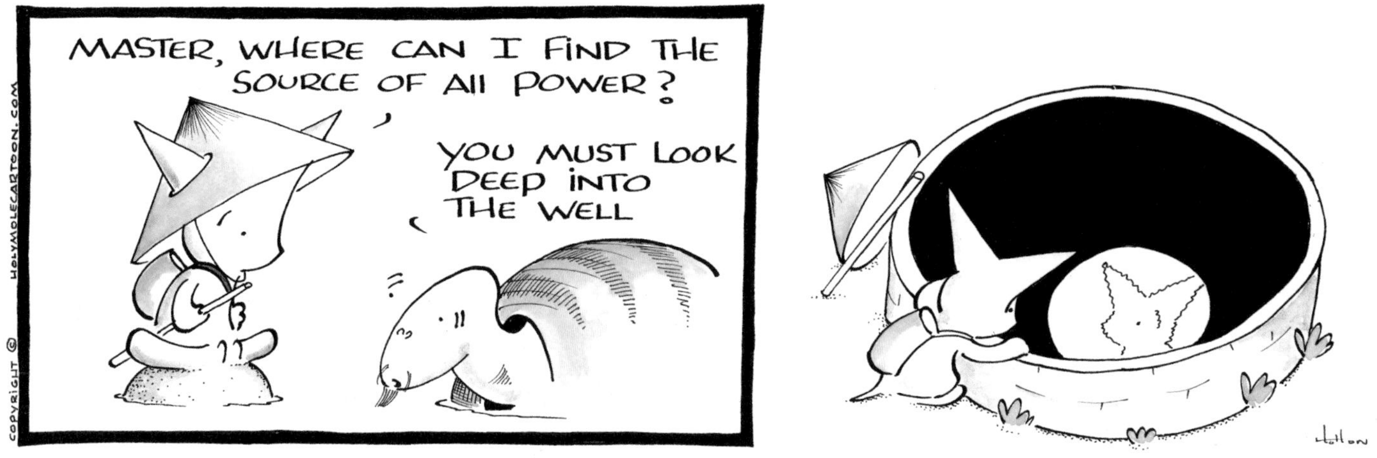
MASTER, WHERE CAN I FIND THE SOURCE OF All POWER?
YOU MUST LOOK DEEP INTO THE WELL
COPYRIGHT © HOLYMOLECARTOON.COM

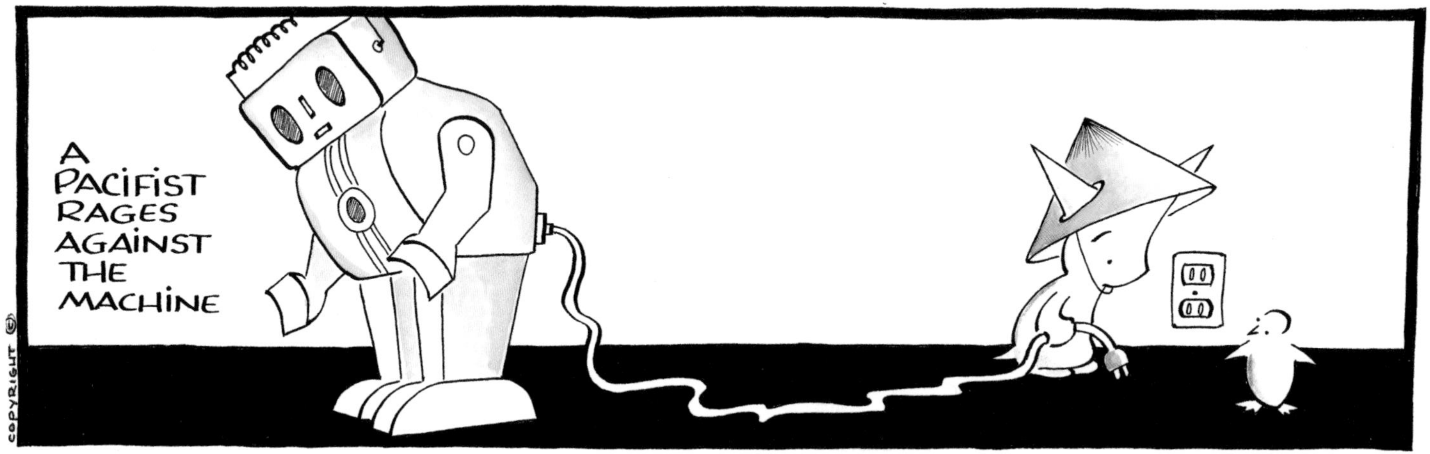
A PACIFIST RAGES AGAINST THE MACHINE
COPYRIGHT ©

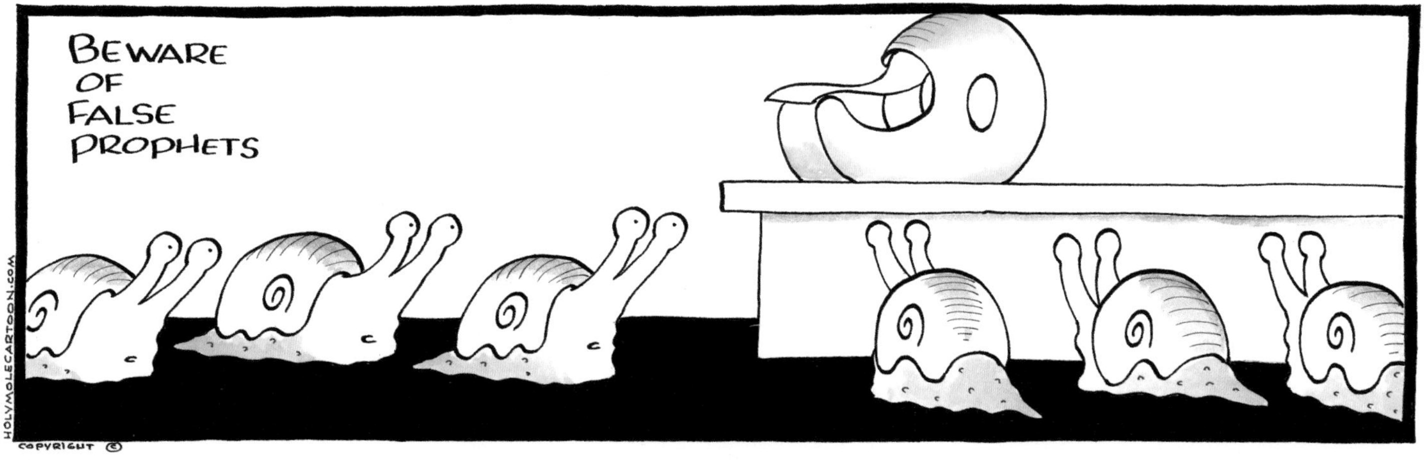
BEWARE OF FALSE PROPHETS
HOLYMOLECARTOON.COM
COPYRIGHT ©

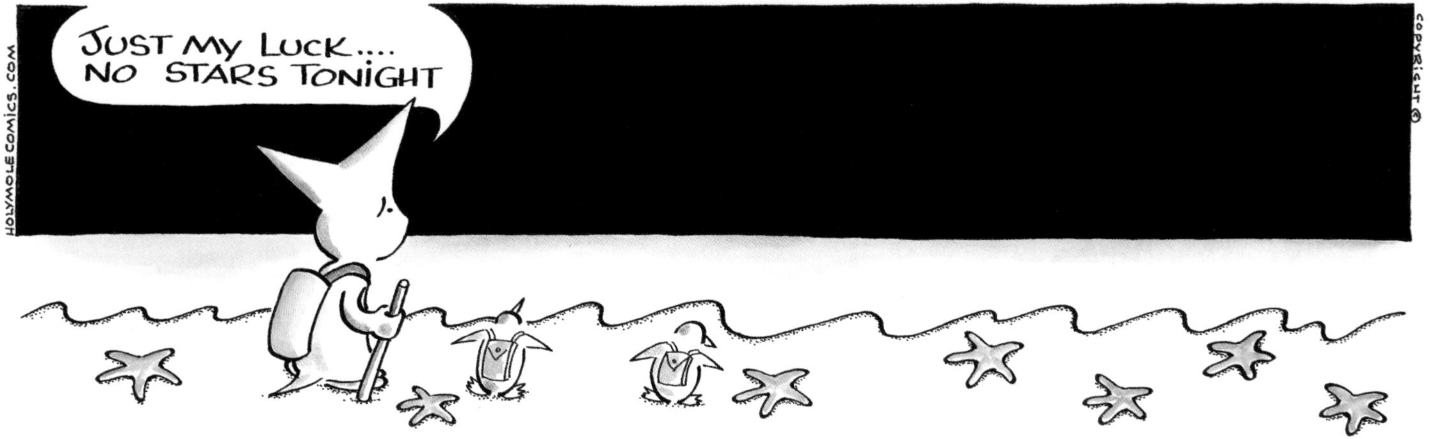
JUST MY LUCK.... NO STARS TONIGHT
HOLYMOLECOMICS.COM
COPYRIGHT ©

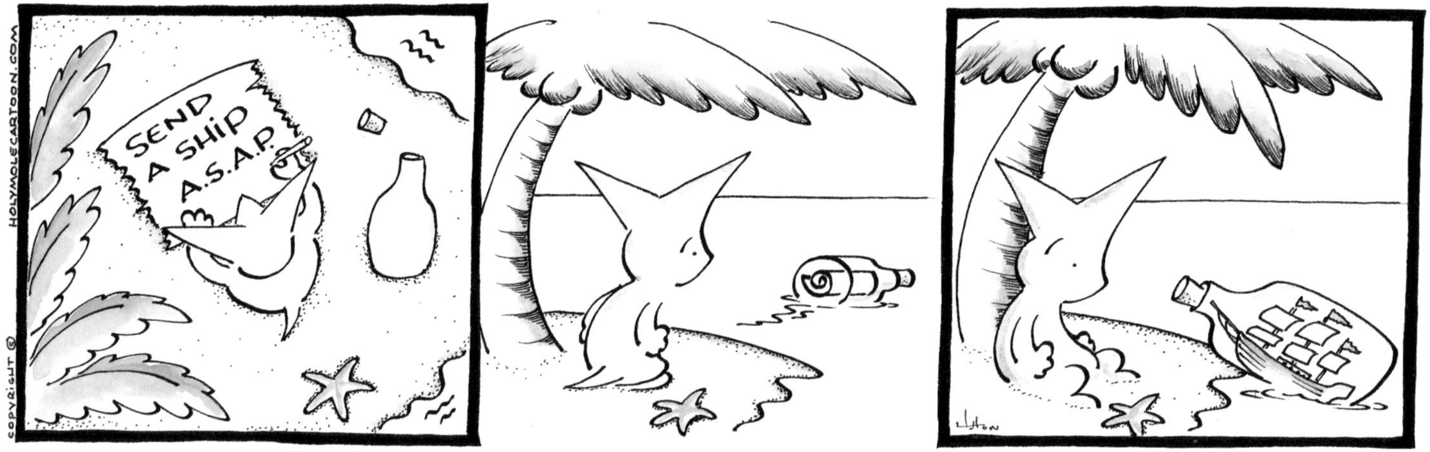
HOLYMOLECARTOON.COM
COPYRIGHT ©
SEND A SHIP A.S.A.P.

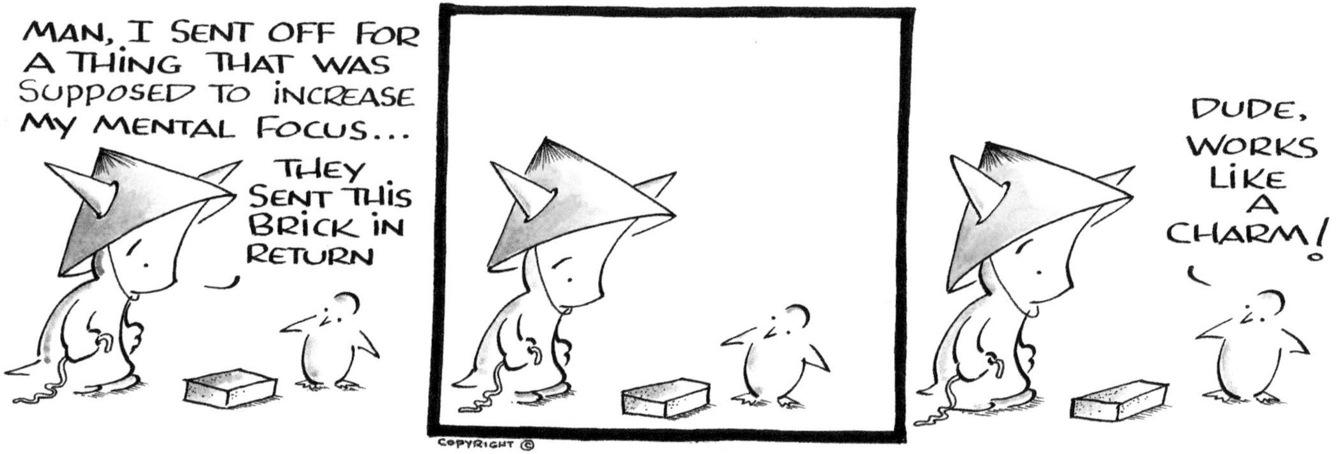
MAN, I SENT OFF FOR A THING THAT WAS SUPPOSED TO INCREASE MY MENTAL FOCUS...
THEY SENT THIS BRICK IN RETURN
DUDE, WORKS LIKE A CHARM!
COPYRIGHT ©

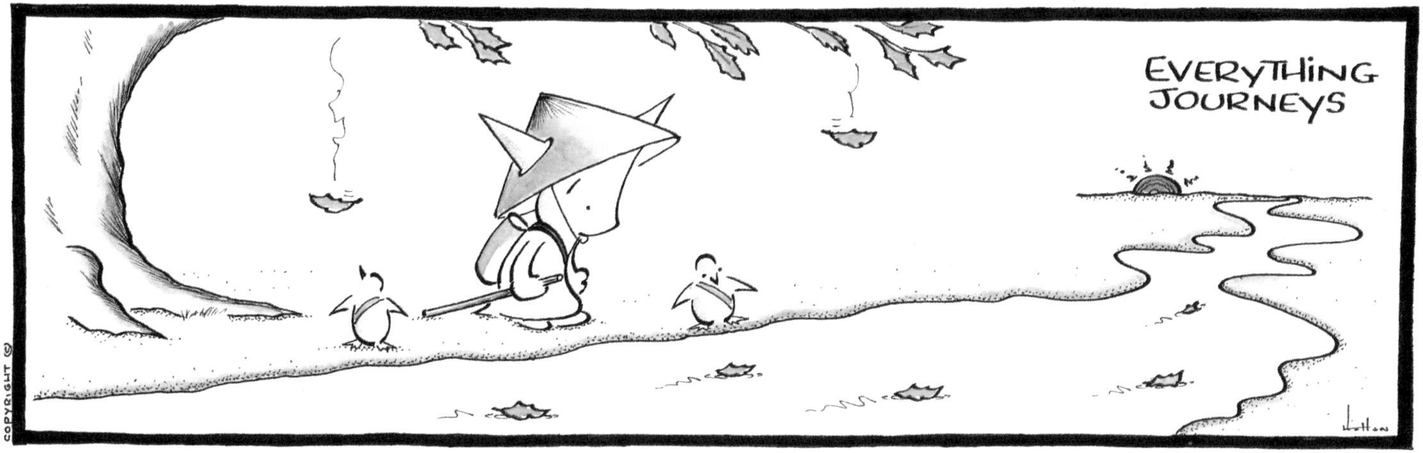
EVERYTHING
JOURNEYS
COPYRIGHT ©

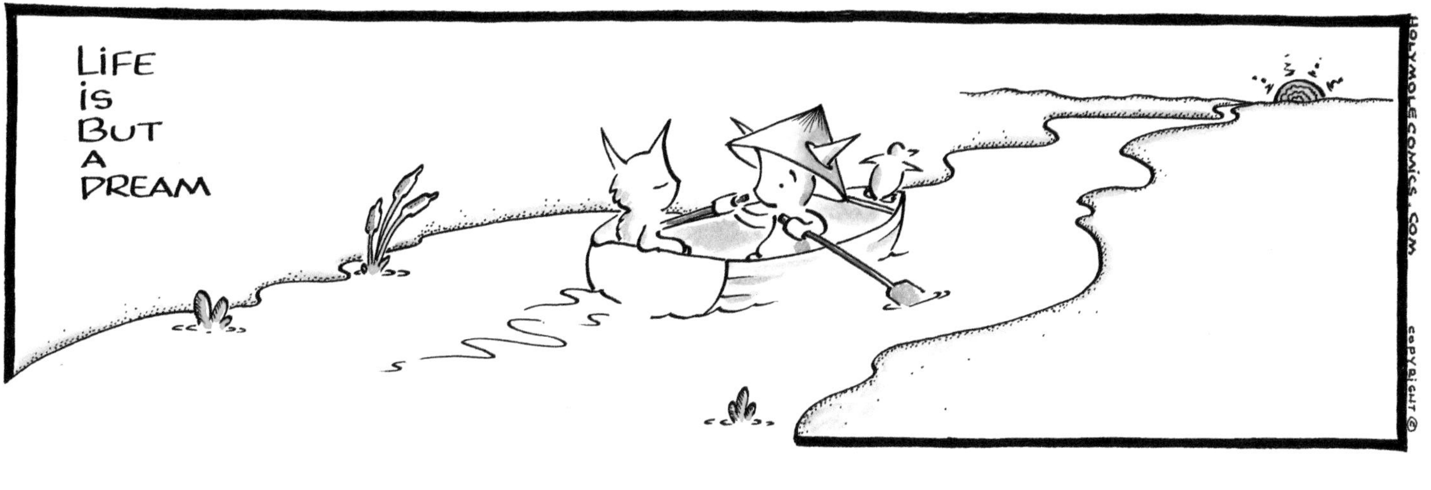
LIFE
IS
BUT
A
DREAM
HOLYMOLECOMICS.COM
COPYRIGHT ©

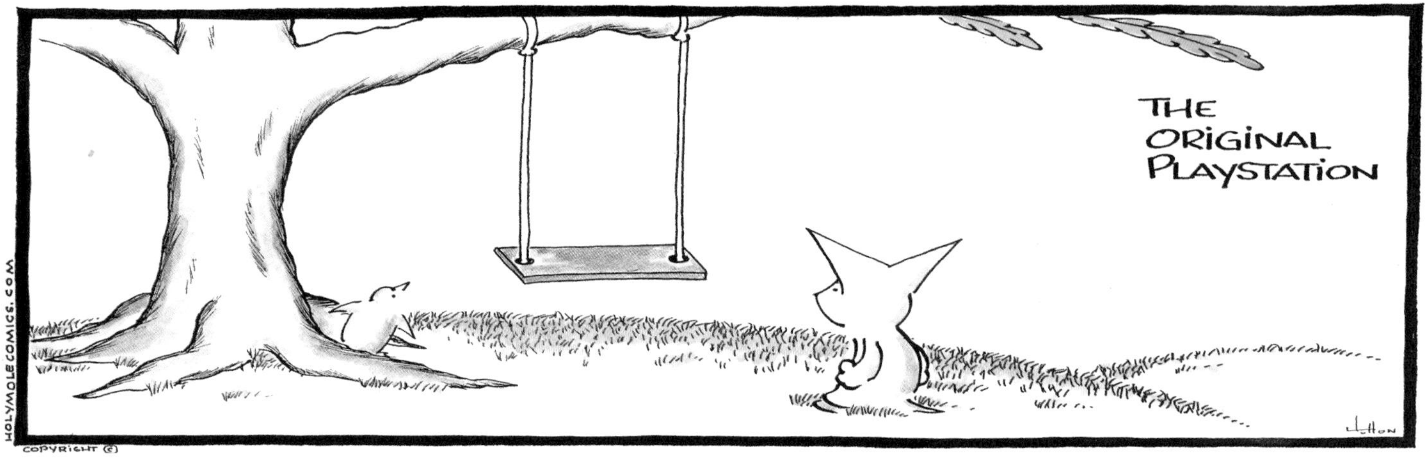
THE ORIGINAL PLAYSTATION
HOLYMOLECOMICS.COM
COPYRIGHT ©

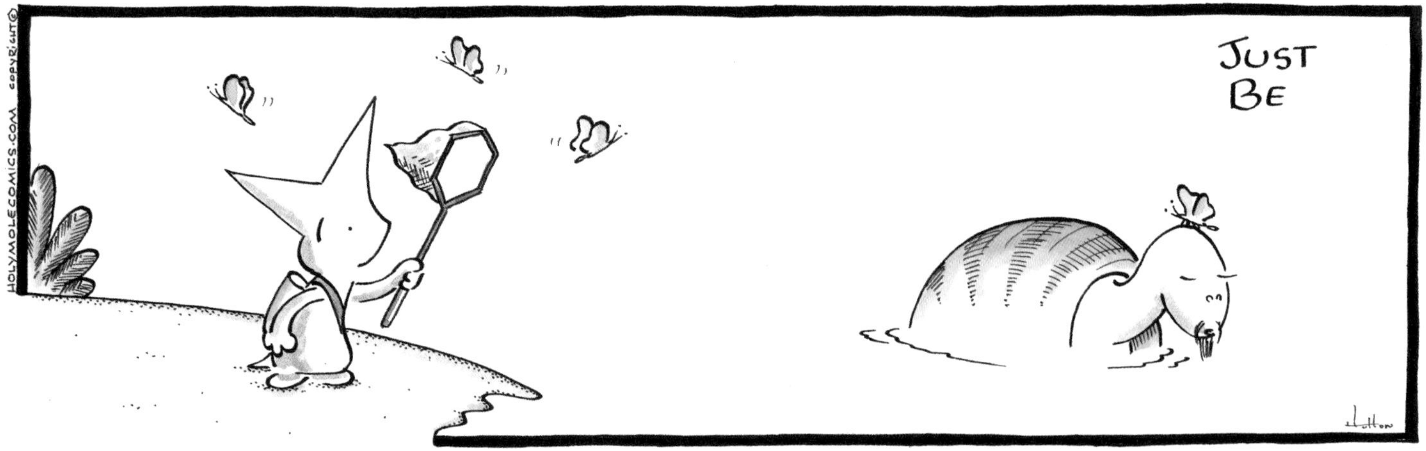
JUST BE
HOLYMOLECOMICS.COM COPYRIGHT ©

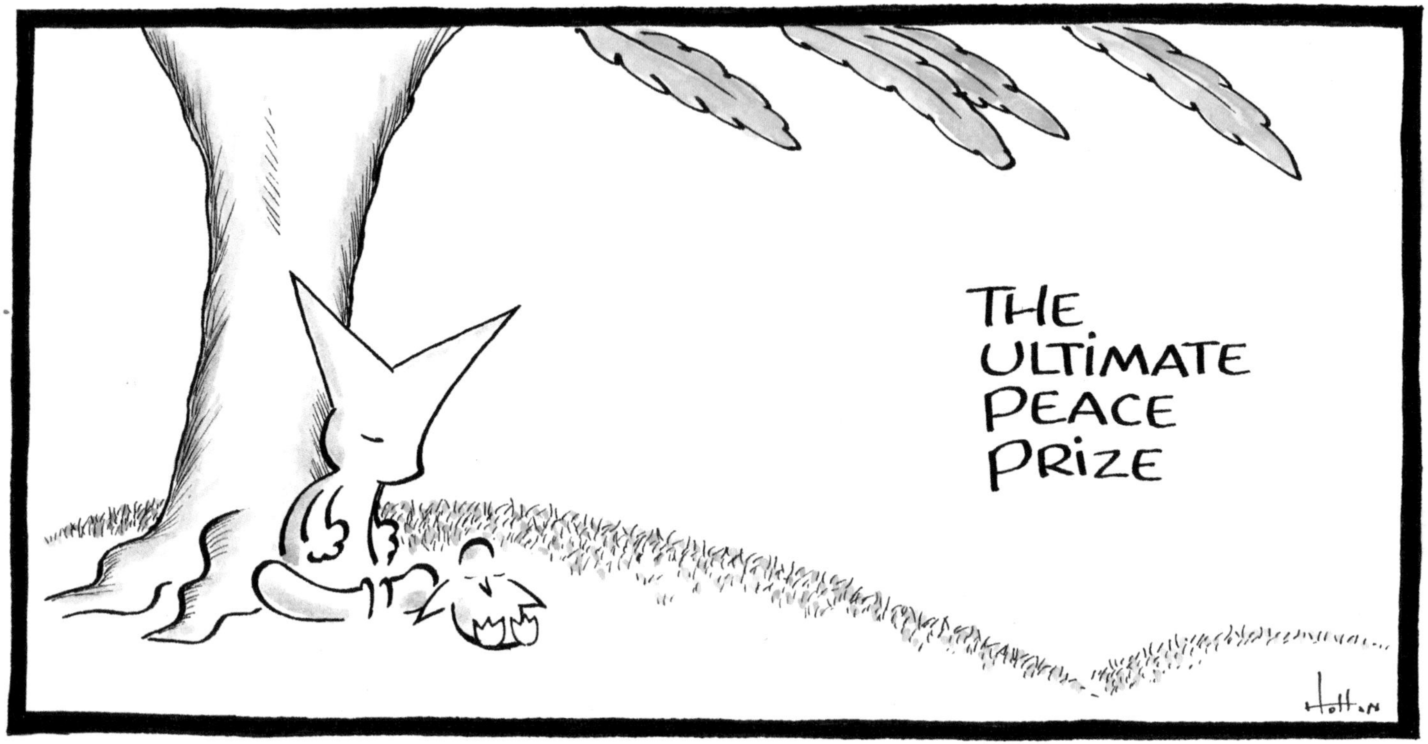
THE ULTIMATE PEACE PRIZE
Holton

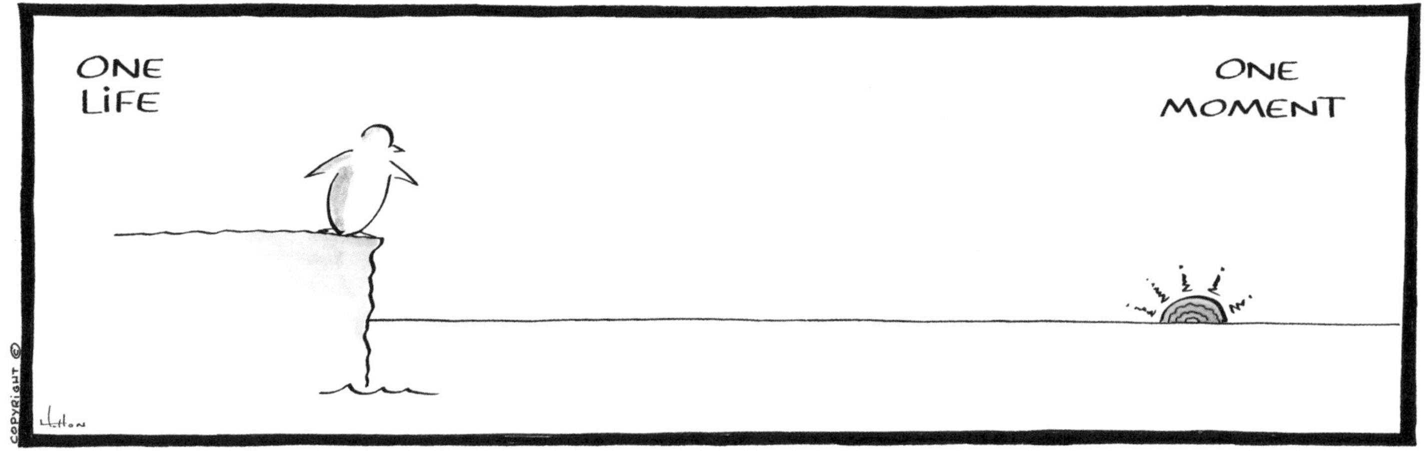
ONE LIFE
ONE MOMENT
COPYRIGHT ©

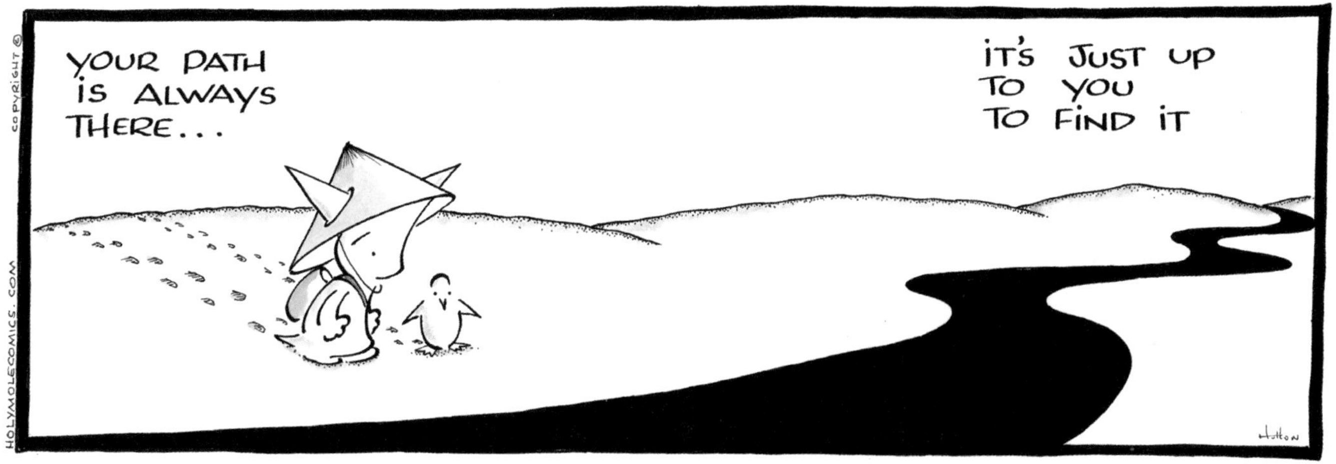
YOUR PATH IS ALWAYS THERE...
IT'S JUST UP TO YOU TO FIND IT
COPYRIGHT ©
HOLYMOLECOMICS.COM

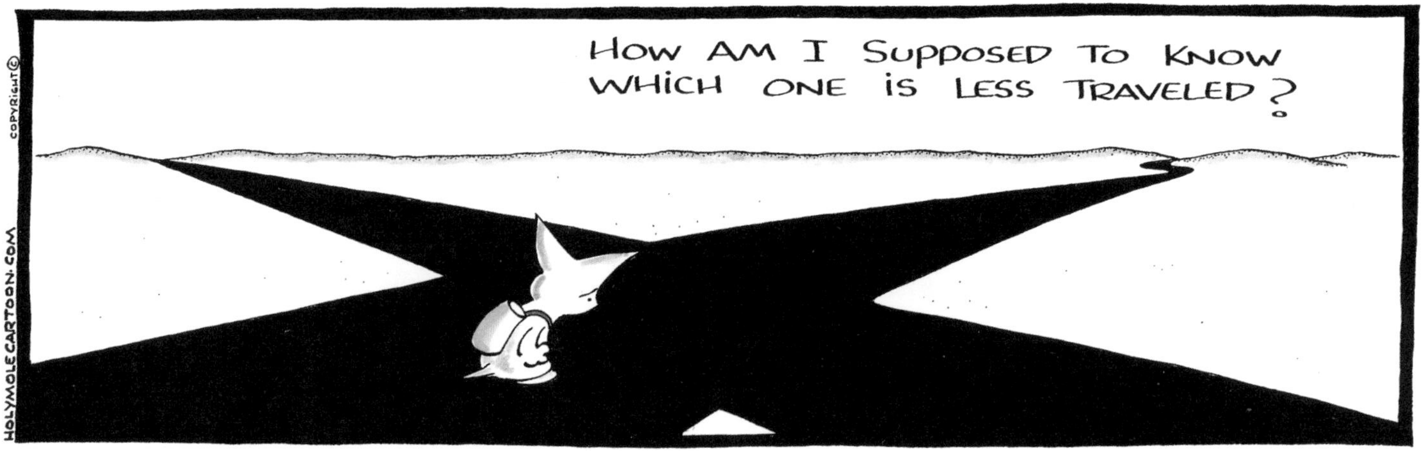
HOLYMOLECARTOON.COM COPYRIGHT ©
HOW AM I SUPPOSED TO KNOW WHICH ONE IS LESS TRAVELED?

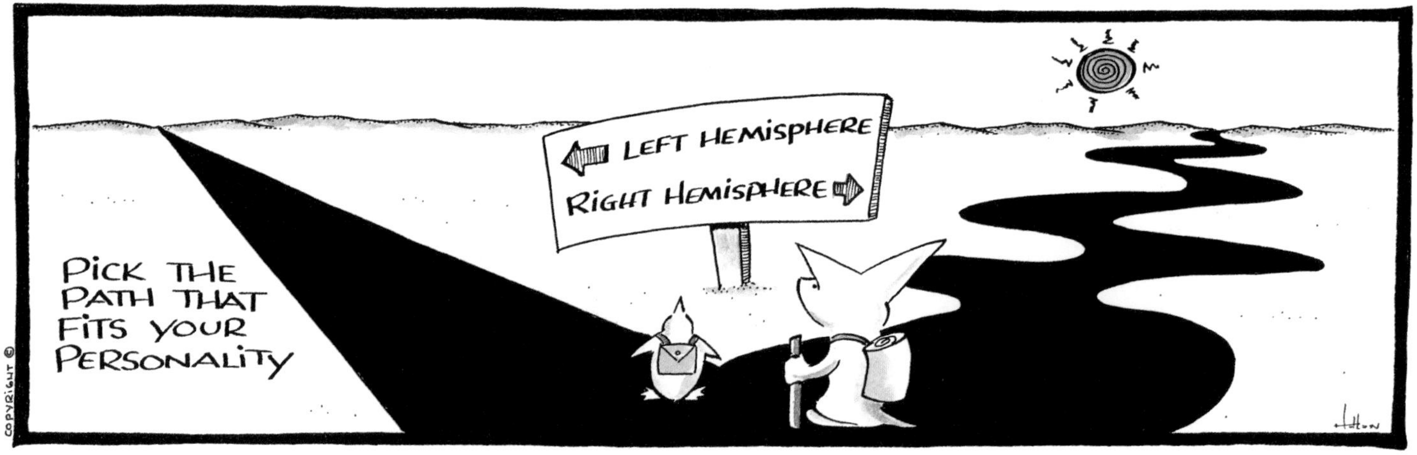
COPYRIGHT ©
LEFT HEMISPHERE
RIGHT HEMISPHERE
PICK THE PATH THAT FITS YOUR PERSONALITY

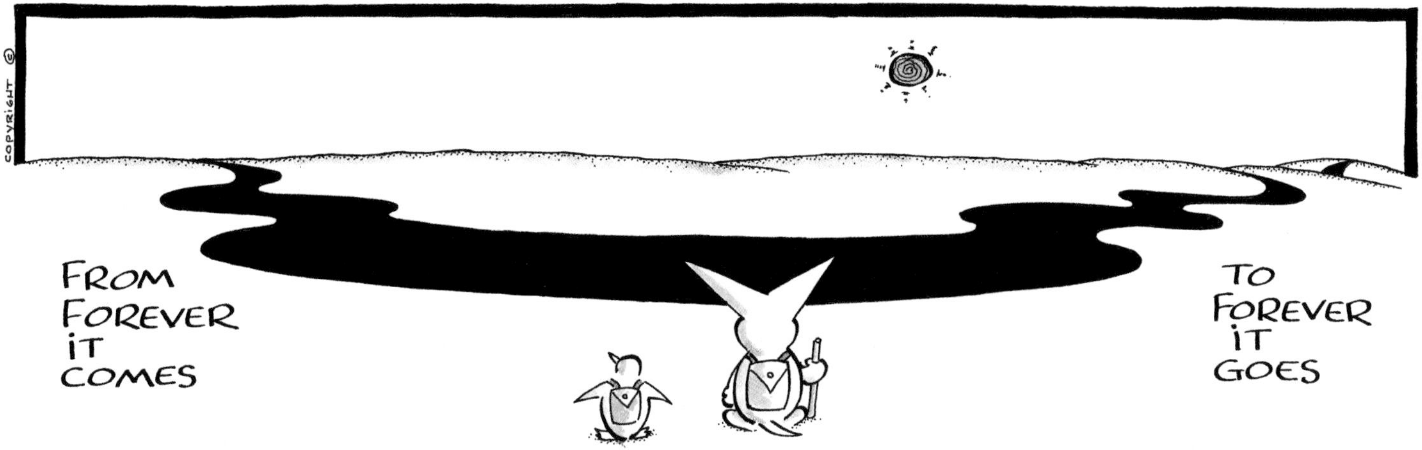
COPYRIGHT ©
FROM FOREVER IT COMES
TO FOREVER IT GOES

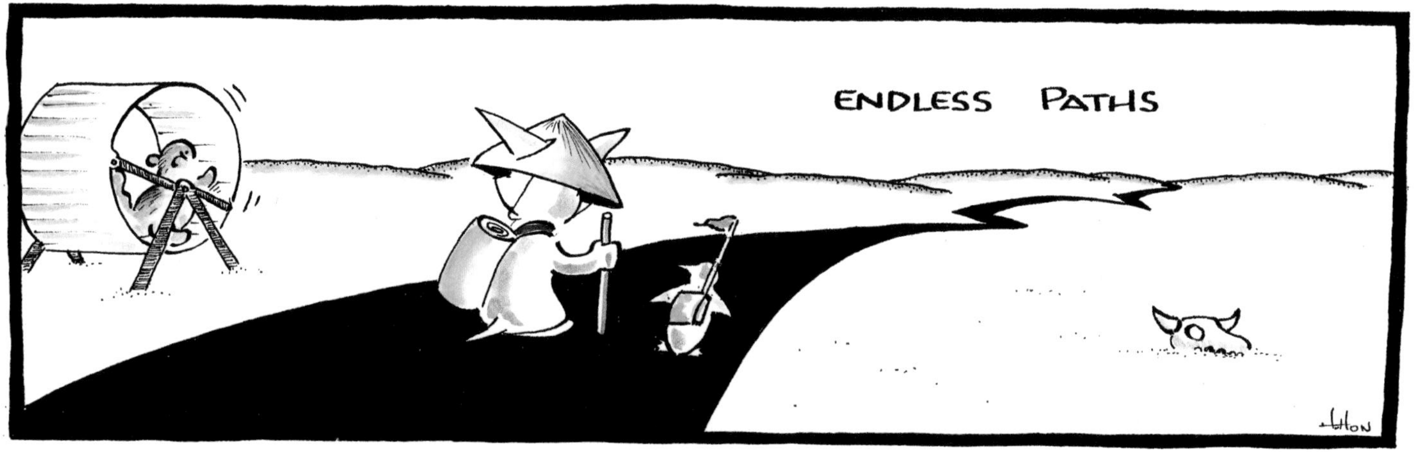
ENDLESS PATHS

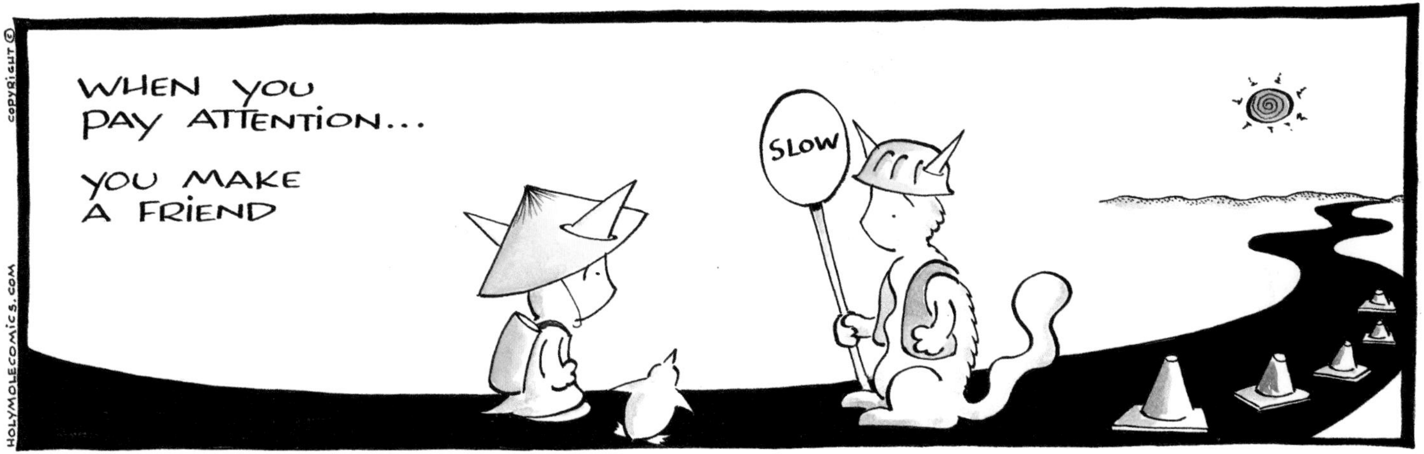
WHEN YOU PAY ATTENTION...
YOU MAKE A FRIEND
SLOW
COPYRIGHT © HOLYMOLECOMICS.COM

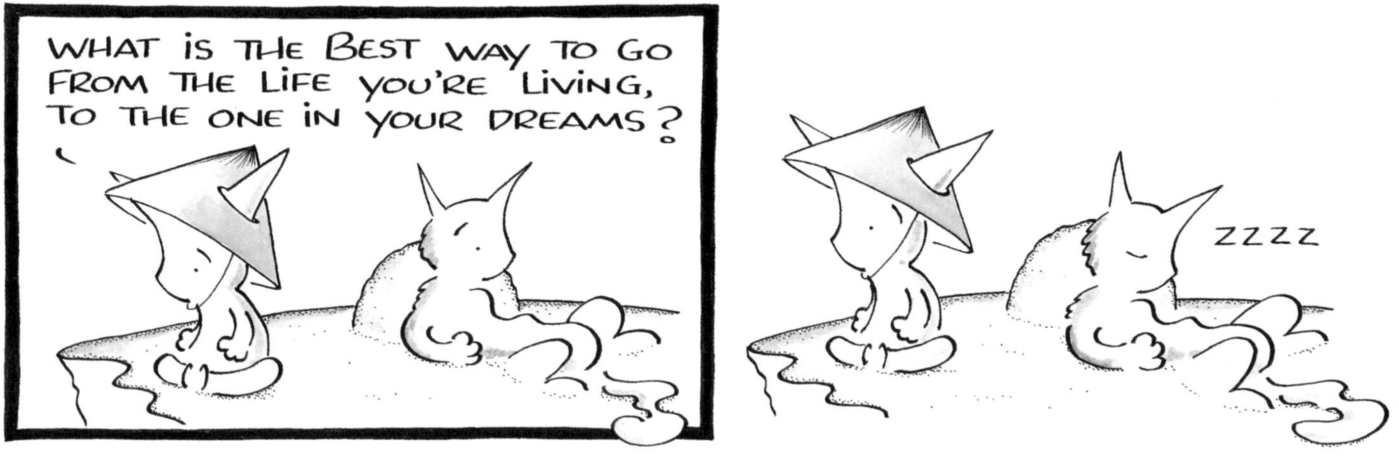
WHAT IS THE BEST WAY TO GO FROM THE LIFE YOU'RE LIVING, TO THE ONE IN YOUR DREAMS?
ZZZZ

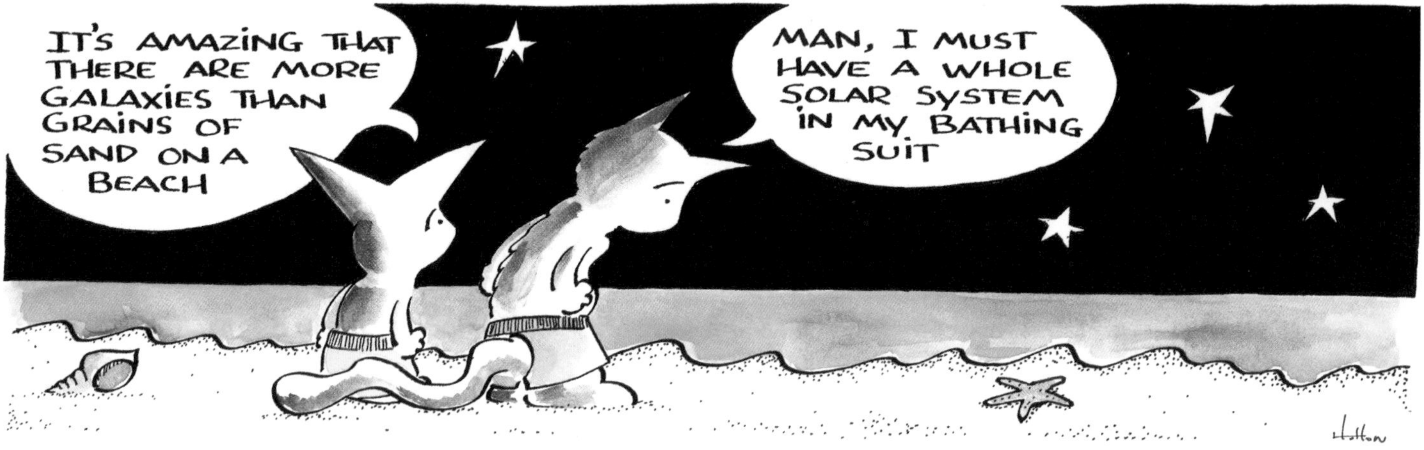
IT'S AMAZING THAT THERE ARE MORE GALAXIES THAN GRAINS OF SAND ON A BEACH
MAN, I MUST HAVE A WHOLE SOLAR SYSTEM IN MY BATHING SUIT

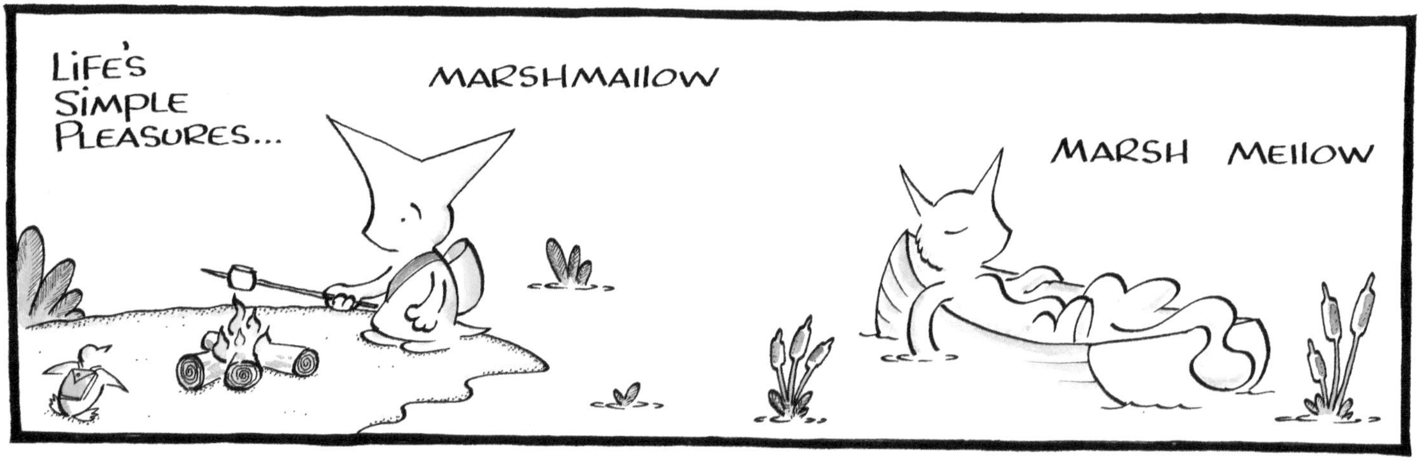
LIFE'S SIMPLE PLEASURES...
MARSHMALLOW
MARSH MELLOW

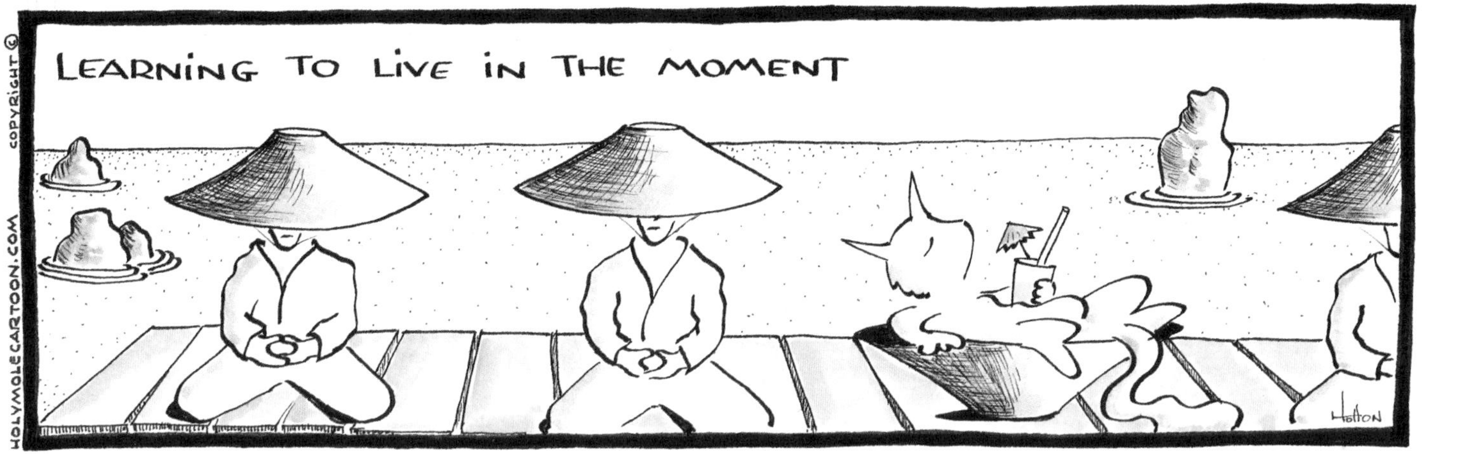
COPYRIGHT ©
HOLYMOLECARTOON.COM
LEARNING TO LIVE IN THE MOMENT
Hatton

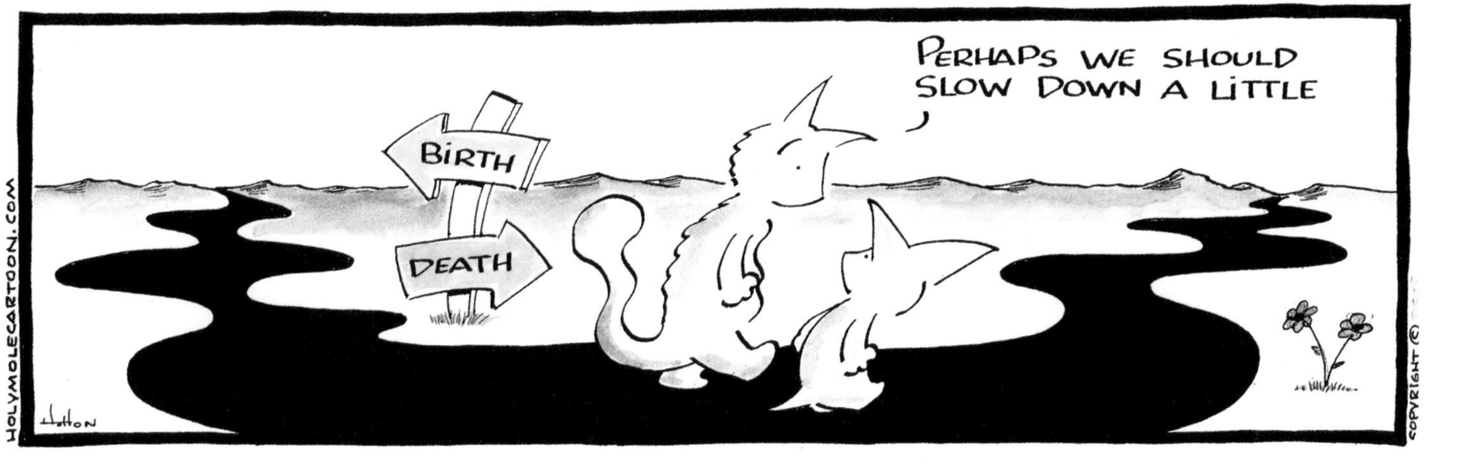
HOLYMOLECARTOON.COM
PERHAPS WE SHOULD SLOW DOWN A LITTLE
BIRTH
DEATH
Hatton
COPYRIGHT ©

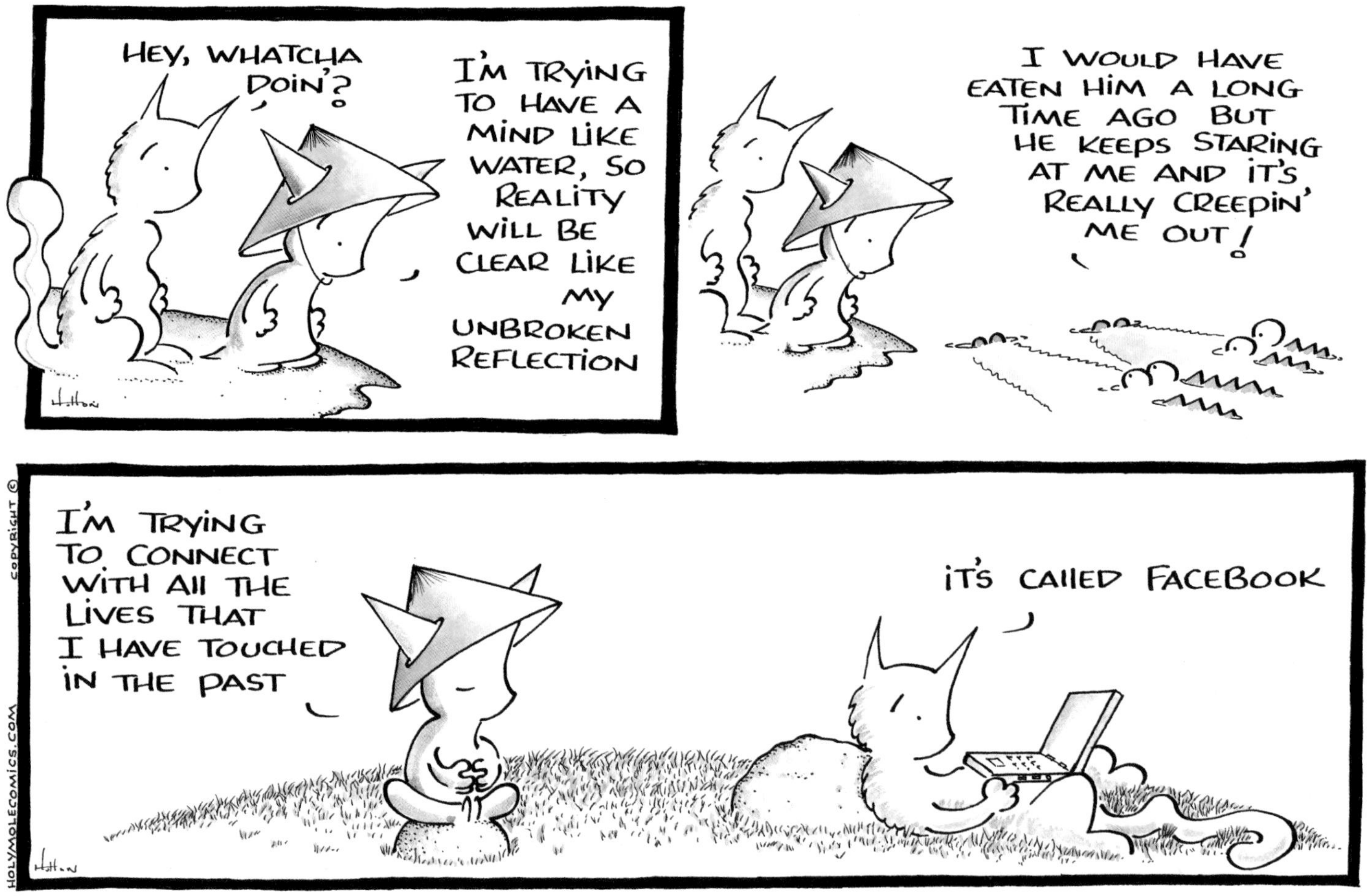
HEY, WHATCHA DOIN'?
I'M TRYING TO HAVE A MIND LIKE WATER, SO REALITY WILL BE CLEAR LIKE MY UNBROKEN REFLECTION
I WOULD HAVE EATEN HIM A LONG TIME AGO BUT HE KEEPS STARING AT ME AND IT'S REALLY CREEPIN' ME OUT!
I'M TRYING TO CONNECT WITH ALL THE LIVES THAT I HAVE TOUCHED IN THE PAST
IT'S CALLED FACEBOOK
HOLYMOLECOMICS.COM COPYRIGHT ©

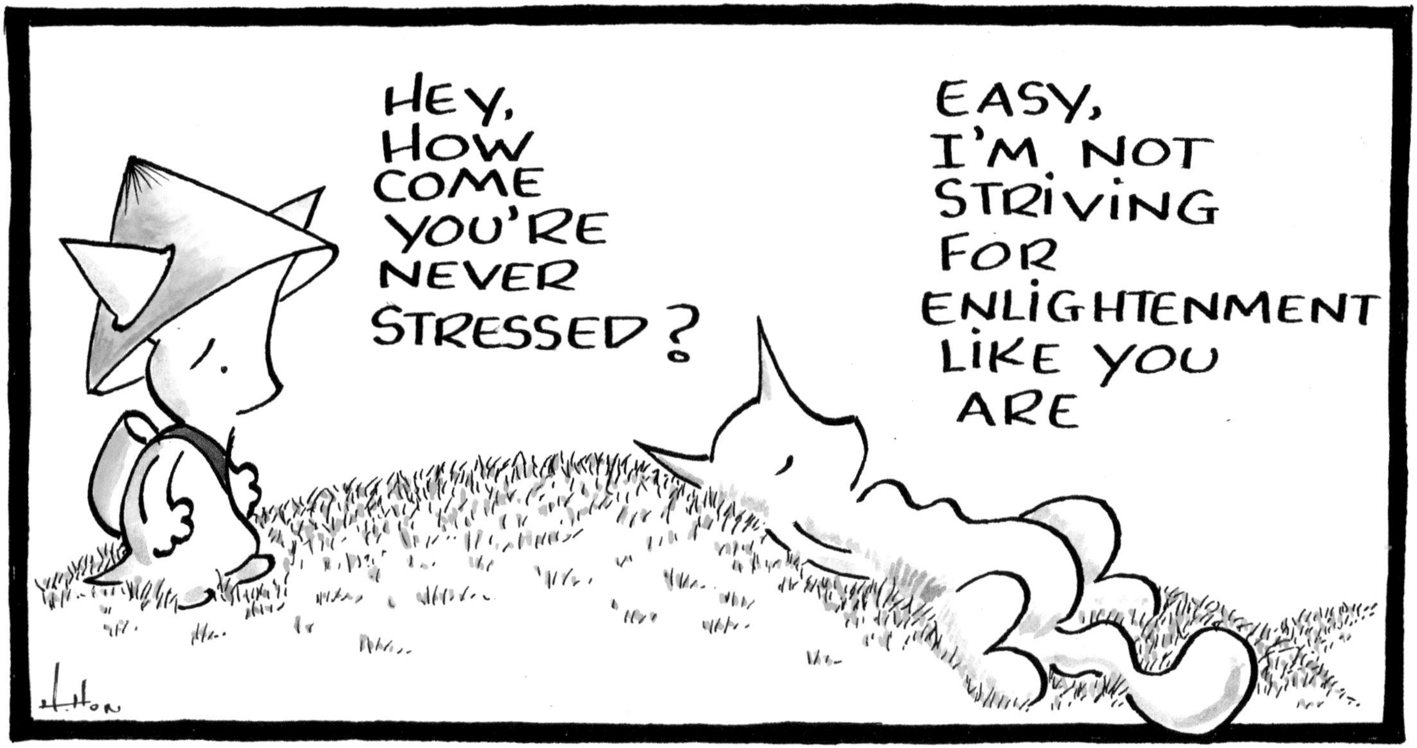
HEY, HOW COME YOU'RE NEVER STRESSED?
EASY, I'M NOT STRIVING FOR ENLIGHTENMENT LIKE YOU ARE

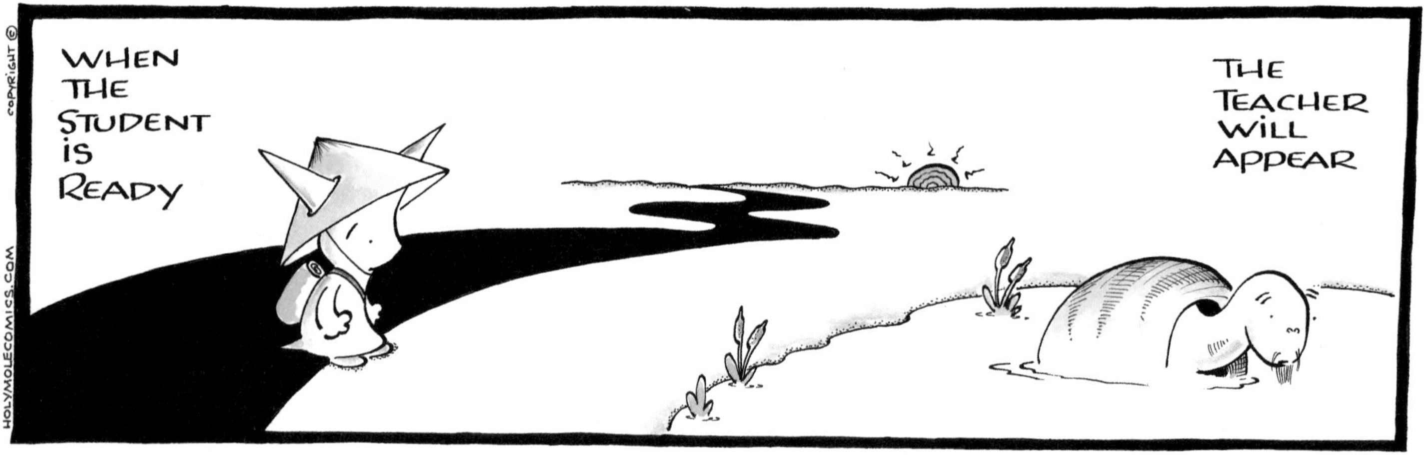
COPYRIGHT ©
HOLYMOLECOMICS.COM
WHEN THE STUDENT IS READY
THE TEACHER WILL APPEAR

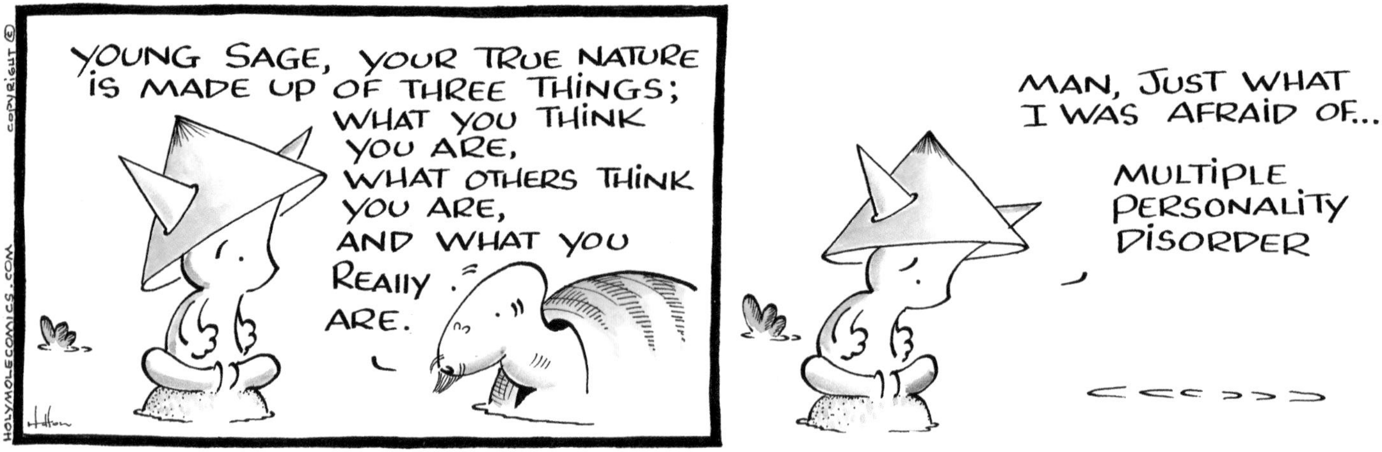
COPYRIGHT ©
HOLYMOLECOMICS.COM
YOUNG SAGE, YOUR TRUE NATURE IS MADE UP OF THREE THINGS; WHAT YOU THINK YOU ARE, WHAT OTHERS THINK YOU ARE, AND WHAT YOU REALLY ARE.
MAN, JUST WHAT I WAS AFRAID OF...
MULTIPLE PERSONALITY DISORDER

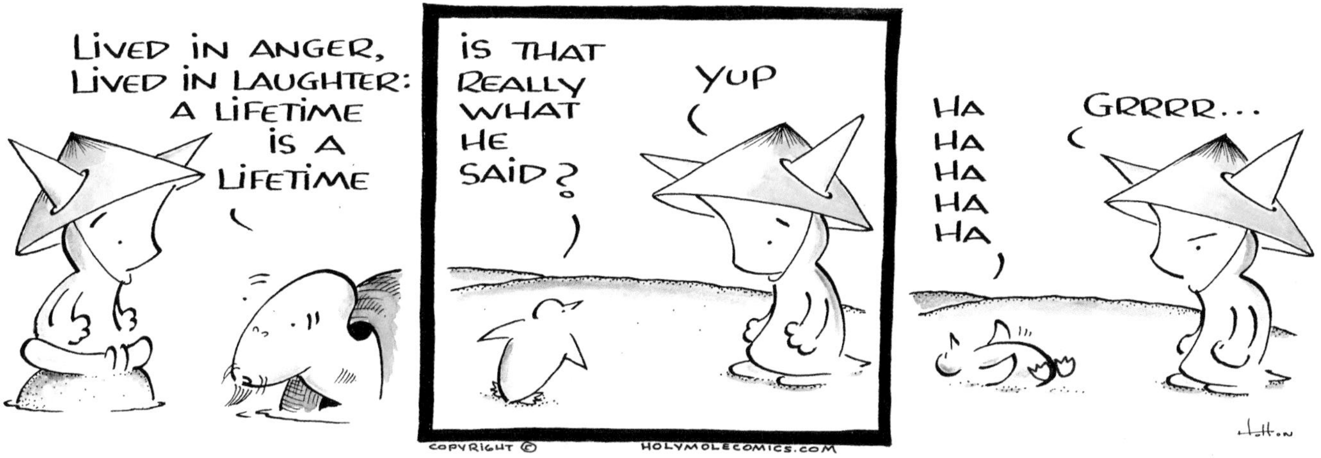
LIVED IN ANGER,
LIVED IN LAUGHTER:
A LIFETIME
IS A
LIFETIME
IS THAT
REALLY
WHAT
HE
SAID?
YUP
HA
HA
HA
HA
HA
GRRRR...
COPYRIGHT ©
HOLYMOLECOMICS.COM

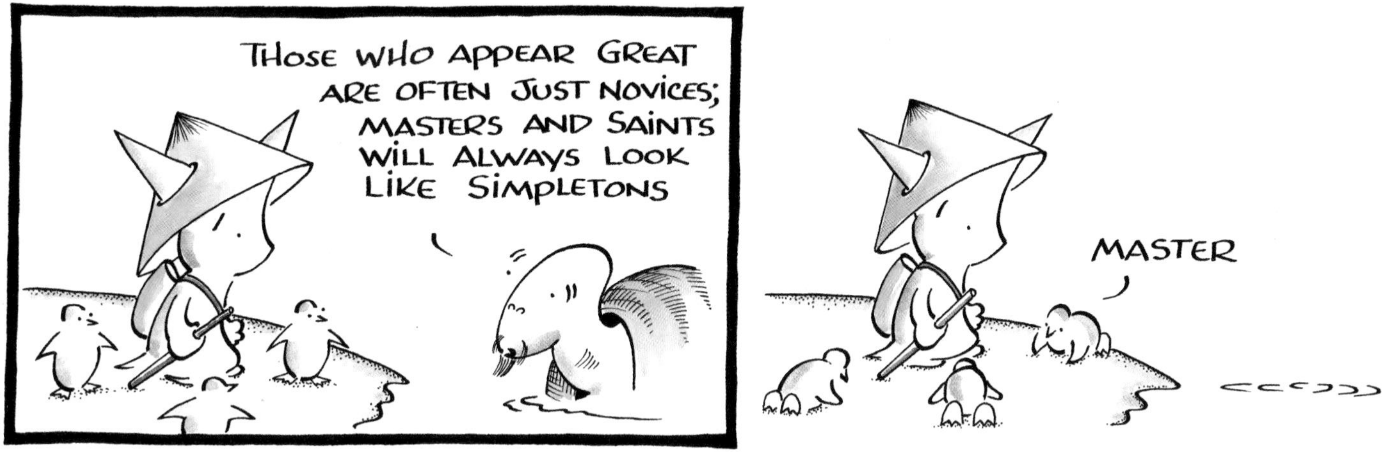
THOSE WHO APPEAR GREAT
ARE OFTEN JUST NOVICES;
MASTERS AND SAINTS
WILL ALWAYS LOOK
LIKE SIMPLETONS
MASTER

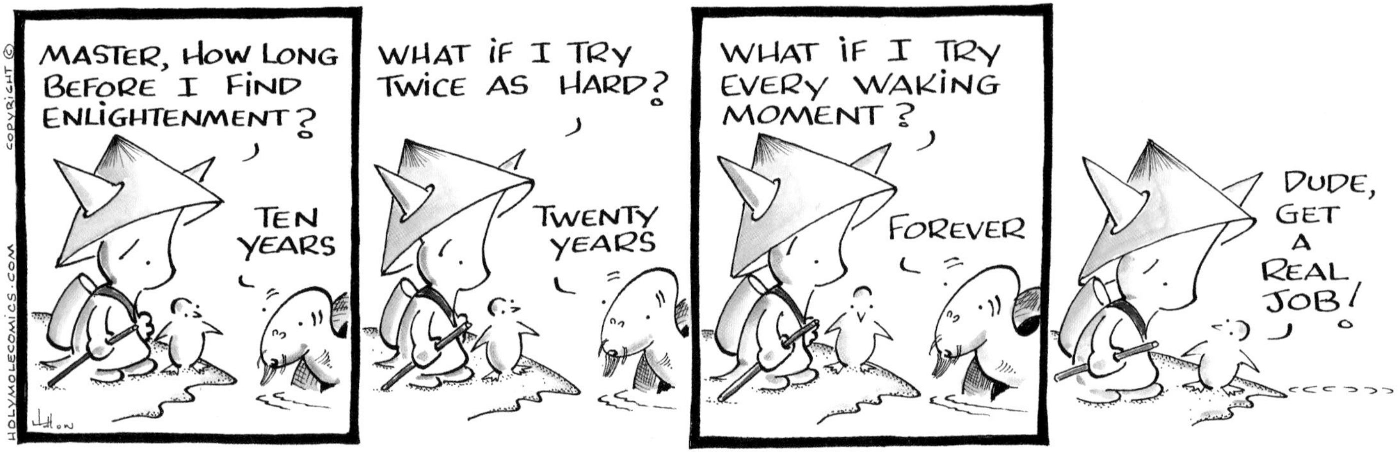
COPYRIGHT ©
HOLYMOLECOMICS.COM
MASTER, HOW LONG BEFORE I FIND ENLIGHTENMENT?
TEN YEARS
WHAT IF I TRY TWICE AS HARD?
TWENTY YEARS
WHAT IF I TRY EVERY WAKING MOMENT?
FOREVER
DUDE, GET A REAL JOB!

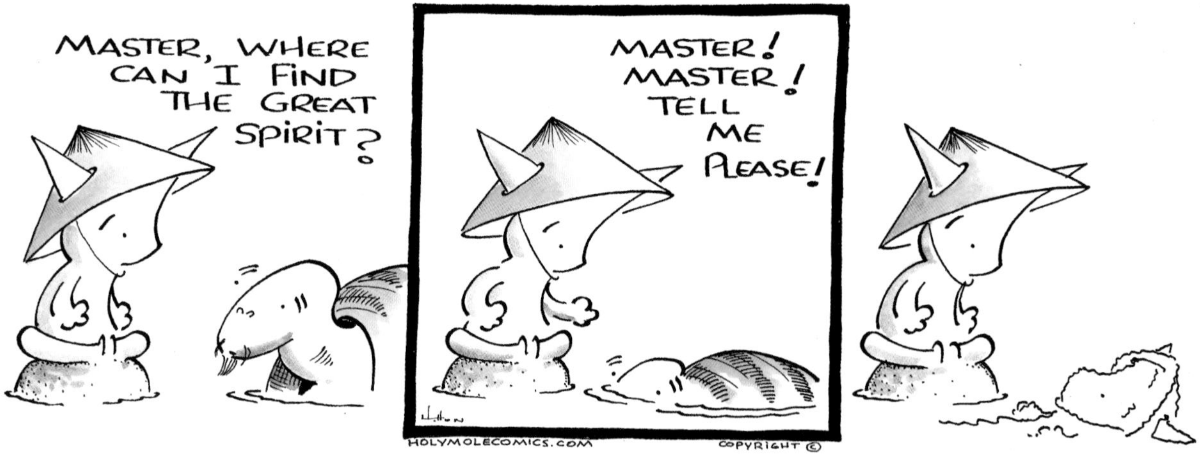
MASTER, WHERE CAN I FIND THE GREAT SPIRIT?
MASTER! MASTER! TELL ME PLEASE!
HOLYMOLECOMICS.COM
COPYRIGHT ©

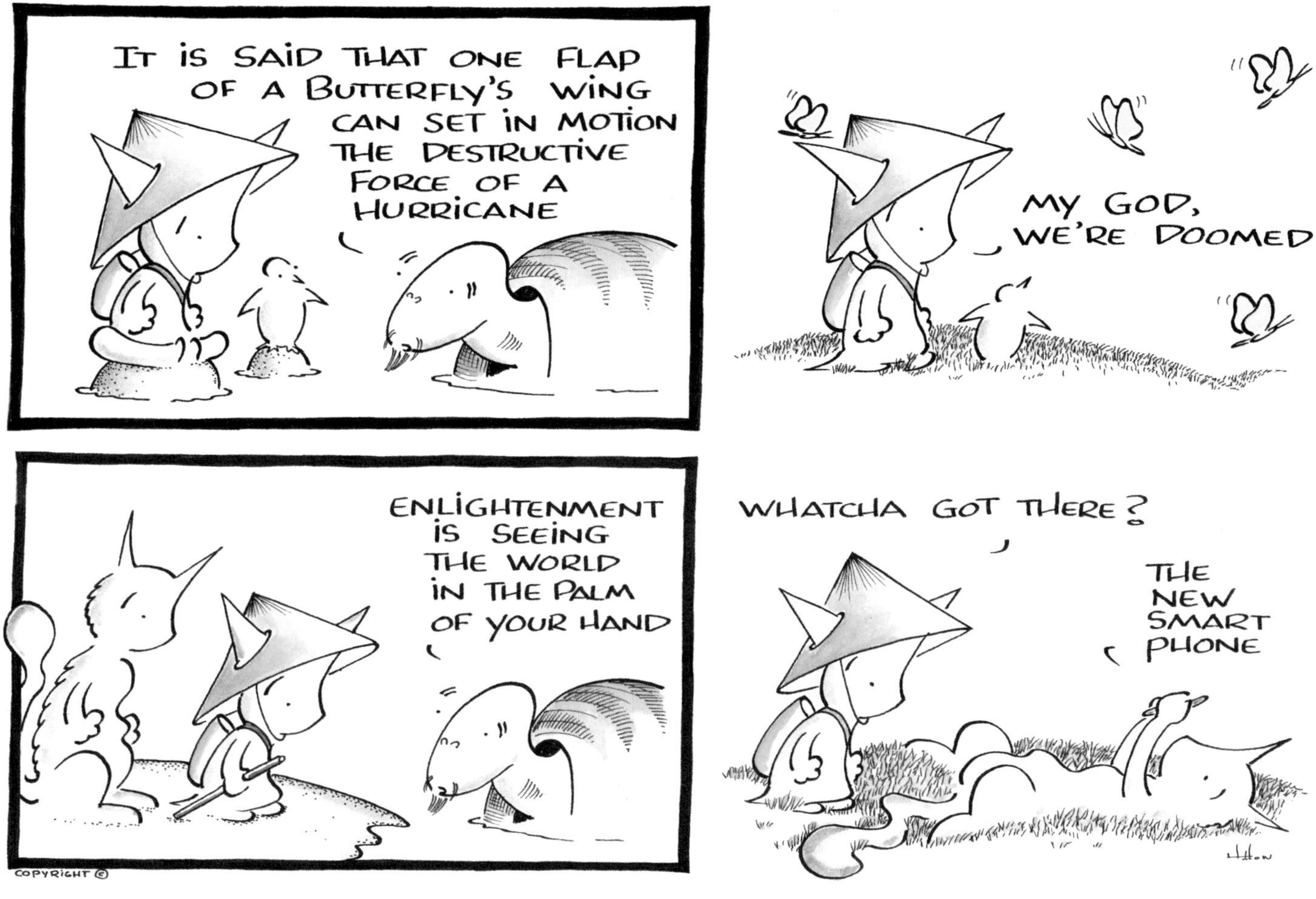
IT IS SAID THAT ONE FLAP OF A BUTTERFLY'S WING CAN SET IN MOTION THE DESTRUCTIVE FORCE OF A HURRICANE
MY GOD, WE'RE DOOMED
ENLIGHTENMENT IS SEEING THE WORLD IN THE PALM OF YOUR HAND
WHATCHA GOT THERE?
THE NEW SMART PHONE
COPYRIGHT ©

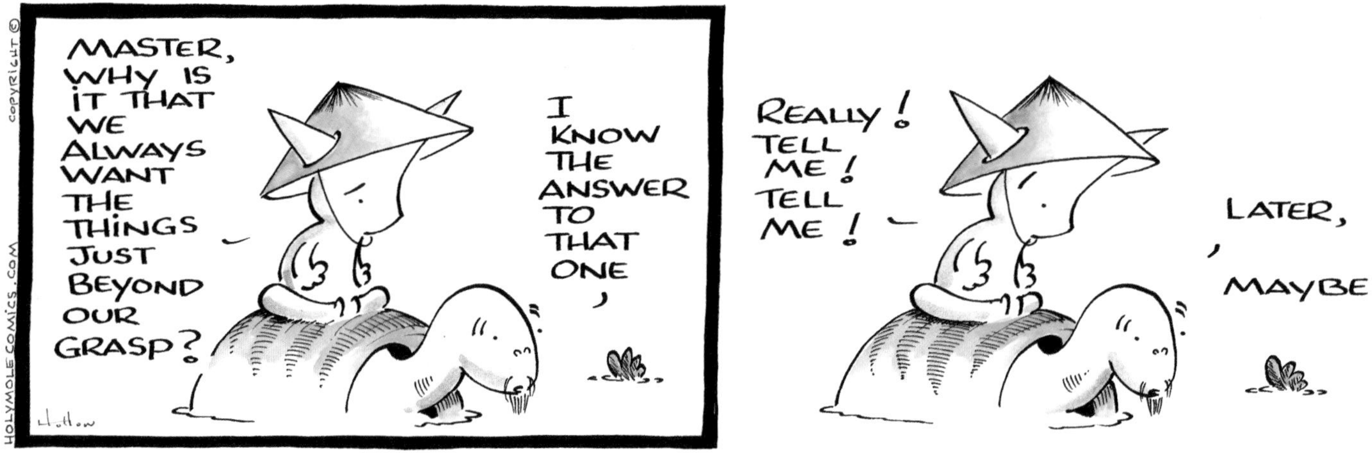
MASTER, WHY IS IT THAT WE ALWAYS WANT THE THINGS JUST BEYOND OUR GRASP?
I KNOW THE ANSWER TO THAT ONE
REALLY! TELL ME! TELL ME!
LATER, MAYBE
HOLYMOLECOMICS.COM
COPYRIGHT ©

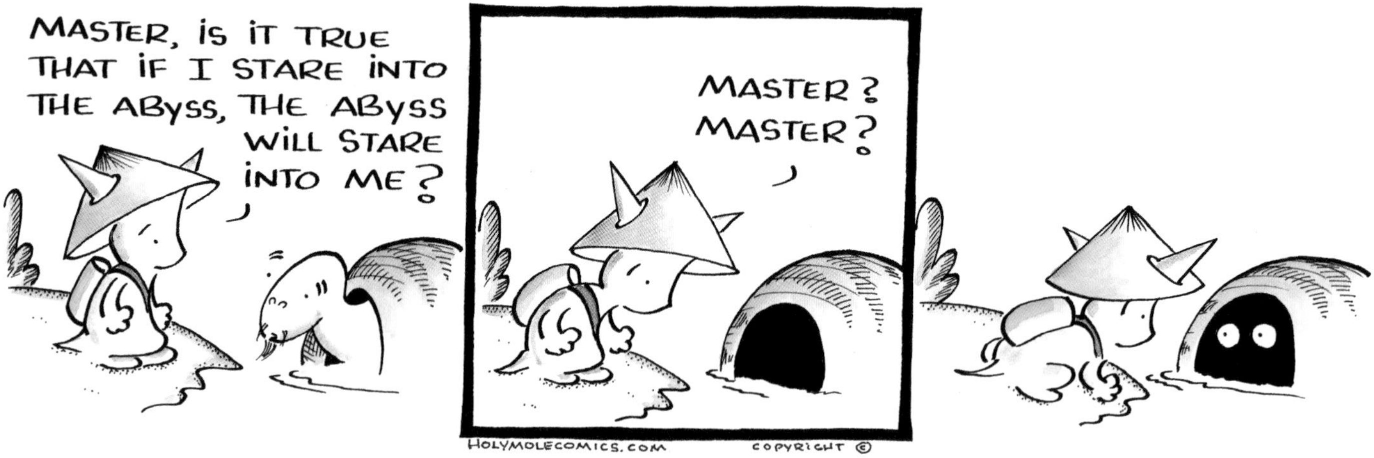
MASTER, IS IT TRUE THAT IF I STARE INTO THE ABYSS, THE ABYSS WILL STARE INTO ME?
MASTER? MASTER?
HOLYMOLECOMICS.COM
COPYRIGHT ©

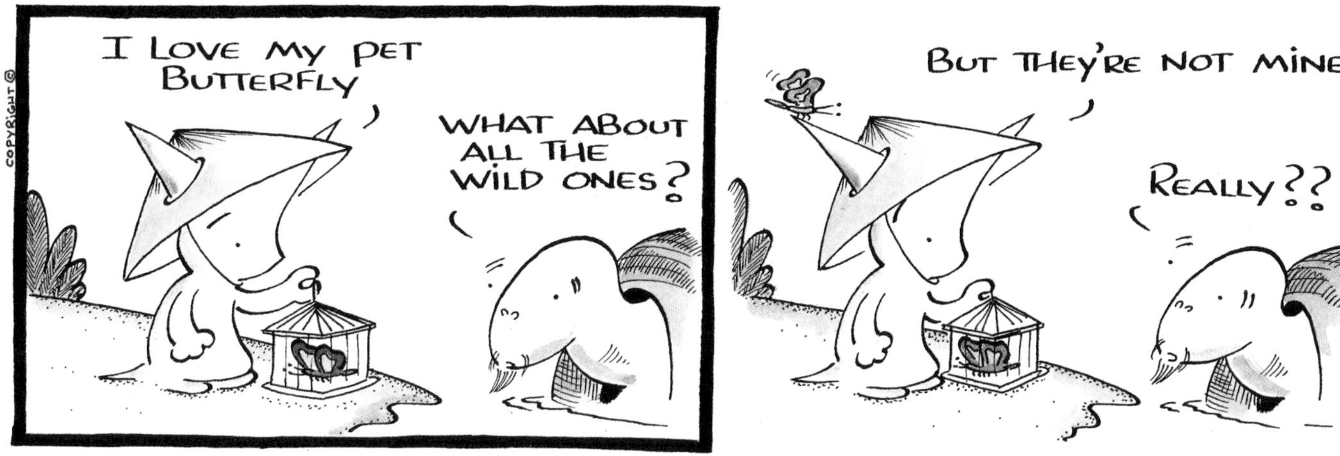
COPYRIGHT ©
I LOVE MY PET BUTTERFLY
WHAT ABOUT ALL THE WILD ONES?
BUT THEY'RE NOT MINE
REALLY??

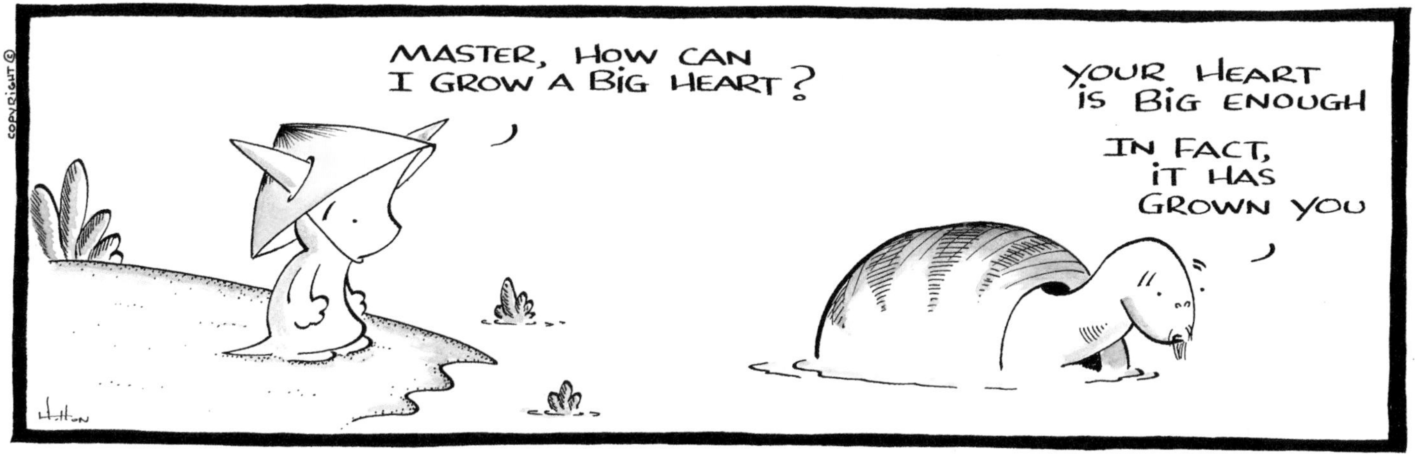
COPYRIGHT ©
MASTER, HOW CAN I GROW A BIG HEART?
YOUR HEART IS BIG ENOUGH
IN FACT, IT HAS GROWN YOU

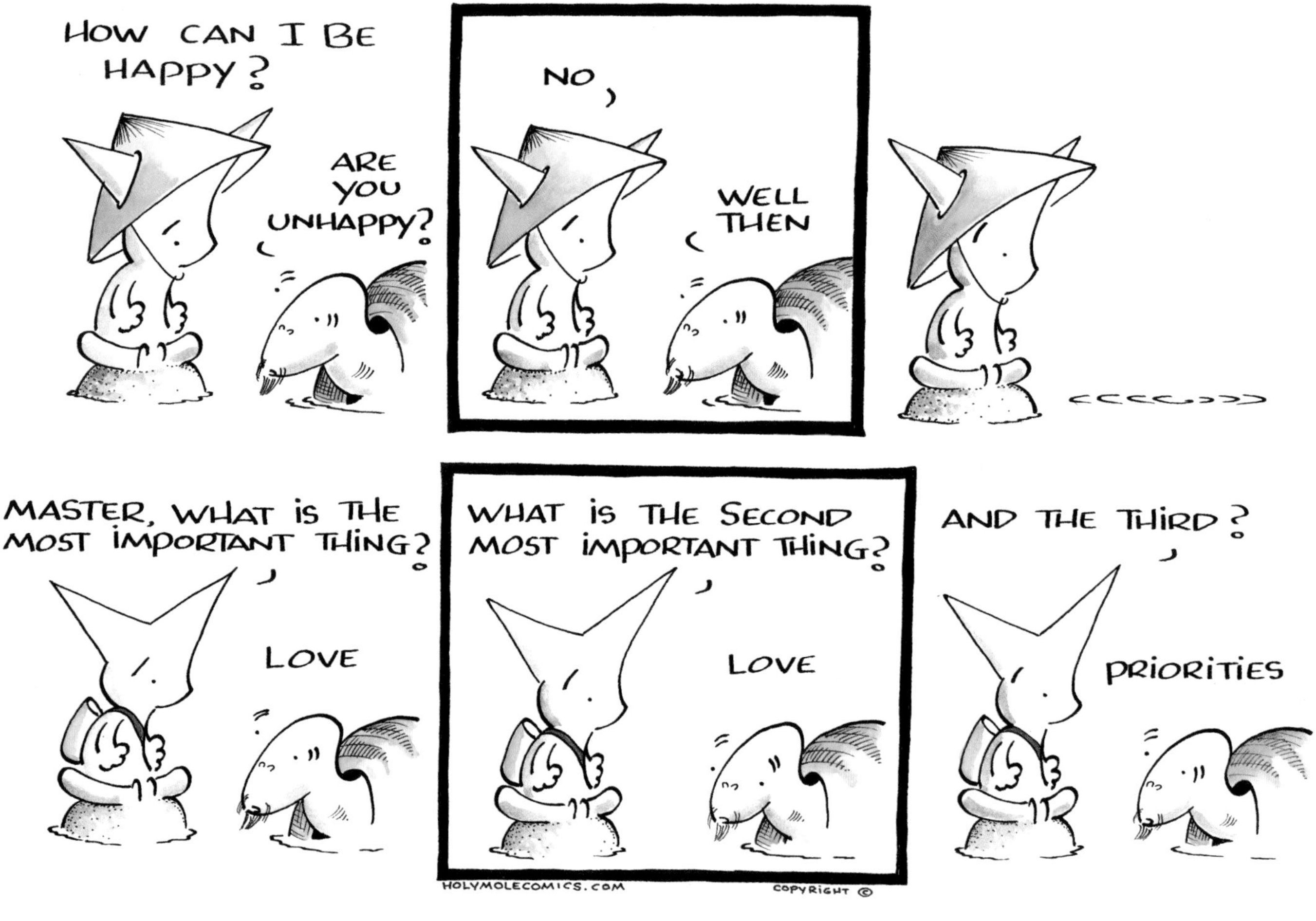

HOW CAN I BE HAPPY?
ARE YOU UNHAPPY?
NO
WELL THEN
MASTER, WHAT IS THE MOST IMPORTANT THING?
LOVE
WHAT IS THE SECOND MOST IMPORTANT THING?
LOVE
AND THE THIRD?
PRIORITIES
HOLYMOLECOMICS.COM
COPYRIGHT ©

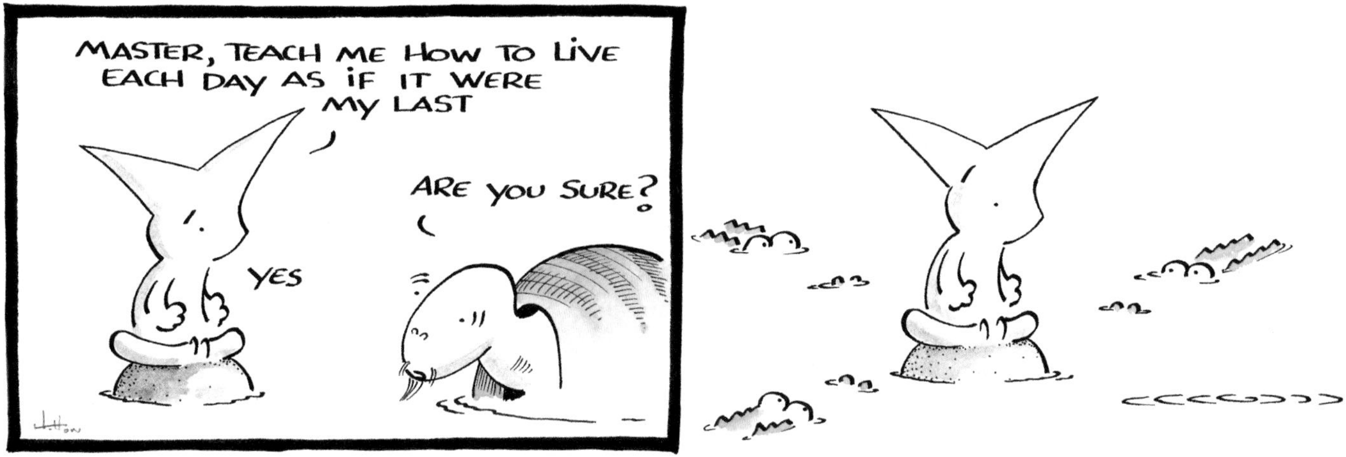
MASTER, TEACH ME HOW TO LIVE EACH DAY AS IF IT WERE MY LAST
ARE YOU SURE?
YES

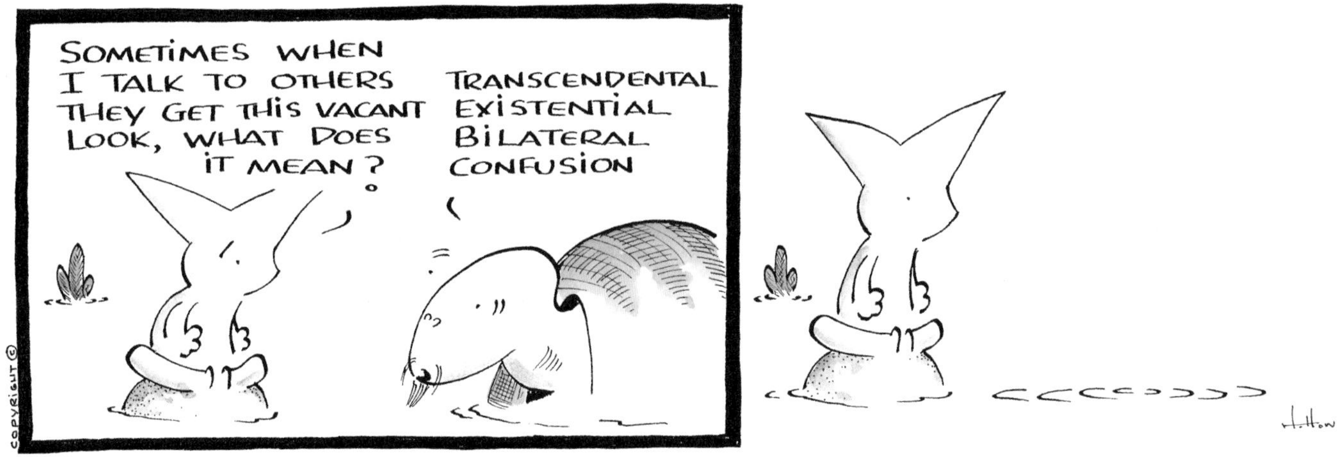
SOMETIMES WHEN I TALK TO OTHERS THEY GET THIS VACANT LOOK, WHAT DOES IT MEAN?
TRANSCENDENTAL EXISTENTIAL BILATERAL CONFUSION
COPYRIGHT ©

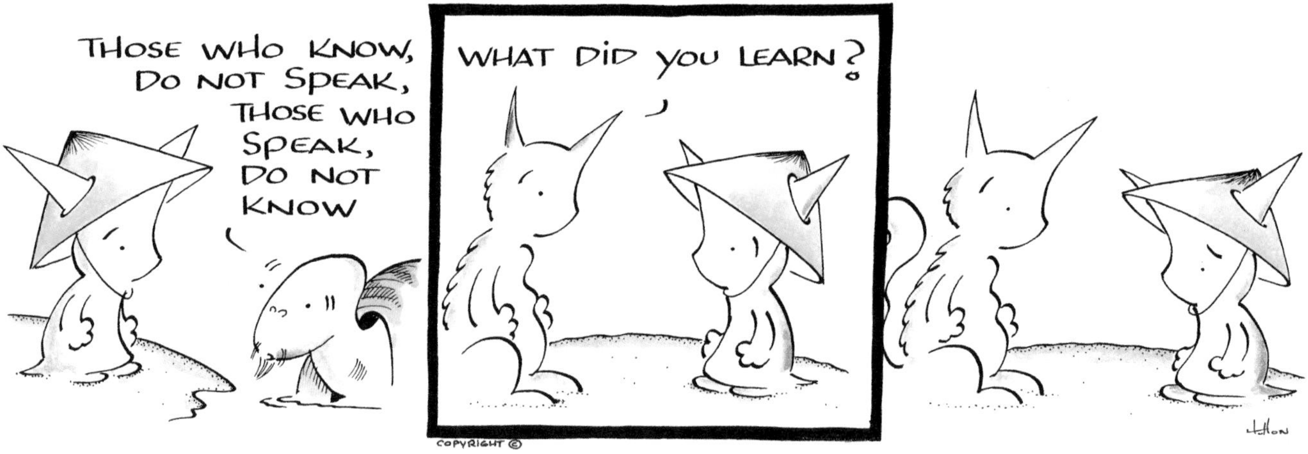
THOSE WHO KNOW, DO NOT SPEAK, THOSE WHO SPEAK, DO NOT KNOW
WHAT DID YOU LEARN?
COPYRIGHT ©
Hutton

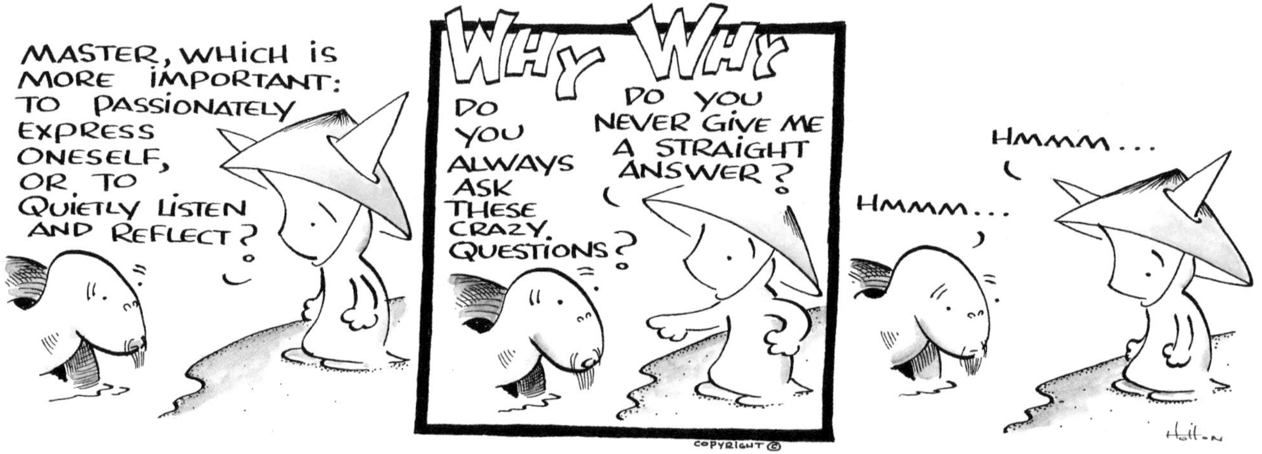
MASTER, WHICH IS MORE IMPORTANT: TO PASSIONATELY EXPRESS ONESELF, OR TO QUIETLY LISTEN AND REFLECT?
WHY
DO YOU ALWAYS ASK THESE CRAZY QUESTIONS?
WHY
DO YOU NEVER GIVE ME A STRAIGHT ANSWER?
HMMM...
HMMM...
COPYRIGHT ©
Hutton

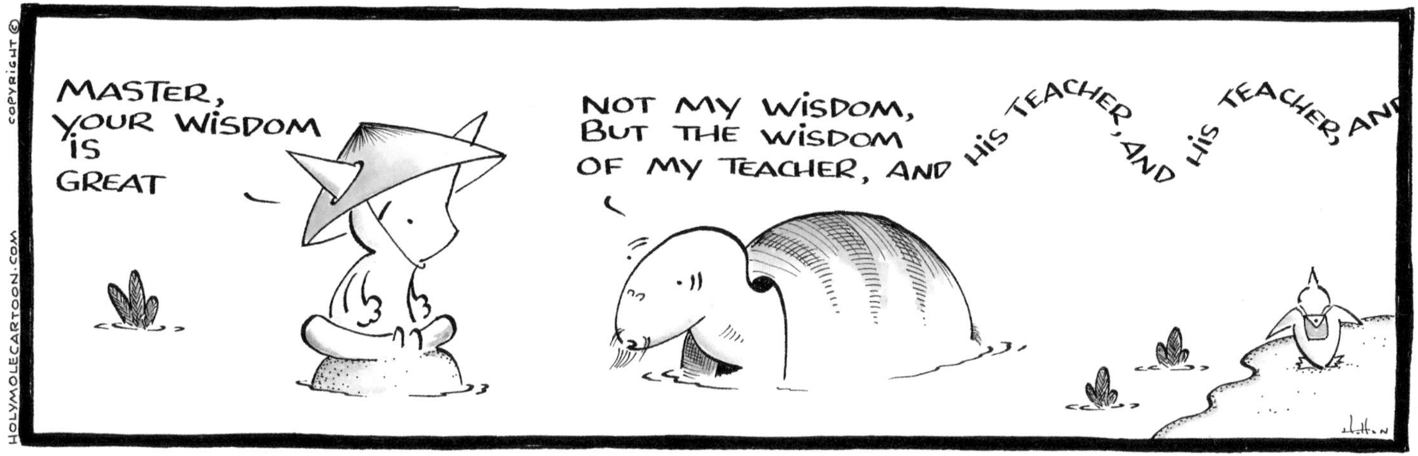
COPYRIGHT © HOLYMOLECARTOON.COM
MASTER, YOUR WISDOM IS GREAT
NOT MY WISDOM, BUT THE WISDOM OF MY TEACHER, AND HIS TEACHER, AND HIS TEACHER, AND

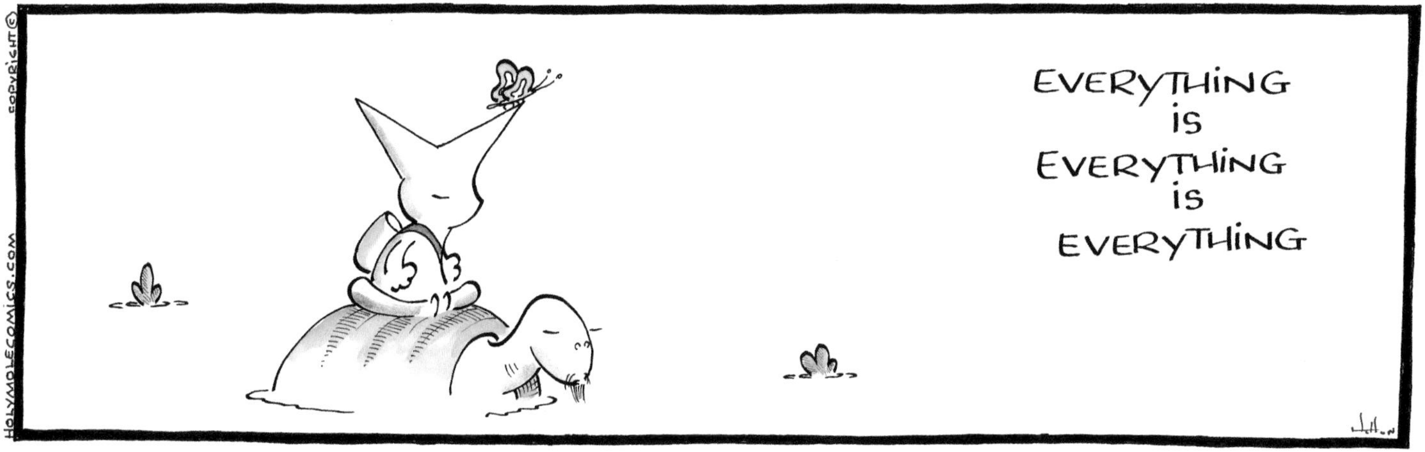
COPYRIGHT © HOLYMOLECOMICS.COM
EVERYTHING IS EVERYTHING IS EVERYTHING

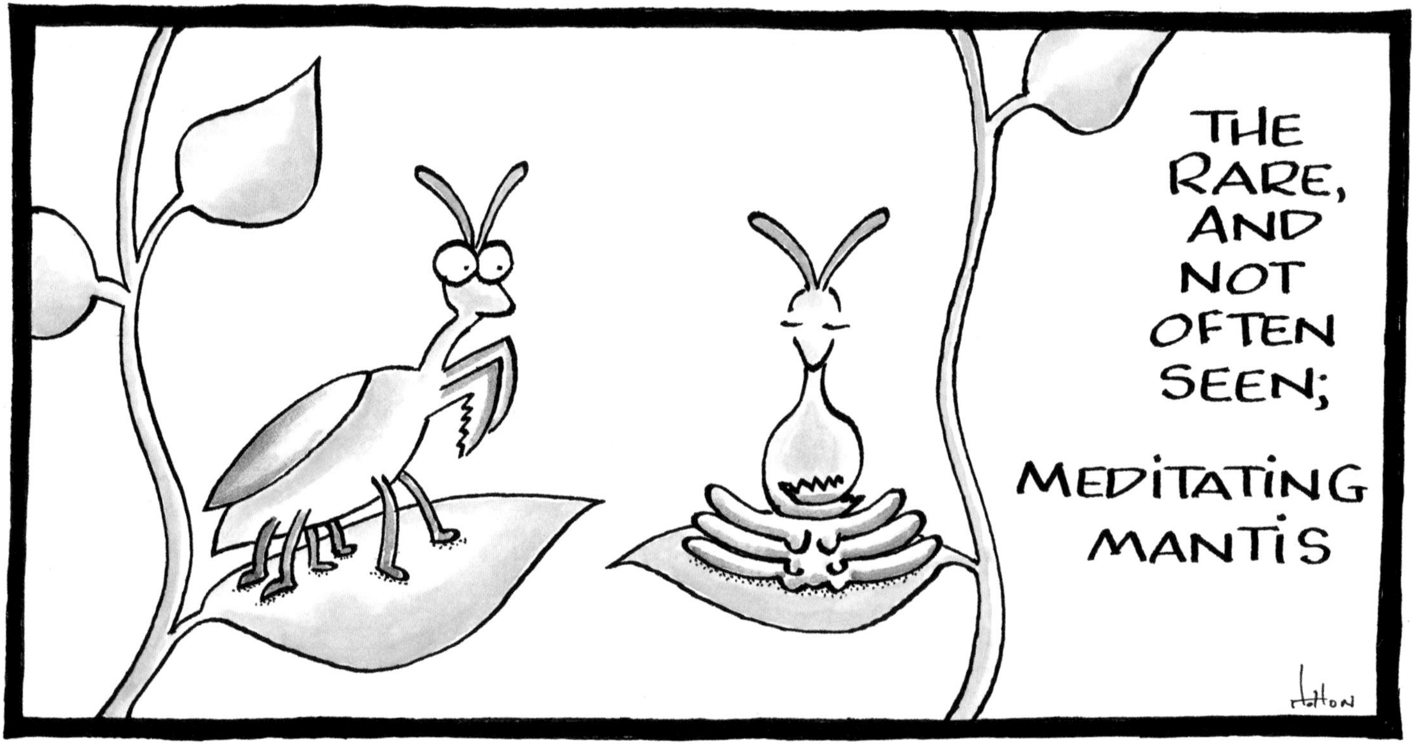
THE RARE, AND NOT OFTEN SEEN;
MEDITATING MANTIS
Hatton

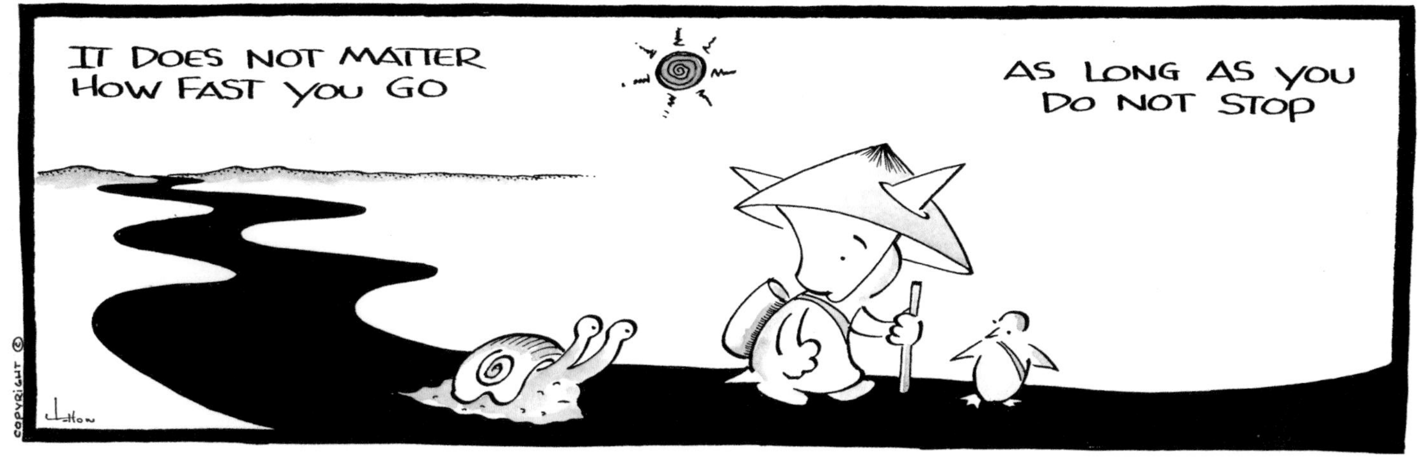
IT DOES NOT MATTER HOW FAST YOU GO
AS LONG AS YOU DO NOT STOP
COPYRIGHT ©

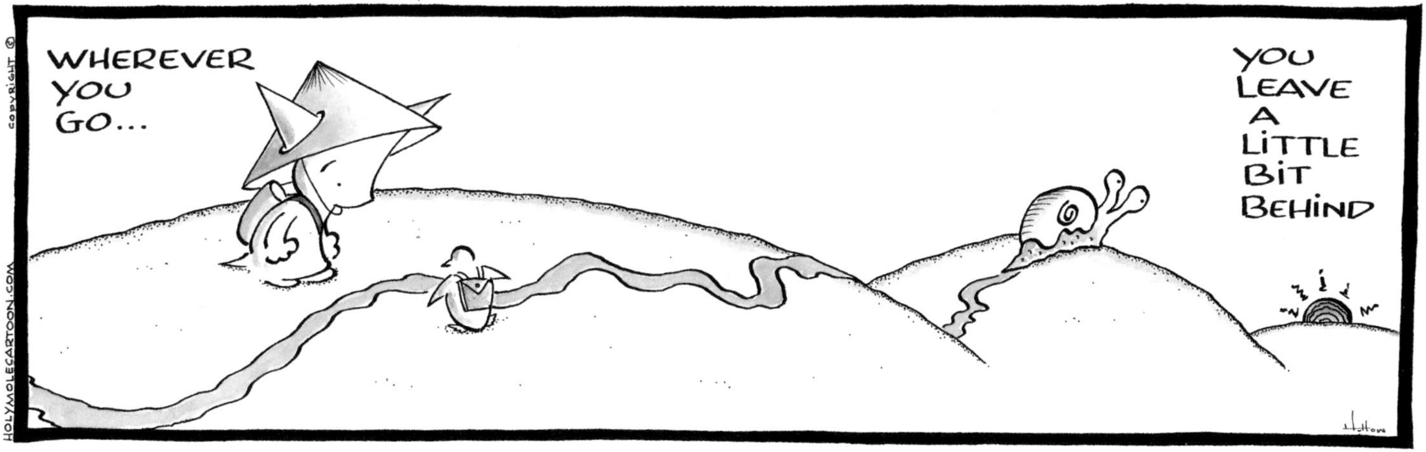
WHEREVER YOU GO...
YOU LEAVE A LITTLE BIT BEHIND
COPYRIGHT ©
HOLYMOLECARTOON.COM

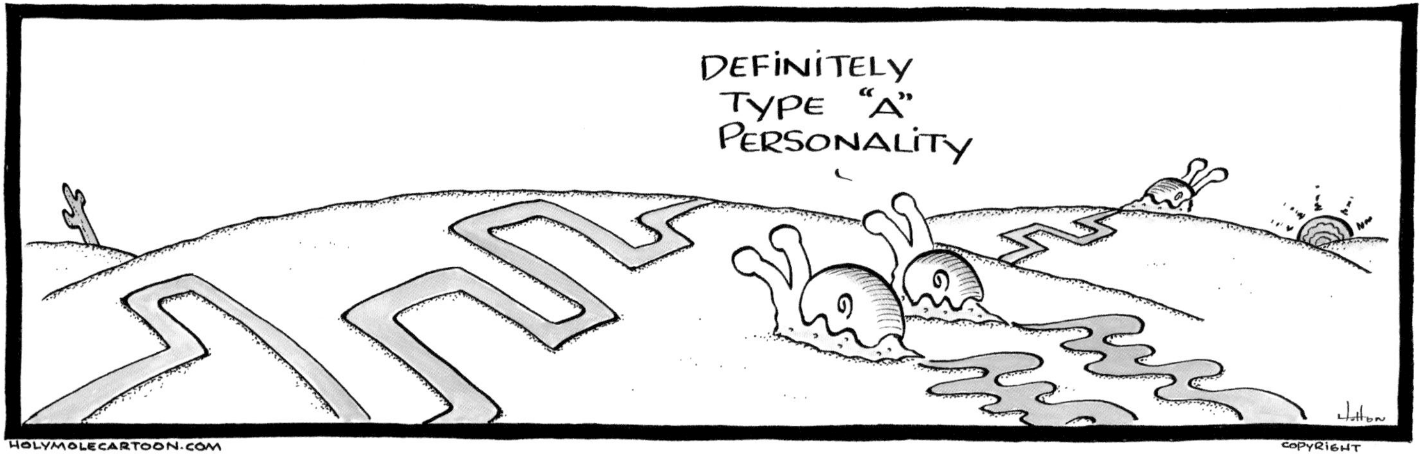
DEFINITELY TYPE "A" PERSONALITY
HOLYMOLECARTOON.COM
COPYRIGHT

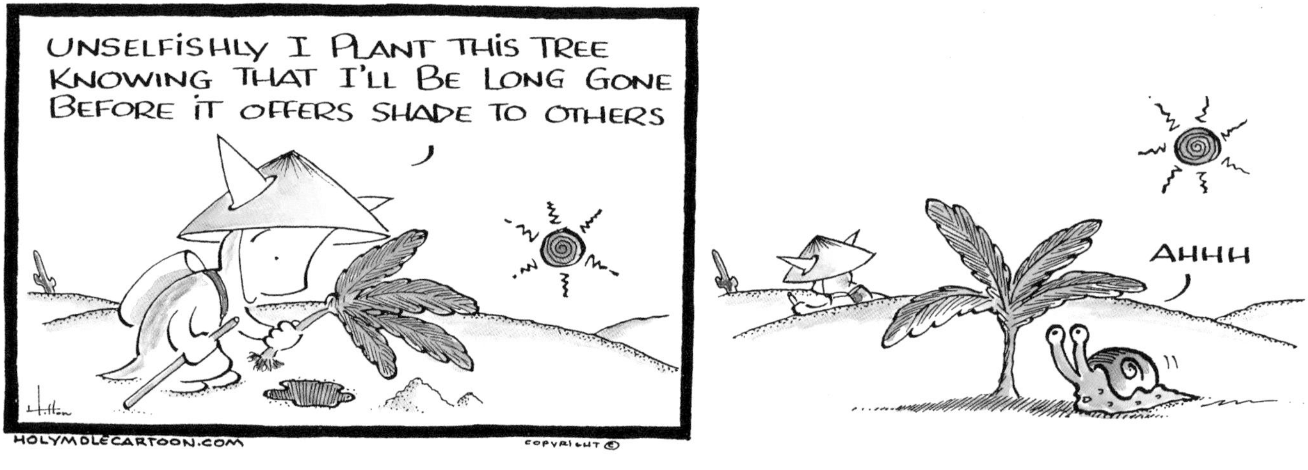
UNSELFISHLY I PLANT THIS TREE KNOWING THAT I'LL BE LONG GONE BEFORE IT OFFERS SHADE TO OTHERS
AHHH
HOLYMOLECARTOON.COM
COPYRIGHT ©

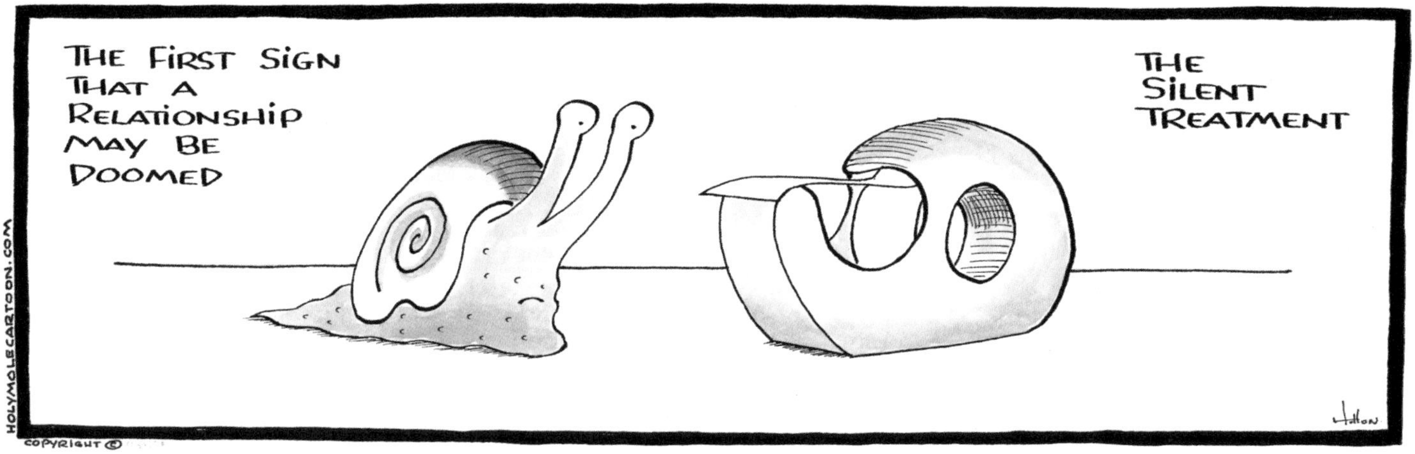
THE FIRST SIGN THAT A RELATIONSHIP MAY BE DOOMED
THE SILENT TREATMENT
HOLYMOLECARTOON.COM
COPYRIGHT ©

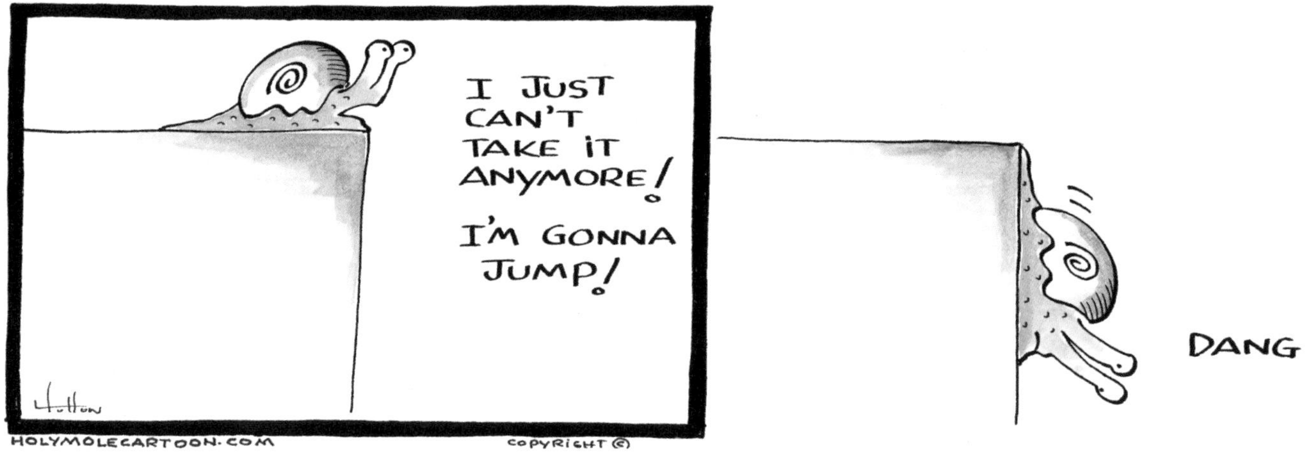
I JUST CAN'T TAKE IT ANYMORE!
I'M GONNA JUMP!
DANG
HOLYMOLECARTOON.COM
COPYRIGHT ©

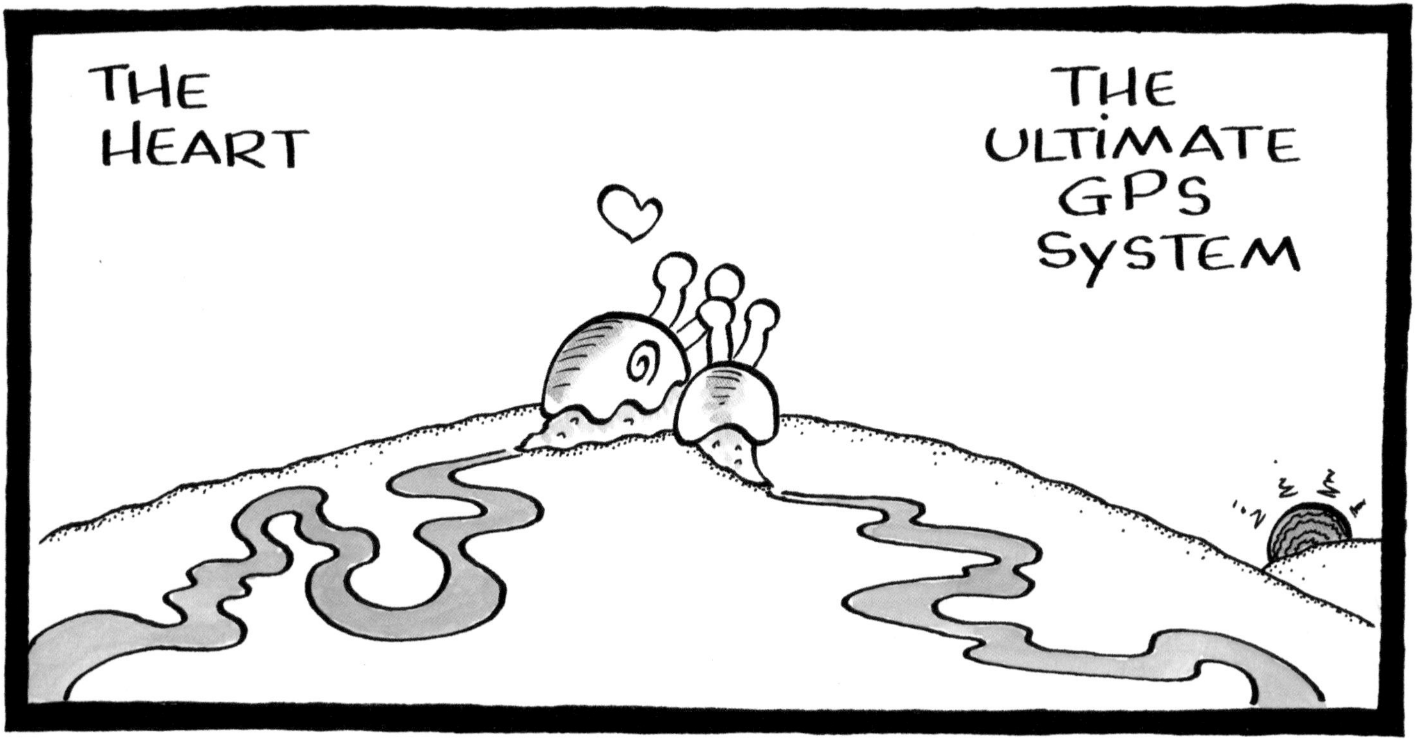
THE HEART
THE ULTIMATE GPS SYSTEM

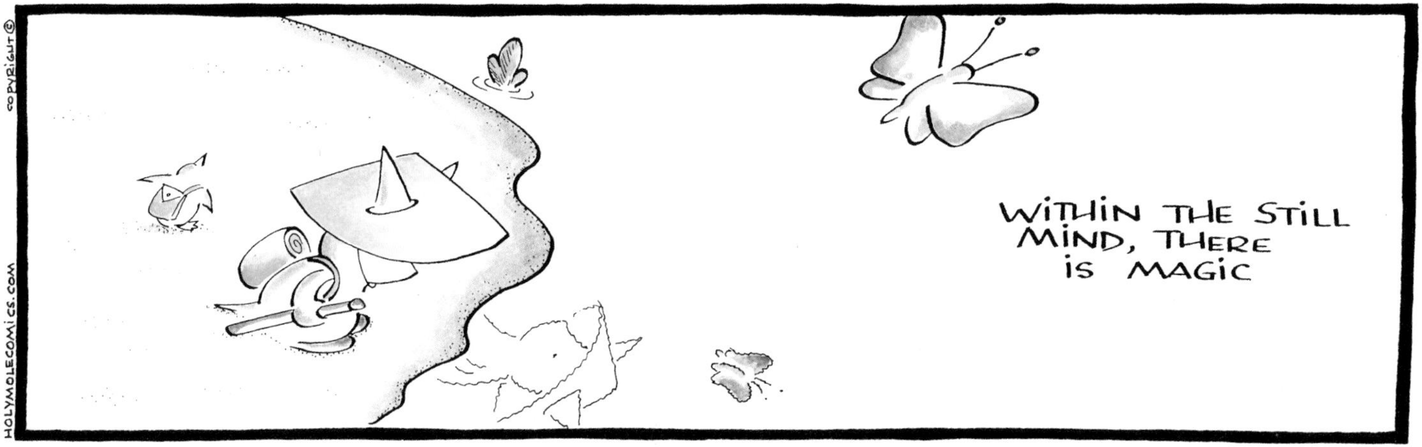
WITHIN THE STILL MIND, THERE IS MAGIC
HOLYMOLECOMICS.COM COPYRIGHT©

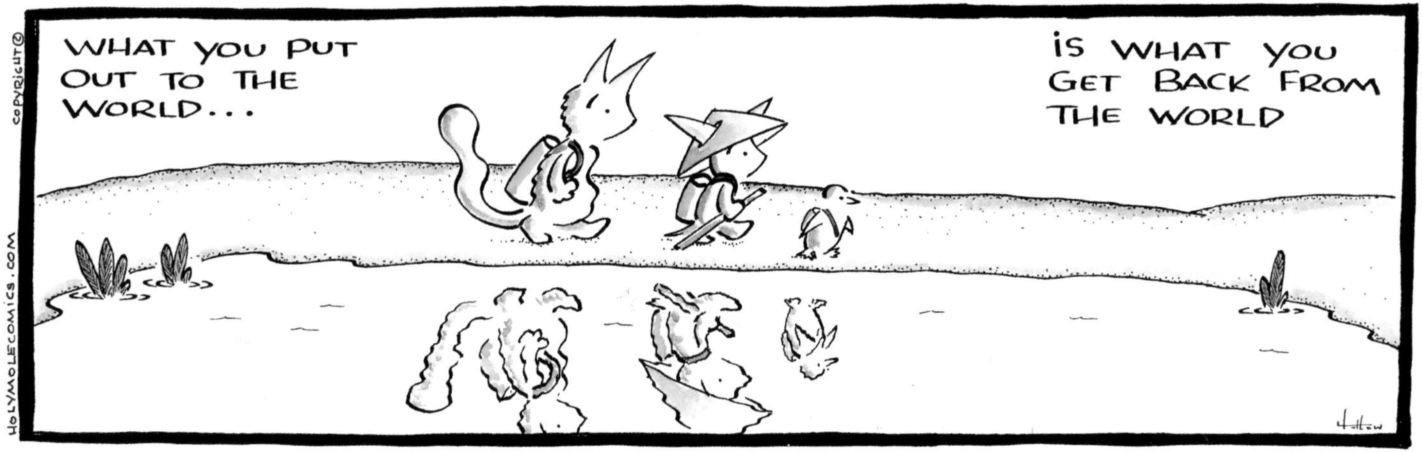
WHAT YOU PUT OUT TO THE WORLD...
IS WHAT YOU GET BACK FROM THE WORLD
HOLYMOLECOMICS.COM COPYRIGHT©

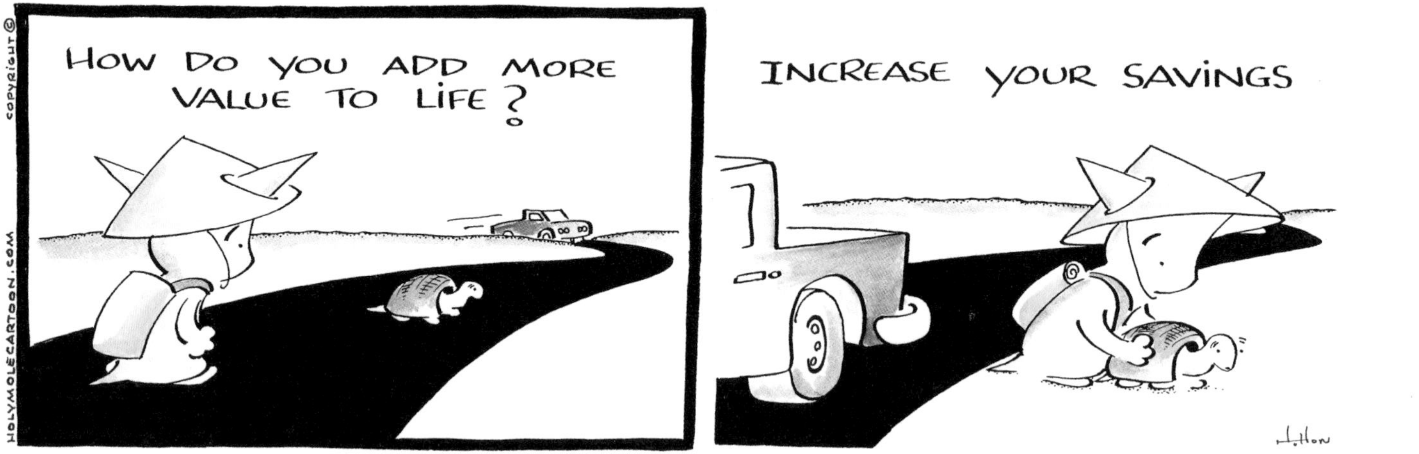
HOW DO YOU ADD MORE VALUE TO LIFE?
INCREASE YOUR SAVINGS
COPYRIGHT ©
HOLYMOLECARTOON.COM

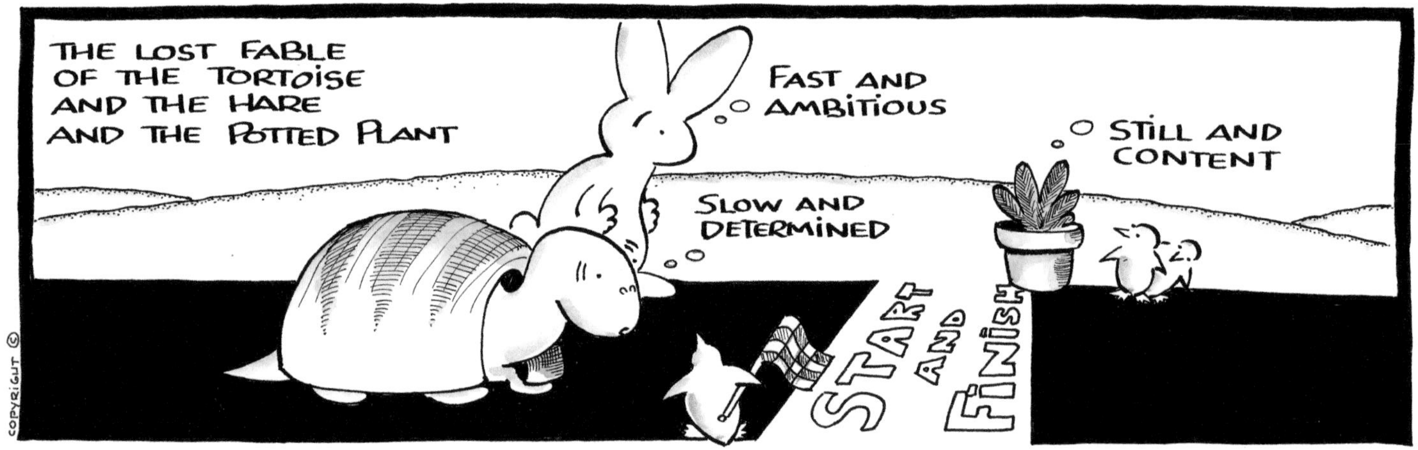
THE LOST FABLE OF THE TORTOISE AND THE HARE AND THE POTTED PLANT
FAST AND AMBITIOUS
SLOW AND DETERMINED
STILL AND CONTENT
START AND FINISH
COPYRIGHT ©

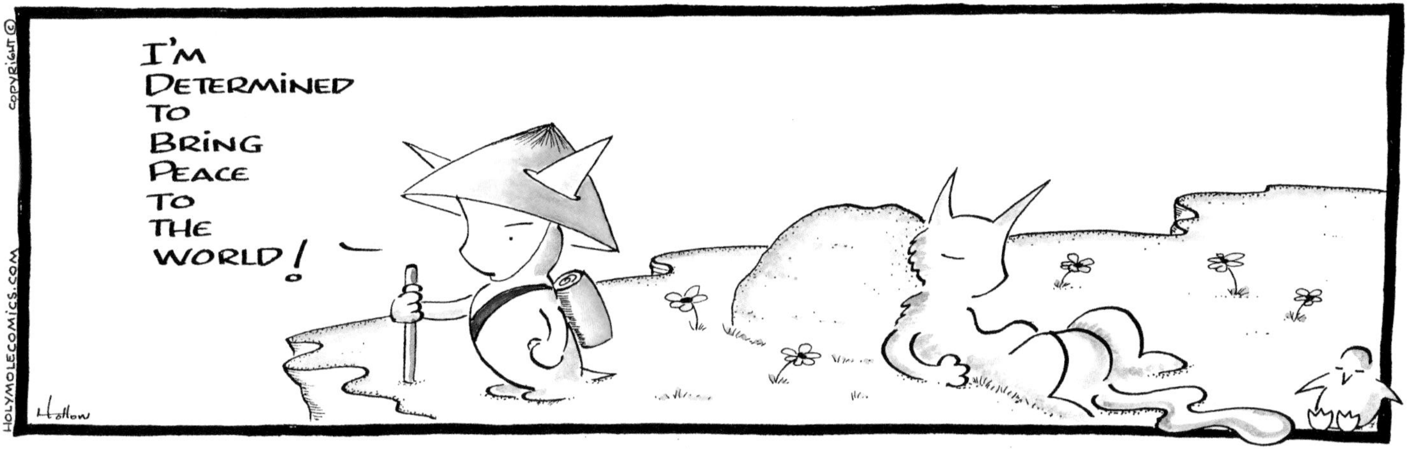
I'M DETERMINED TO BRING PEACE TO THE WORLD!
COPYRIGHT © HOLYMOLECOMICS.COM
Hotton

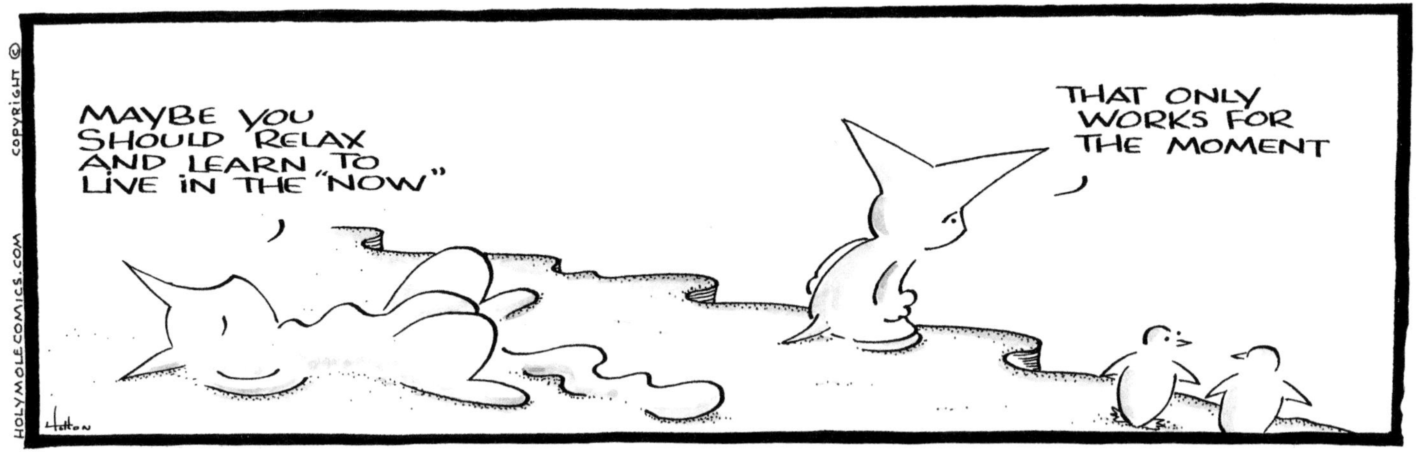
MAYBE YOU SHOULD RELAX AND LEARN TO LIVE IN THE "NOW"
THAT ONLY WORKS FOR THE MOMENT
COPYRIGHT © HOLYMOLECOMICS.COM
Hotton

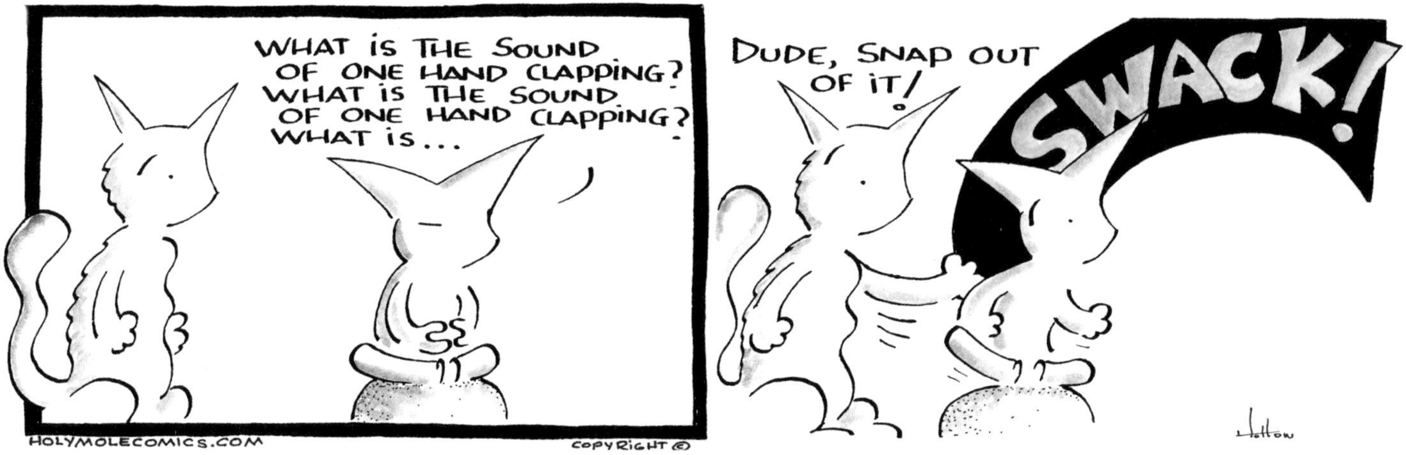
WHAT IS THE SOUND OF ONE HAND CLAPPING? WHAT IS THE SOUND OF ONE HAND CLAPPING? WHAT IS...
DUDE, SNAP OUT OF IT!
SWACK!
HOLYMOLECOMICS.COM
COPYRIGHT ©
Hatton

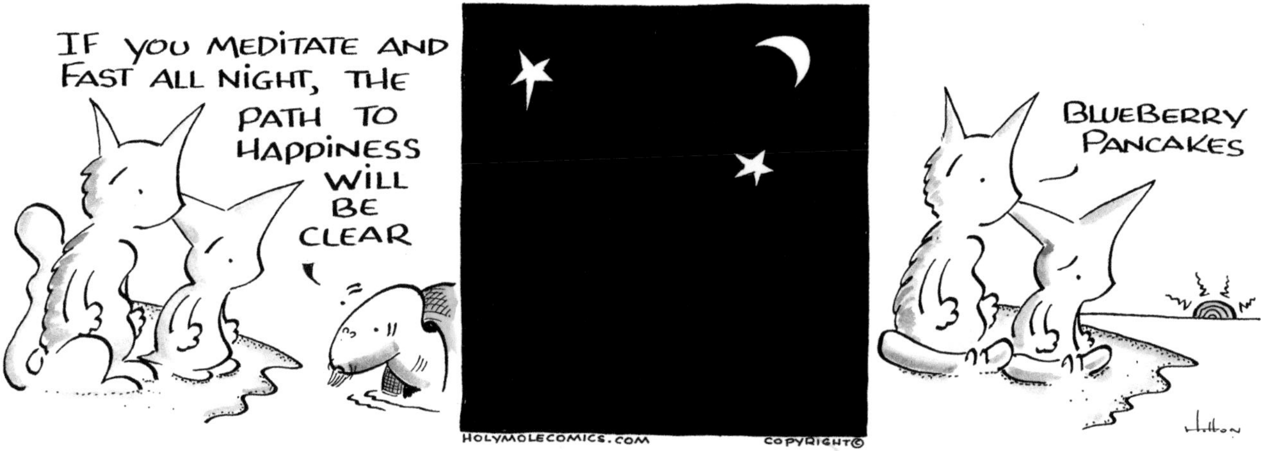
IF YOU MEDITATE AND FAST ALL NIGHT, THE PATH TO HAPPINESS WILL BE CLEAR
BLUEBERRY PANCAKES
HOLYMOLECOMICS.COM
COPYRIGHT©
Hatton

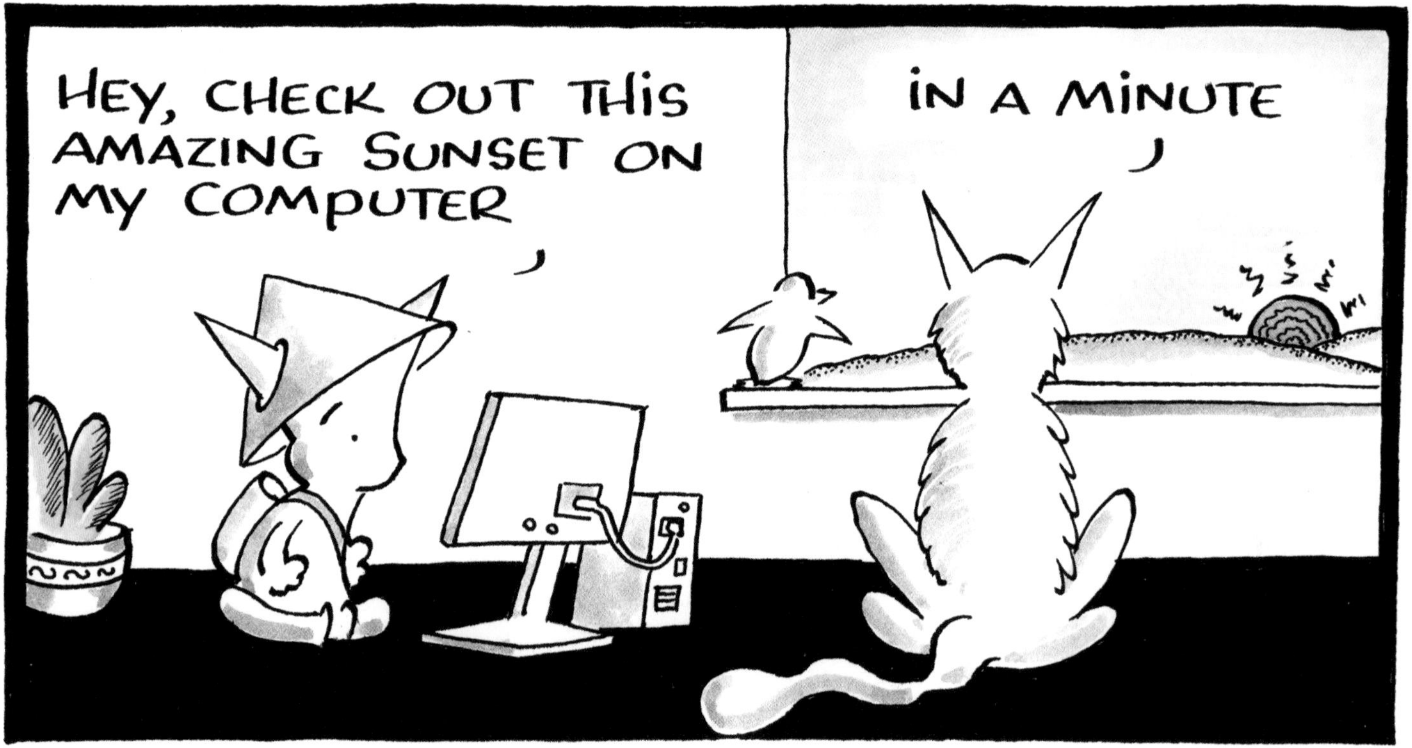
HEY, CHECK OUT THIS AMAZING SUNSET ON MY COMPUTER
IN A MINUTE

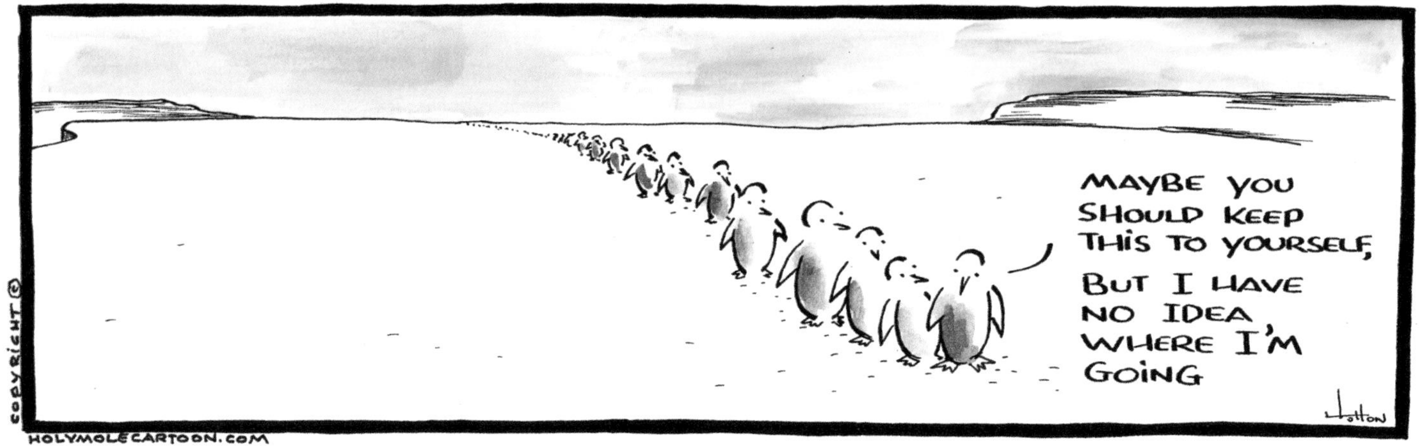
MAYBE YOU SHOULD KEEP THIS TO YOURSELF, BUT I HAVE NO IDEA WHERE I'M GOING
COPYRIGHT ©
HOLYMOLECARTOON.COM

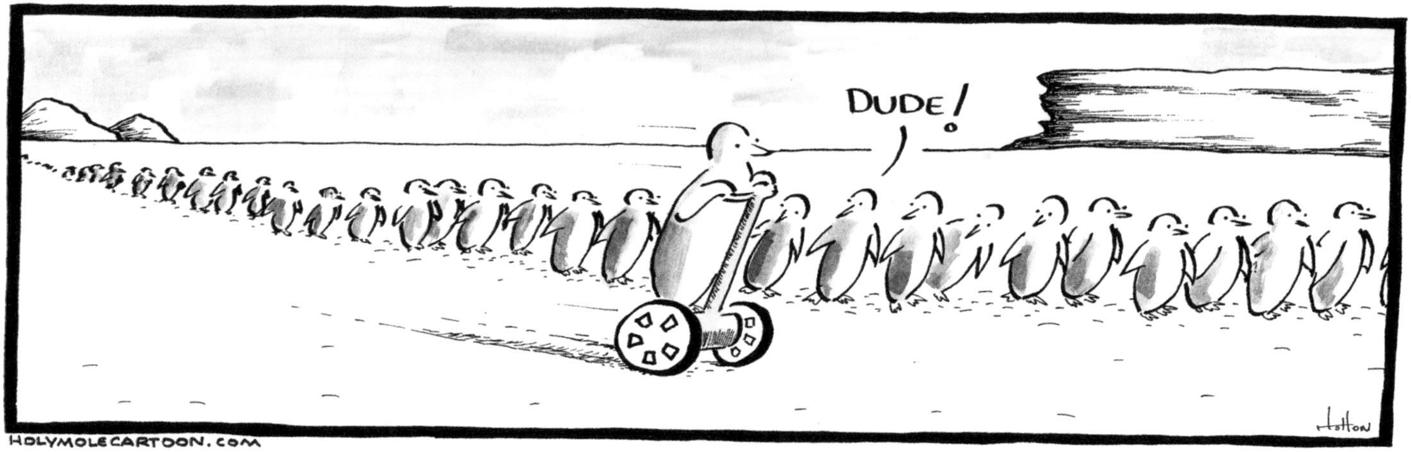
DUDE!
HOLYMOLECARTOON.COM

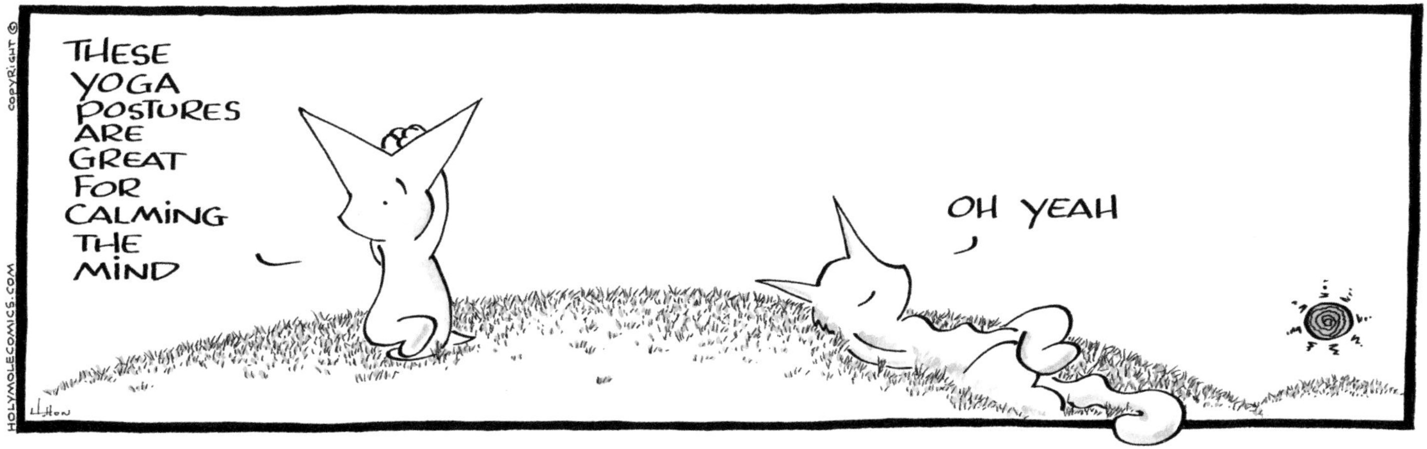
COPYRIGHT ©
HOLYMOLECOMICS.COM
THESE YOGA POSTURES ARE GREAT FOR CALMING THE MIND
OH YEAH

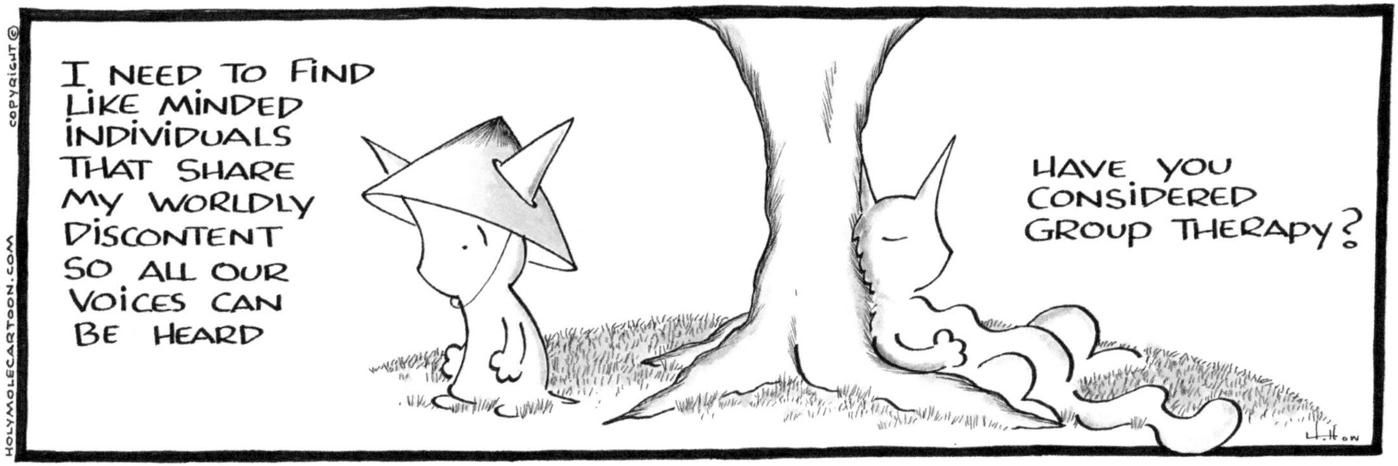
COPYRIGHT ©
HOLYMOLECARTOON.COM
I NEED TO FIND LIKE MINDED INDIVIDUALS THAT SHARE MY WORLDLY DISCONTENT SO ALL OUR VOICES CAN BE HEARD
HAVE YOU CONSIDERED GROUP THERAPY?

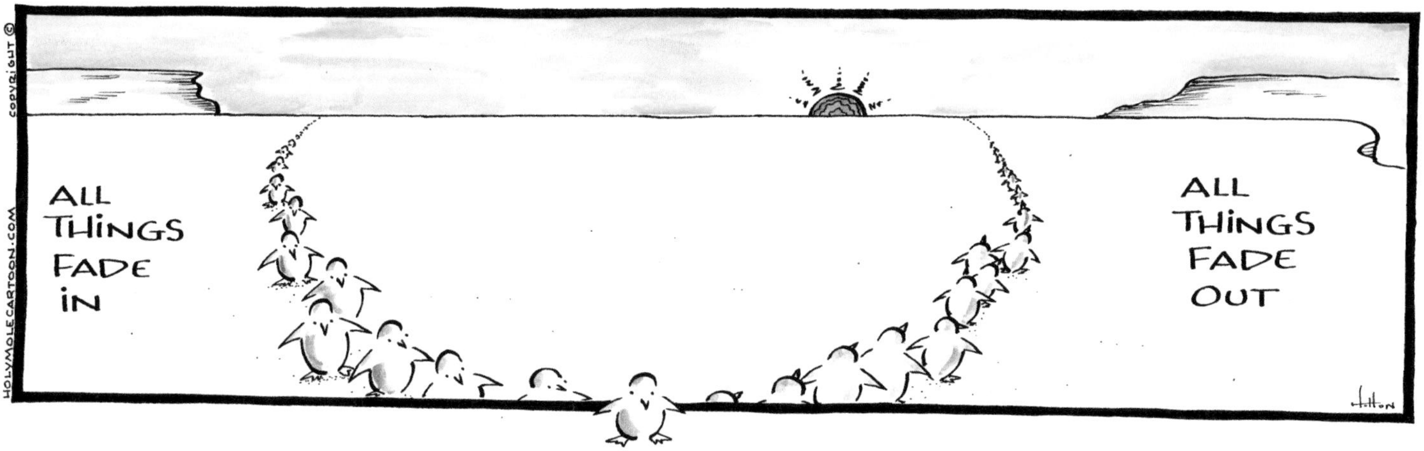
COPYRIGHT ©
HOLYMOLECARTOON.COM
ALL THINGS FADE IN
ALL THINGS FADE OUT

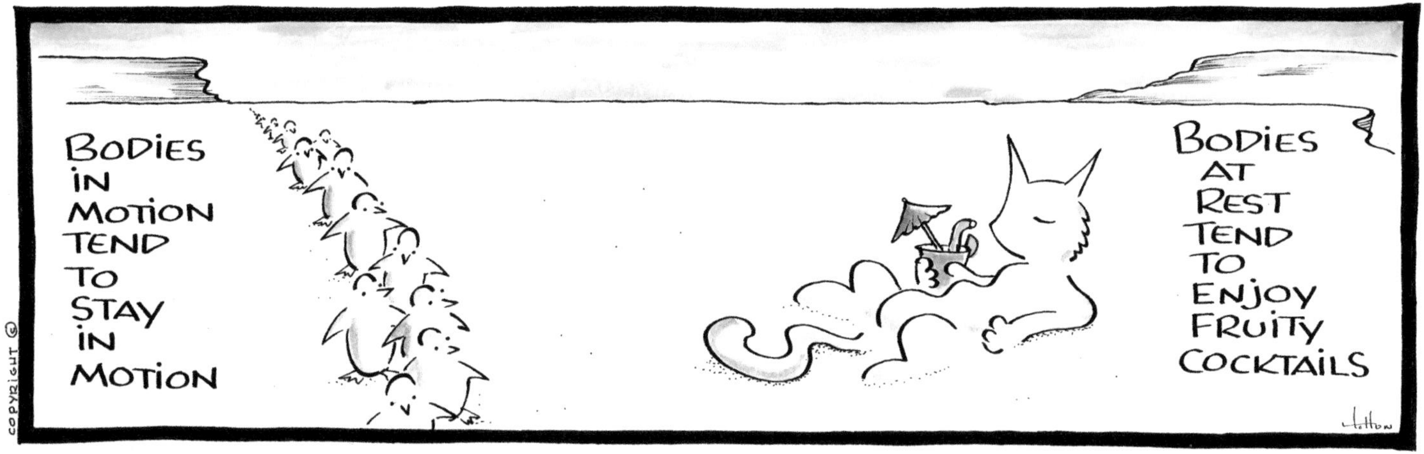
COPYRIGHT ©
BODIES IN MOTION TEND TO STAY IN MOTION
BODIES AT REST TEND TO ENJOY FRUITY COCKTAILS

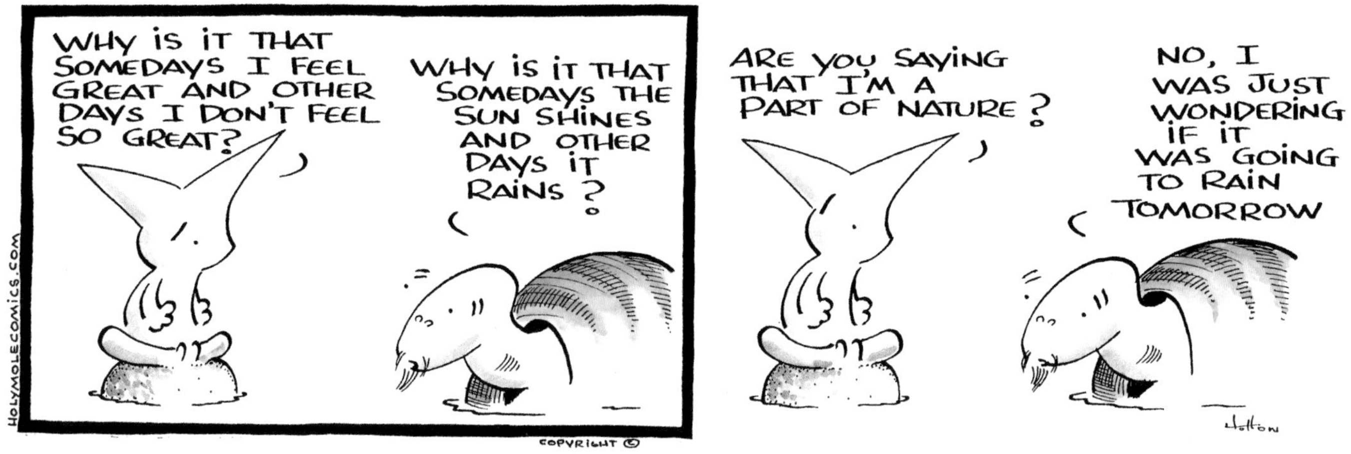
WHY IS IT THAT SOMEDAYS I FEEL GREAT AND OTHER DAYS I DON'T FEEL SO GREAT?
WHY IS IT THAT SOMEDAYS THE SUN SHINES AND OTHER DAYS IT RAINS ?
ARE YOU SAYING THAT I'M A PART OF NATURE ?
NO, I WAS JUST WONDERING IF IT WAS GOING TO RAIN TOMORROW
HOLYMOLECOMICS.COM
COPYRIGHT ©

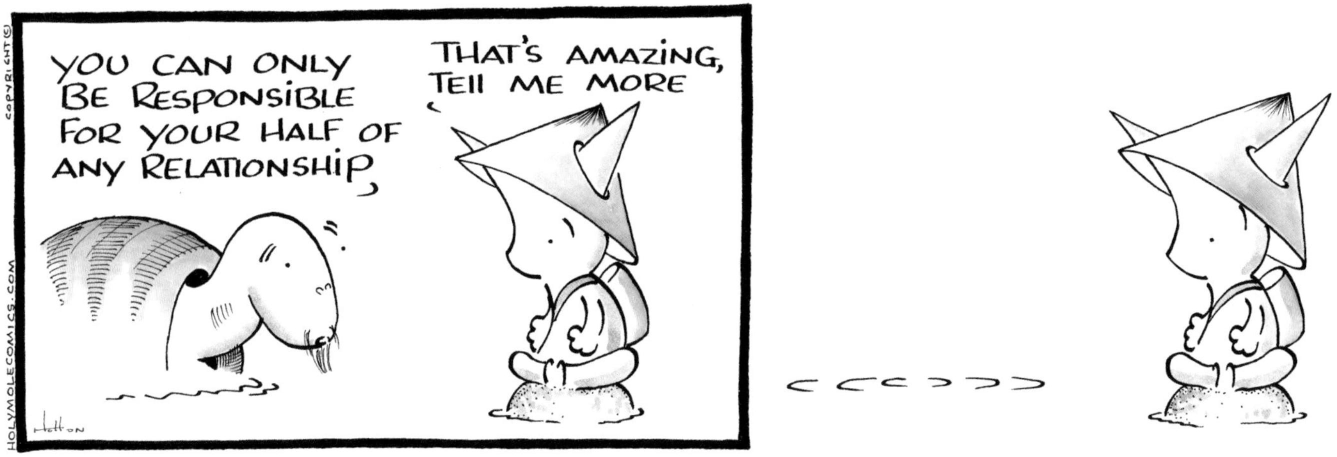
YOU CAN ONLY BE RESPONSIBLE FOR YOUR HALF OF ANY RELATIONSHIP,
THAT'S AMAZING, TEll ME MORE
COPYRIGHT ©
HOLYMOLECOMICS.COM

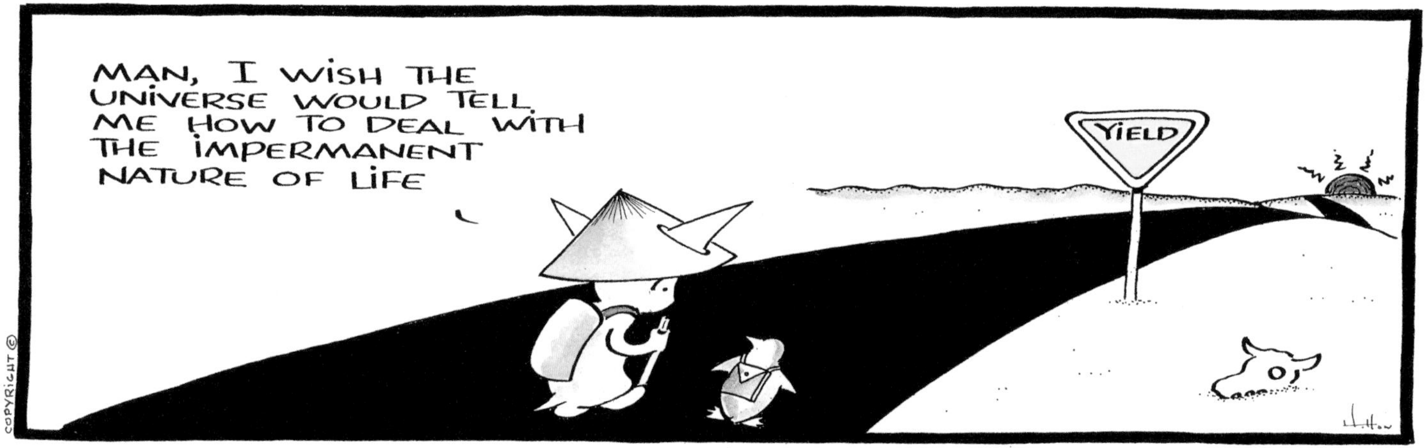
MAN, I WISH THE UNIVERSE WOULD TELL ME HOW TO DEAL WITH THE IMPERMANENT NATURE OF LIFE
YIELD
COPYRIGHT ©

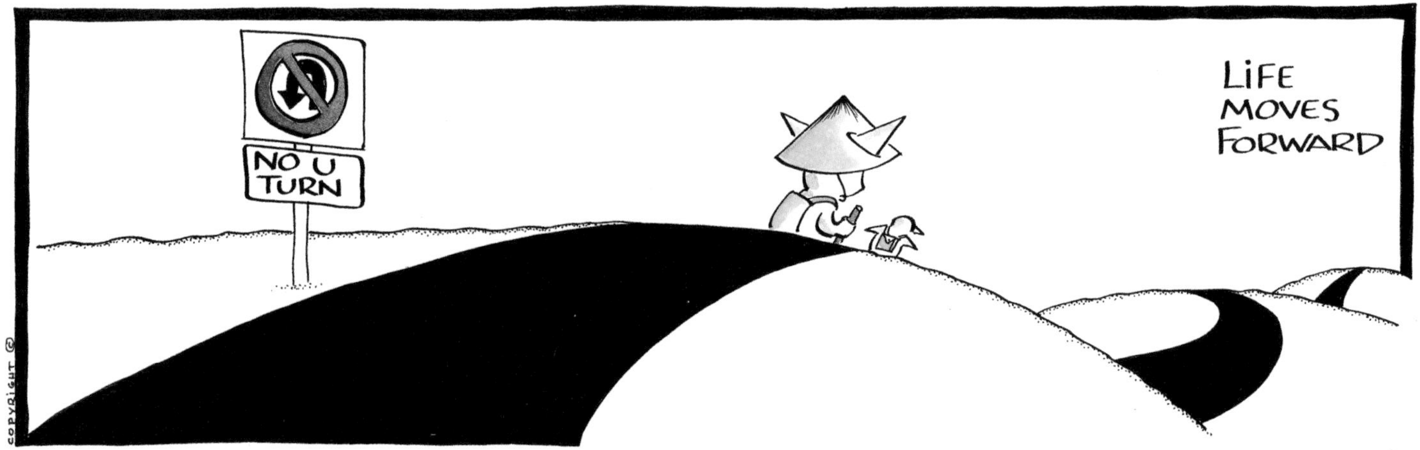
NO U TURN
LIFE MOVES FORWARD
COPYRIGHT ©

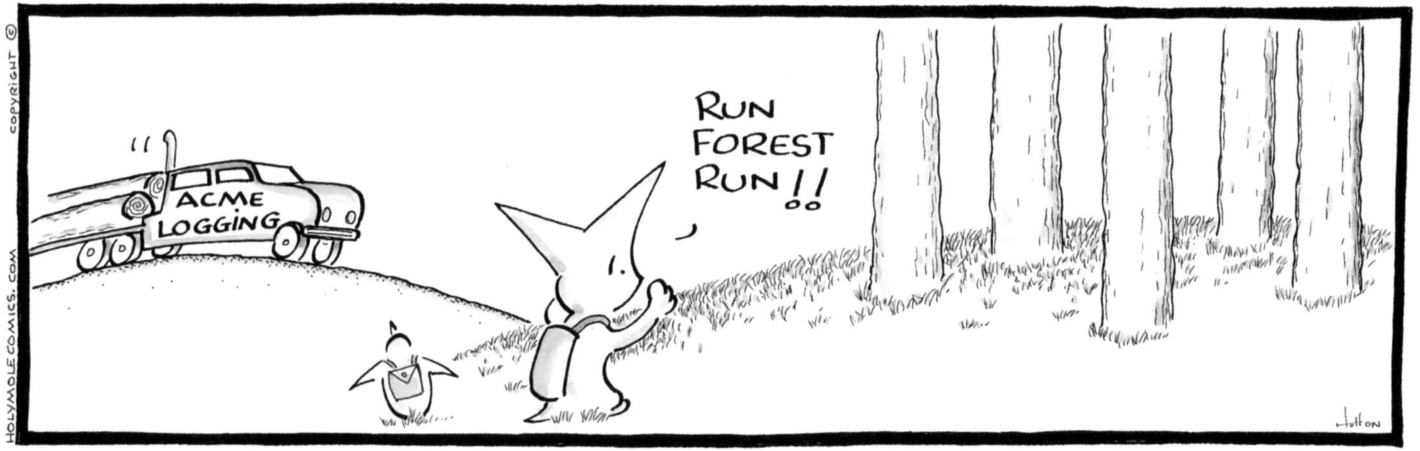
HOLYMOLECOMICS.COM COPYRIGHT ©
ACME LOGGING
RUN FOREST RUN!!

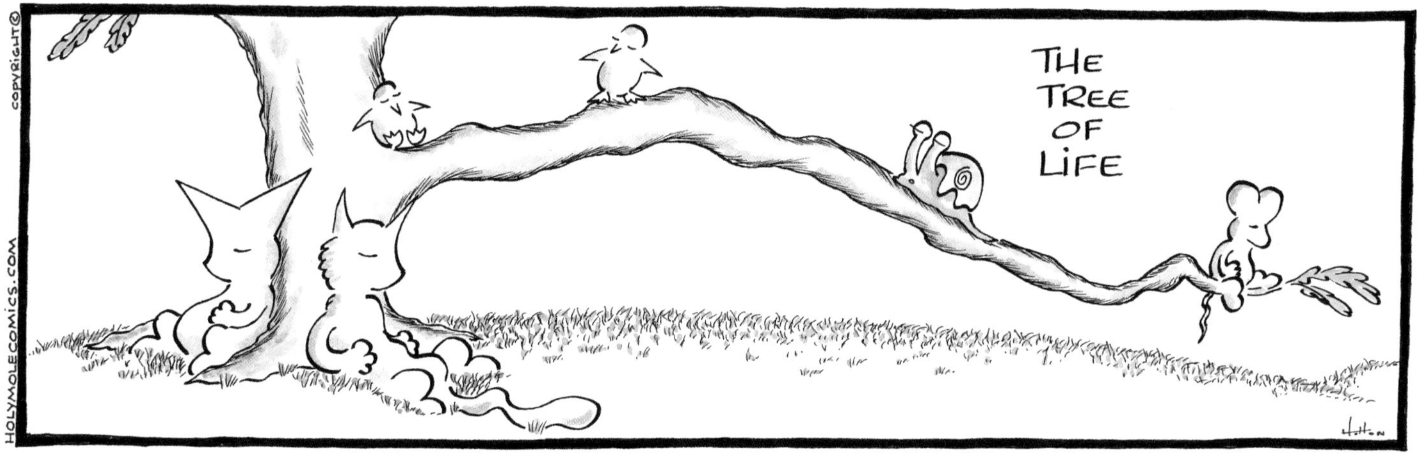
HOLYMOLECOMICS.COM COPYRIGHT ©
THE TREE OF LIFE

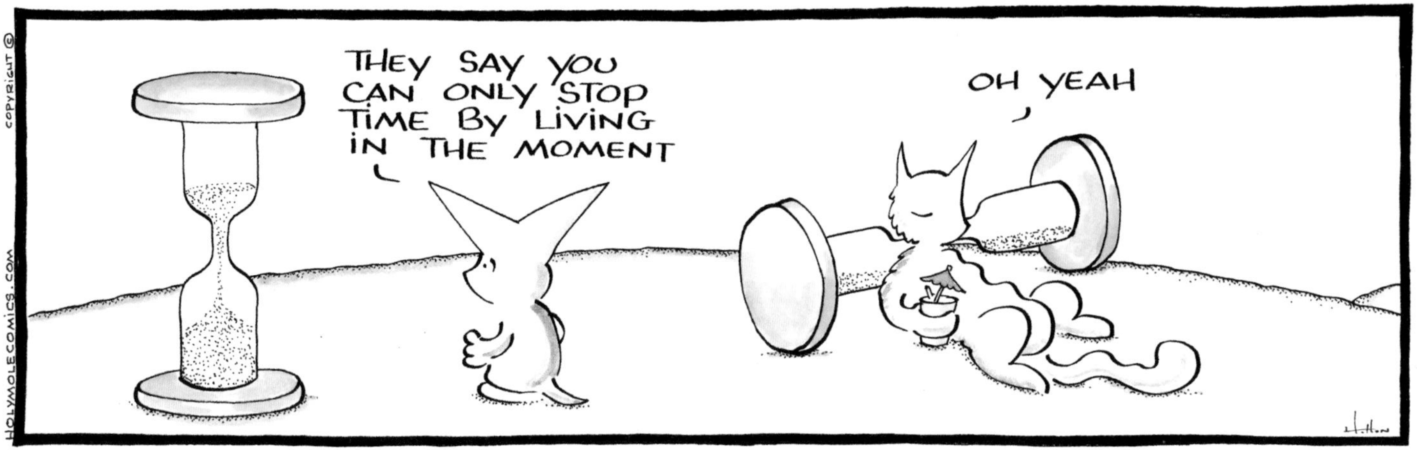
THEY SAY YOU CAN ONLY STOP TIME BY LIVING IN THE MOMENT
OH YEAH
HOLYMOLECOMICS.COM COPYRIGHT ©

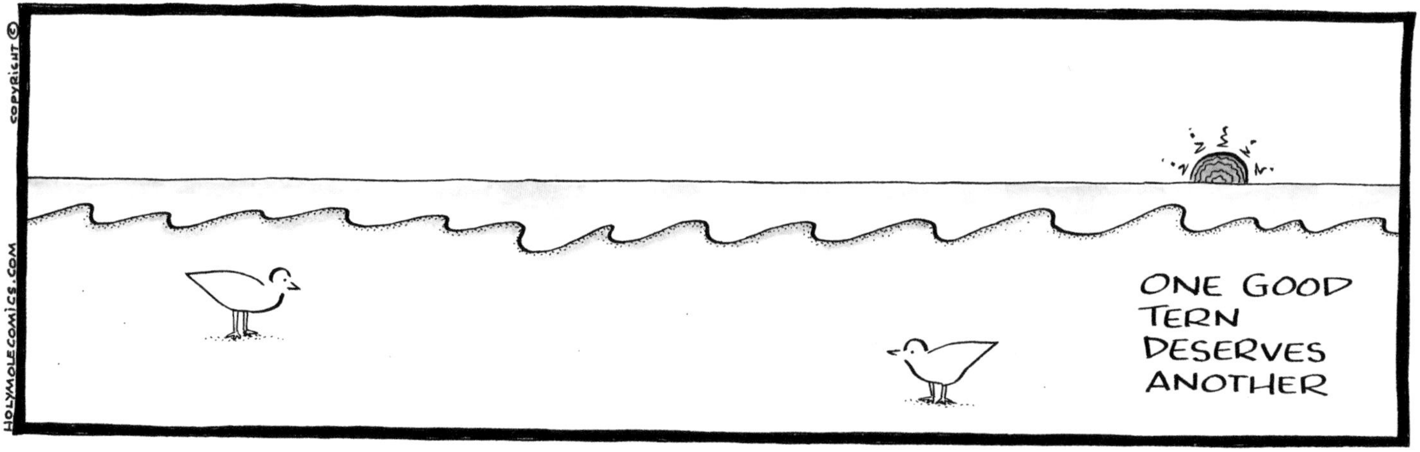
ONE GOOD TERN DESERVES ANOTHER
HOLYMOLECOMICS.COM COPYRIGHT ©

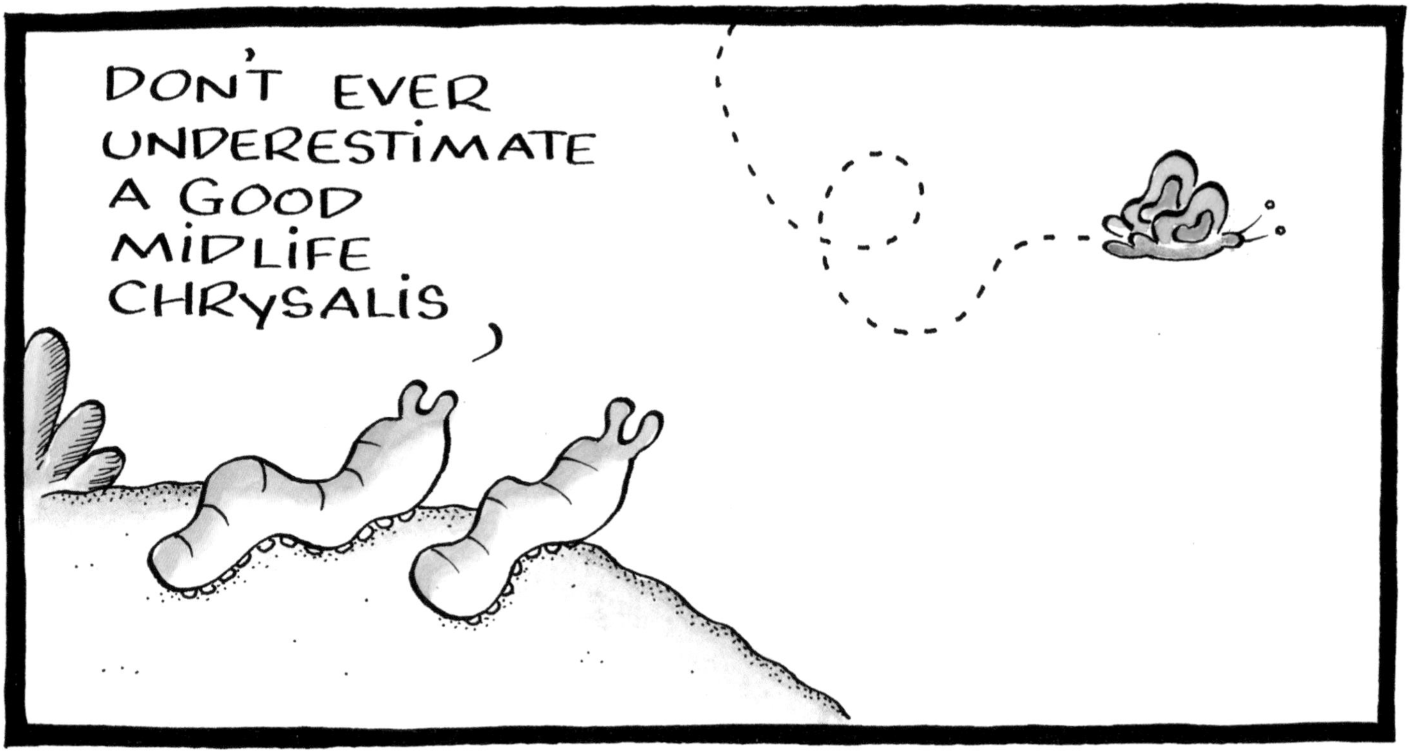
DON'T EVER UNDERESTIMATE A GOOD MIDLIFE CHRYSALIS

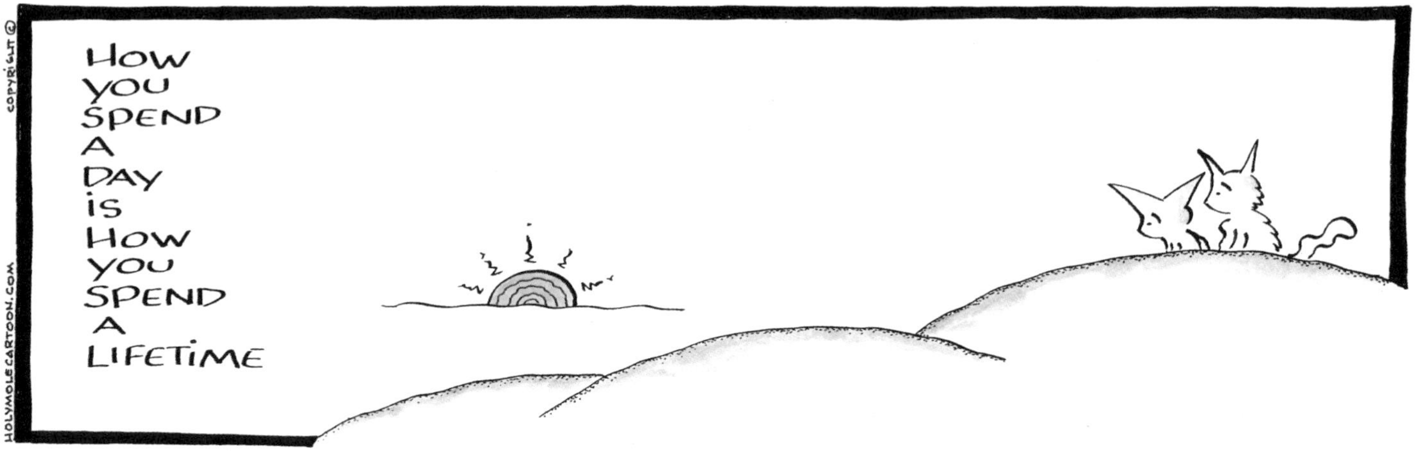
HOW YOU SPEND A DAY IS HOW YOU SPEND A LIFETIME
COPYRIGHT ©
HOLYMOLECARTOON.COM

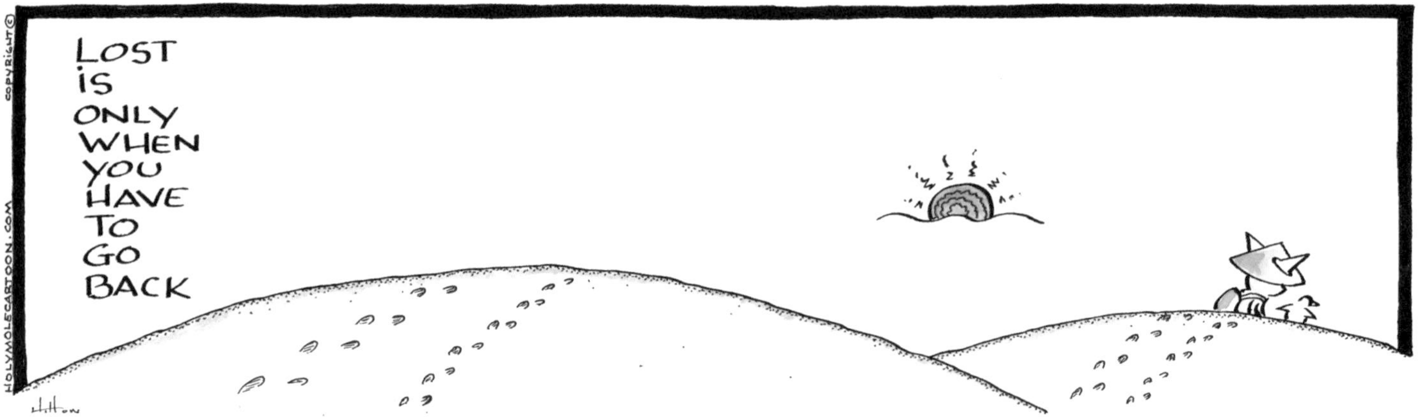
LOST IS ONLY WHEN YOU HAVE TO GO BACK
COPYRIGHT ©
HOLYMOLECARTOON.COM

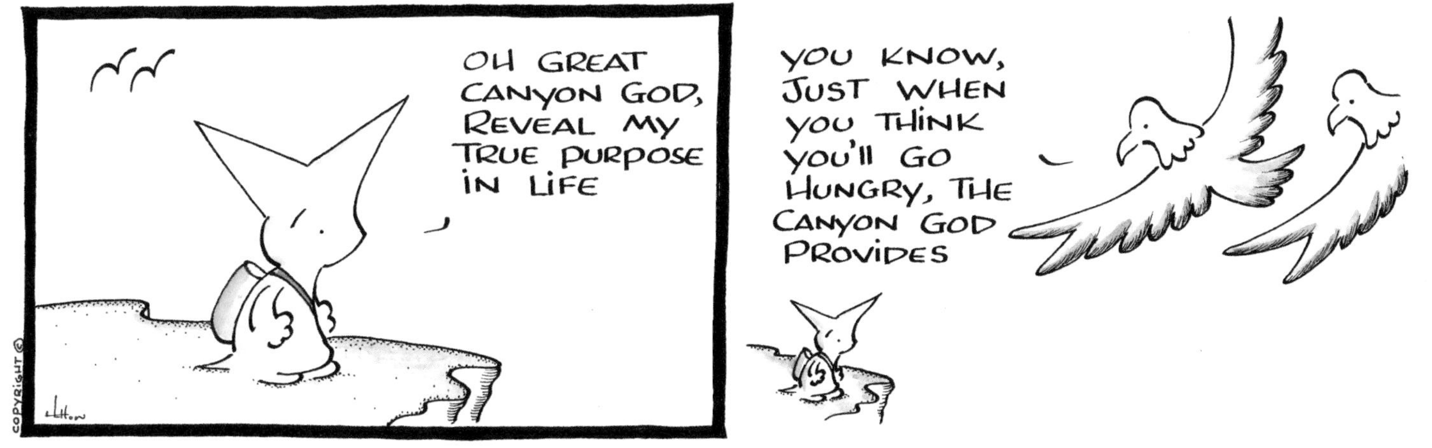
OH GREAT CANYON GOD, REVEAL MY TRUE PURPOSE IN LIFE
YOU KNOW, JUST WHEN YOU THINK YOU'LL GO HUNGRY, THE CANYON GOD PROVIDES
COPYRIGHT ©

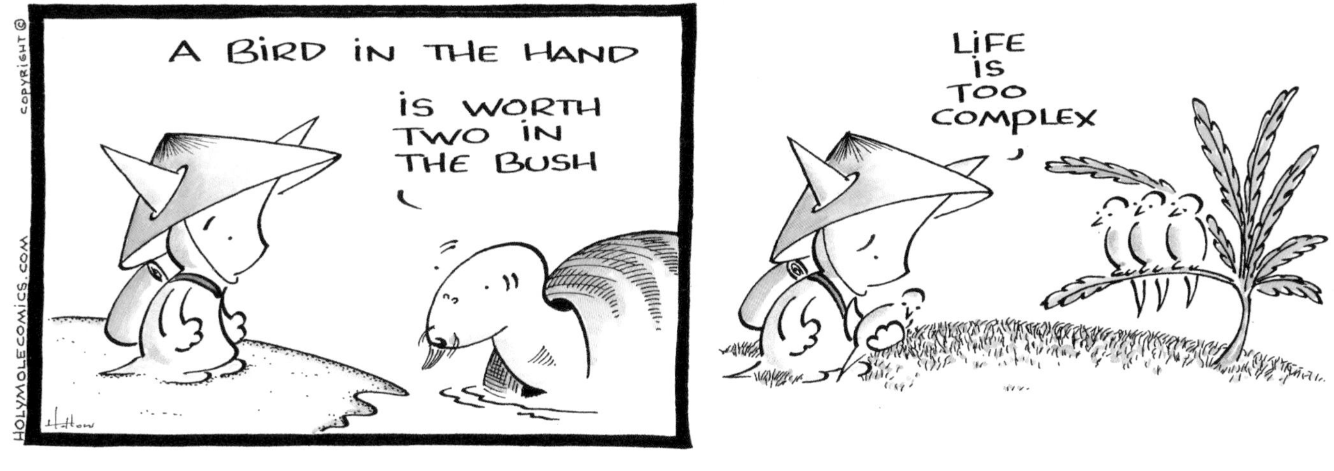
A BIRD IN THE HAND
IS WORTH TWO IN THE BUSH
LIFE IS TOO COMPLEX
COPYRIGHT ©
HOLYMOLECOMICS.COM

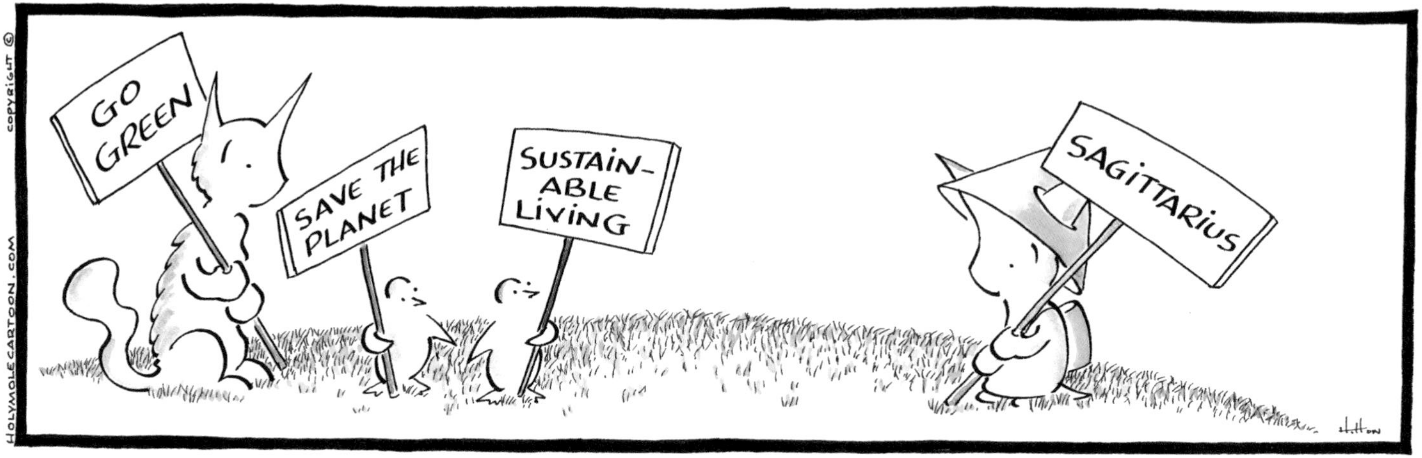
GO GREEN
SAVE THE PLANET
SUSTAIN-ABLE LIVING
SAGITTARIUS
HOLYMOLECARTOON.COM COPYRIGHT ©

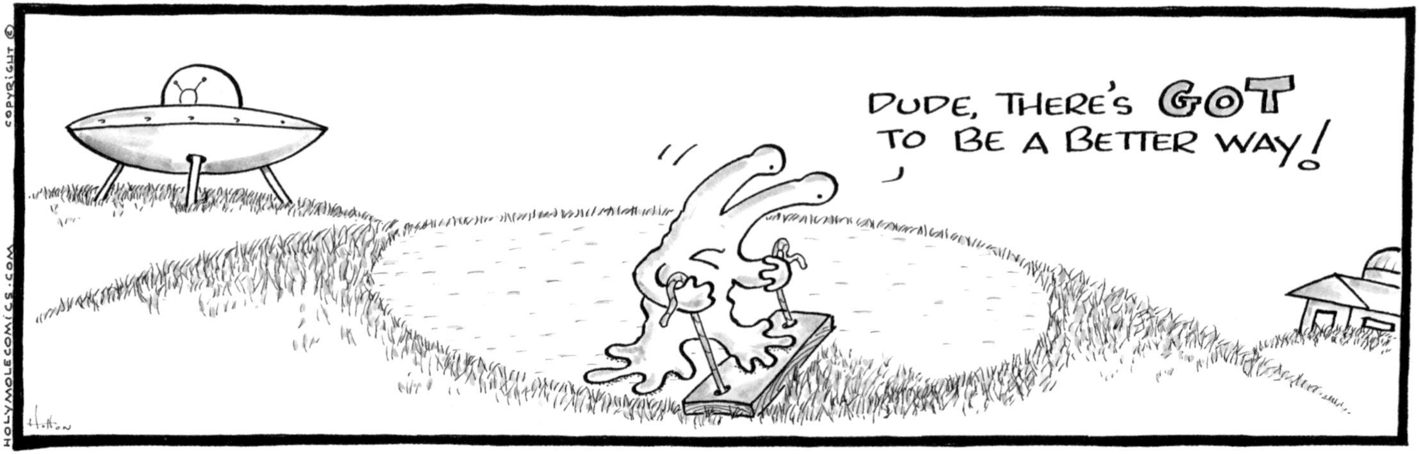
DUDE, THERE'S GOT TO BE A BETTER WAY!
HOLYMOLECOMICS.COM COPYRIGHT ©

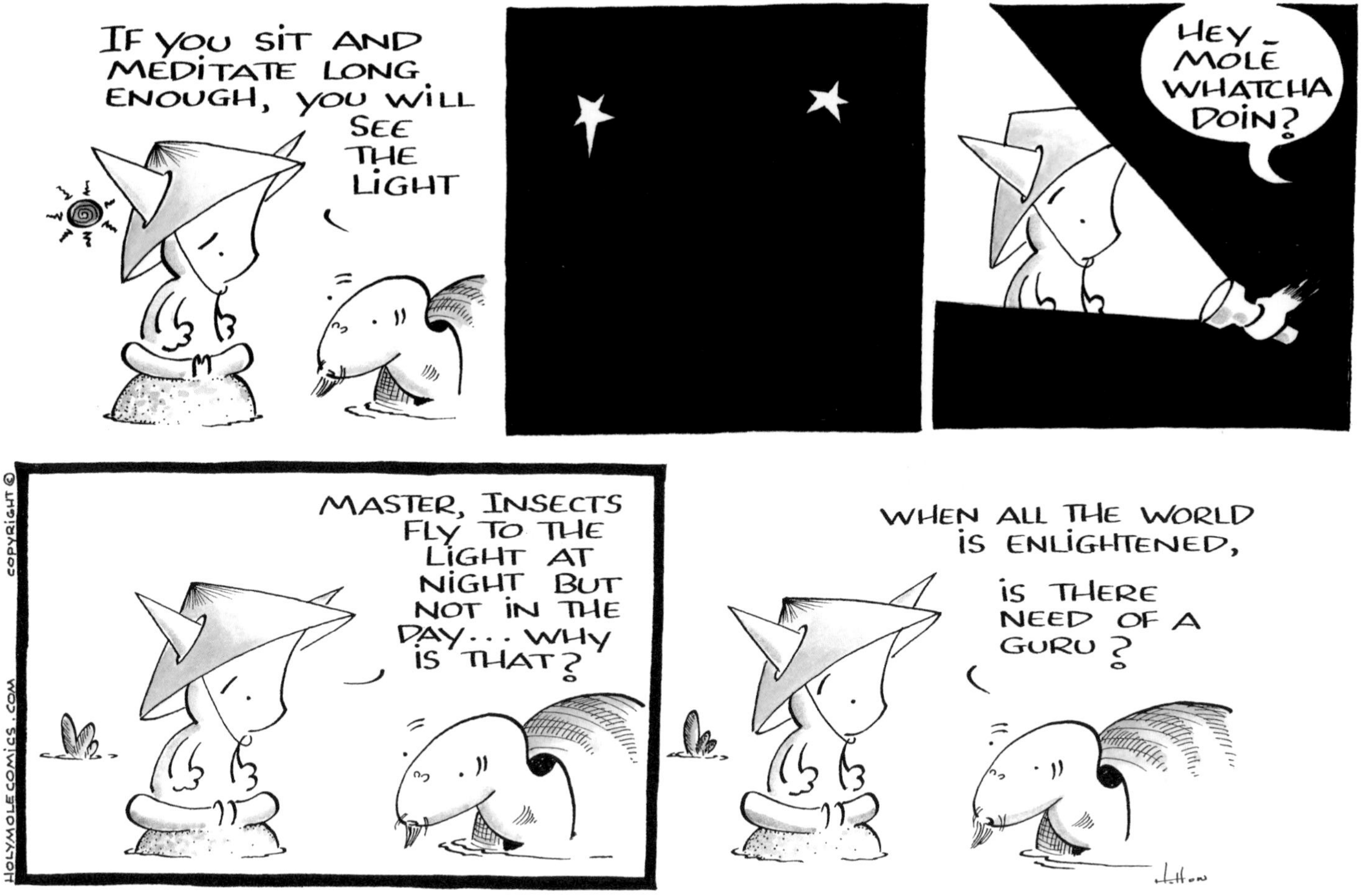
IF YOU SIT AND MEDITATE LONG ENOUGH, YOU WILL SEE THE LIGHT
HEY - MOLE WHATCHA DOIN?
MASTER, INSECTS FLY TO THE LIGHT AT NIGHT BUT NOT IN THE DAY... WHY IS THAT?
WHEN ALL THE WORLD IS ENLIGHTENED,
IS THERE NEED OF A GURU?
HOLYMOLECOMICS.COM COPYRIGHT ©

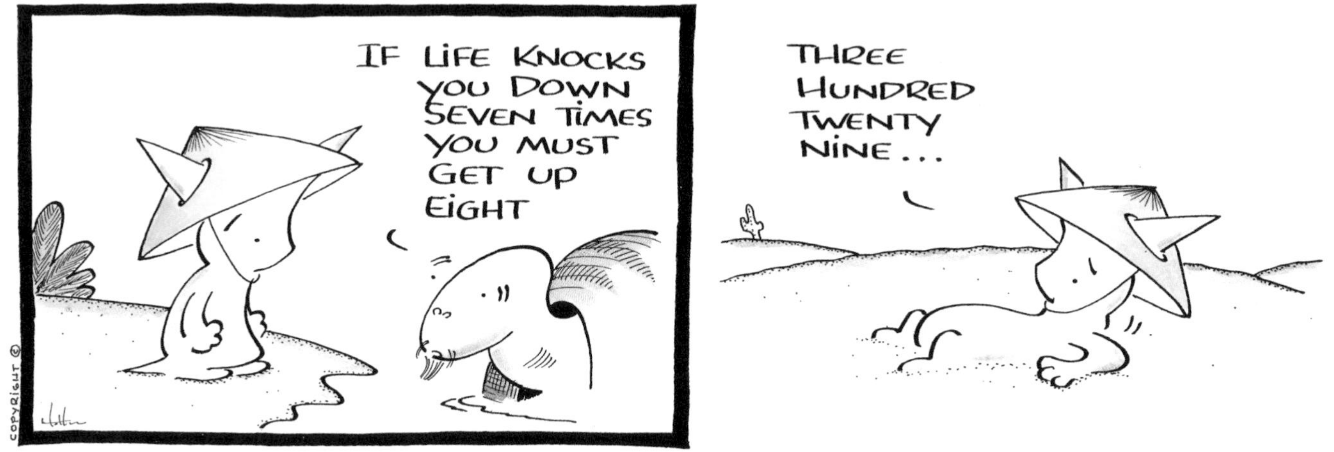
COPYRIGHT ©
IF LIFE KNOCKS YOU DOWN SEVEN TIMES YOU MUST GET UP EIGHT
THREE HUNDRED TWENTY NINE...

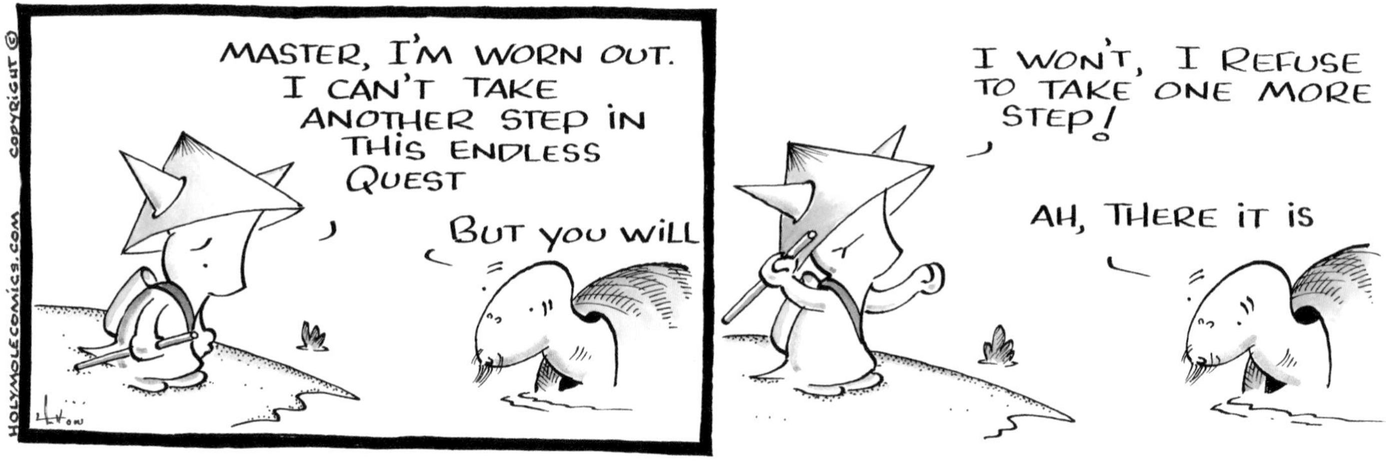
HOLYMOLECOMICS.COM COPYRIGHT ©
MASTER, I'M WORN OUT. I CAN'T TAKE ANOTHER STEP IN THIS ENDLESS QUEST
BUT YOU WILL
I WON'T, I REFUSE TO TAKE ONE MORE STEP!
AH, THERE IT IS

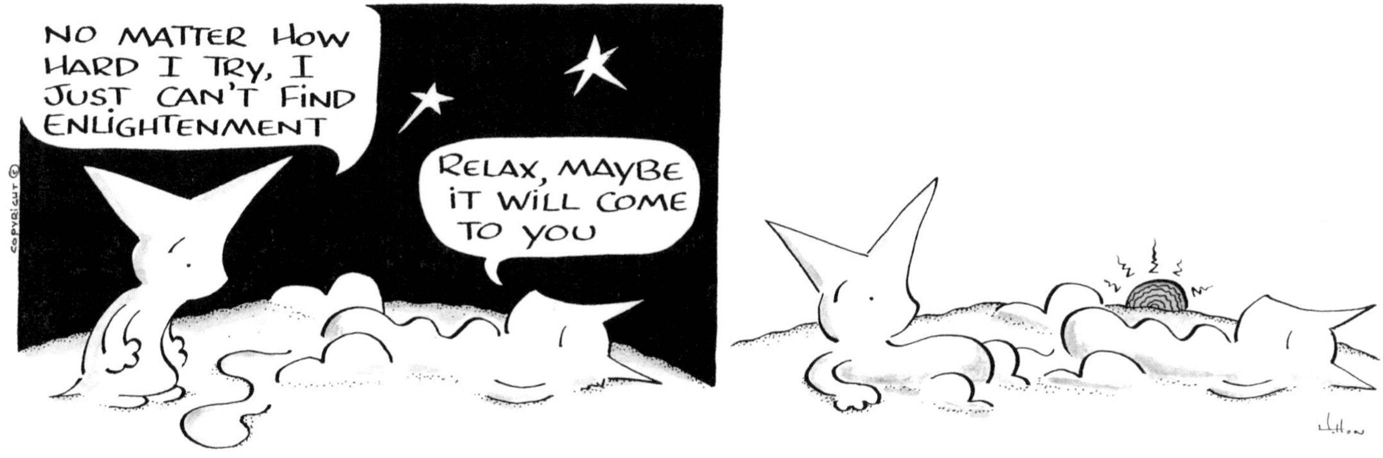
COPYRIGHT ©
NO MATTER HOW HARD I TRY, I JUST CAN'T FIND ENLIGHTENMENT
RELAX, MAYBE IT WILL COME TO YOU

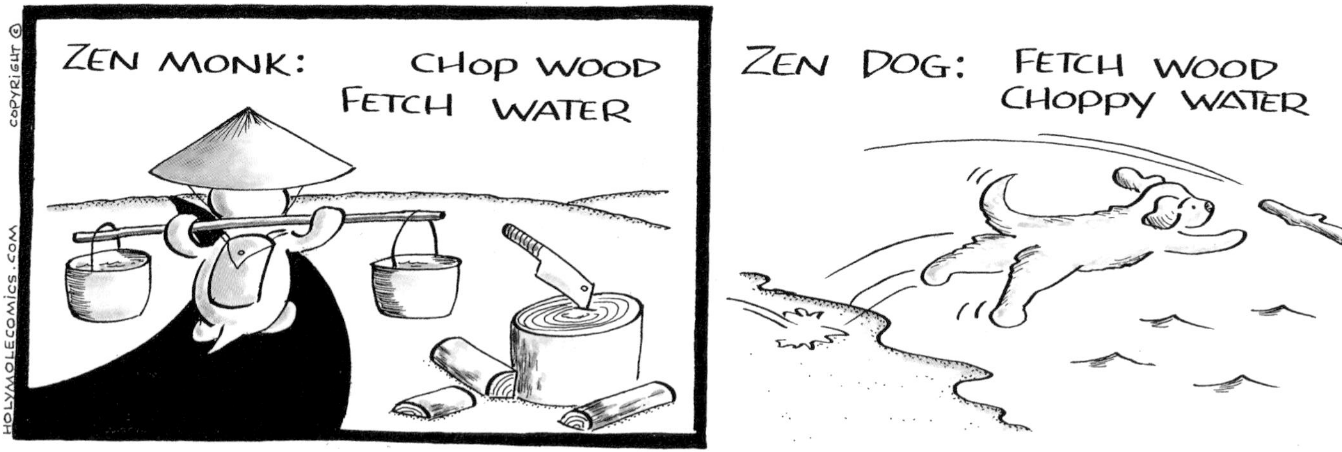
HOLYMOLECOMICS.COM COPYRIGHT ©
ZEN MONK: CHOP WOOD FETCH WATER
ZEN DOG: FETCH WOOD CHOPPY WATER

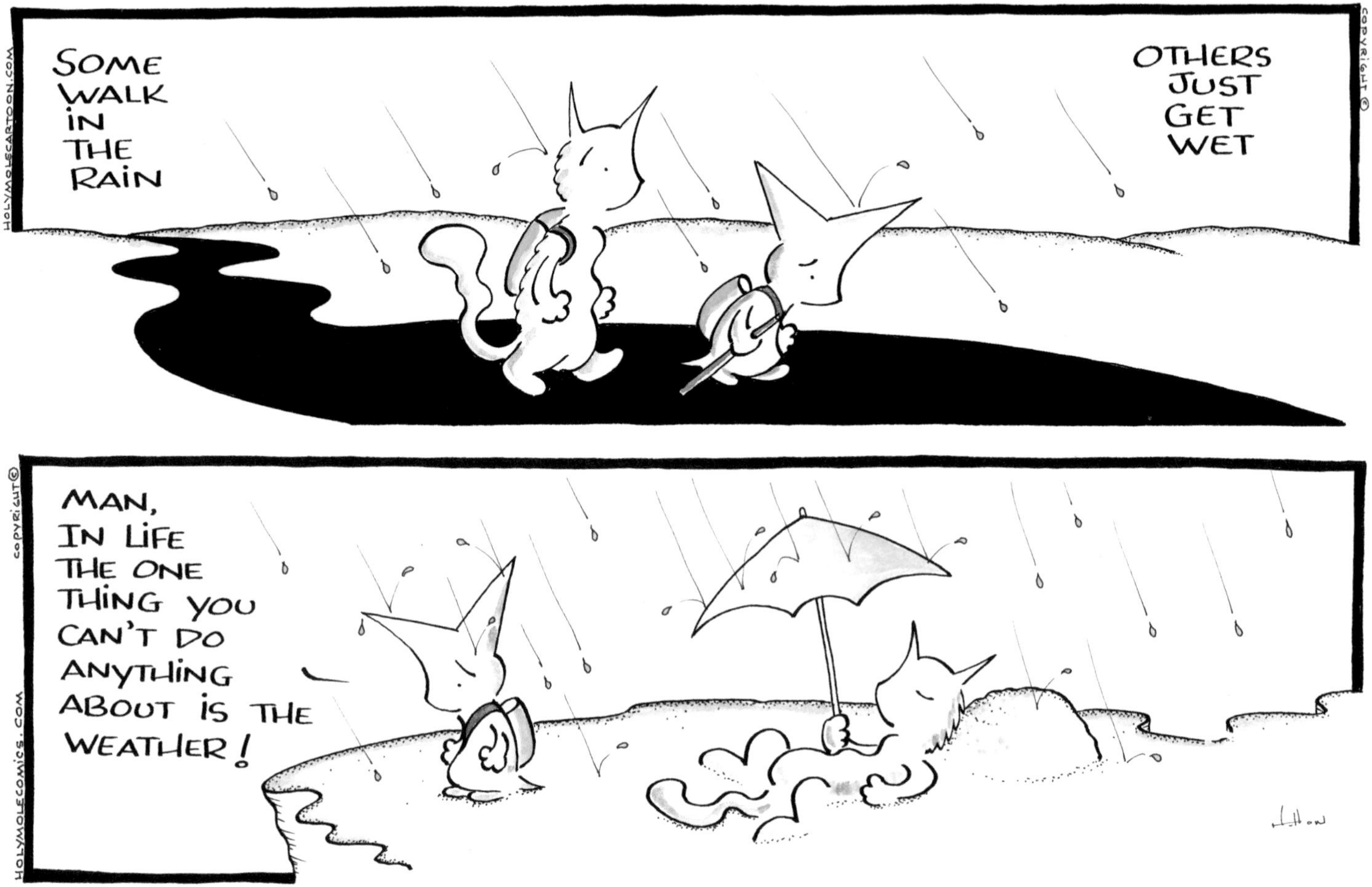
HOLYMOLECARTOON.COM
SOME WALK IN THE RAIN
OTHERS JUST GET WET
COPYRIGHT ©
COPYRIGHT ©
HOLYMOLECOMICS.COM
MAN, IN LIFE THE ONE THING YOU CAN'T DO ANYTHING ABOUT IS THE WEATHER!

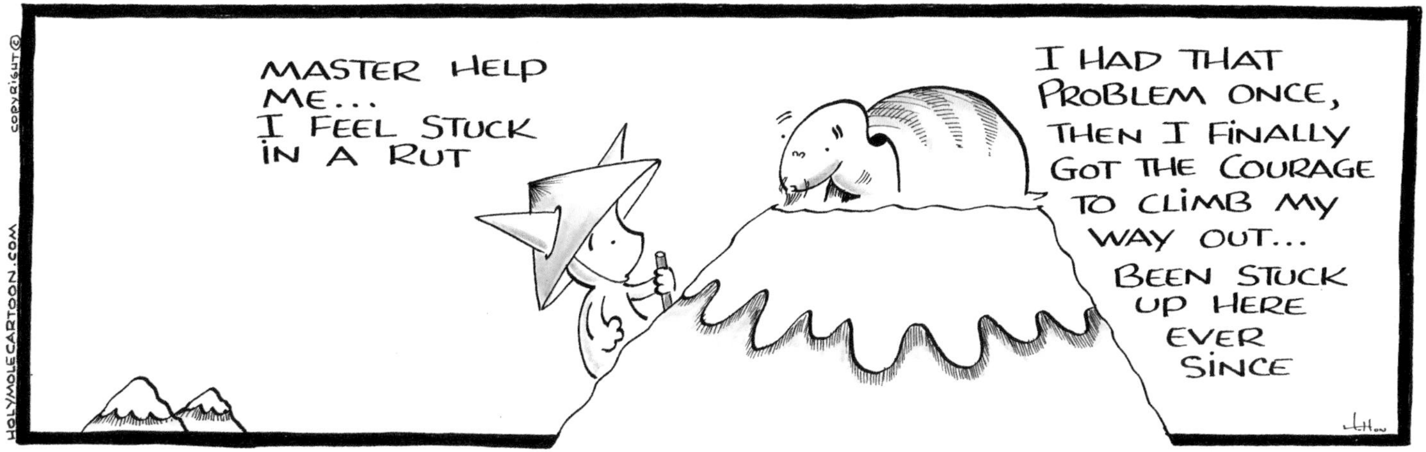
MASTER HELP ME... I FEEL STUCK IN A RUT
I HAD THAT PROBLEM ONCE, THEN I FINALLY GOT THE COURAGE TO CLIMB MY WAY OUT...
BEEN STUCK UP HERE EVER SINCE
HOLYMOLECARTOON.COM COPYRIGHT ©

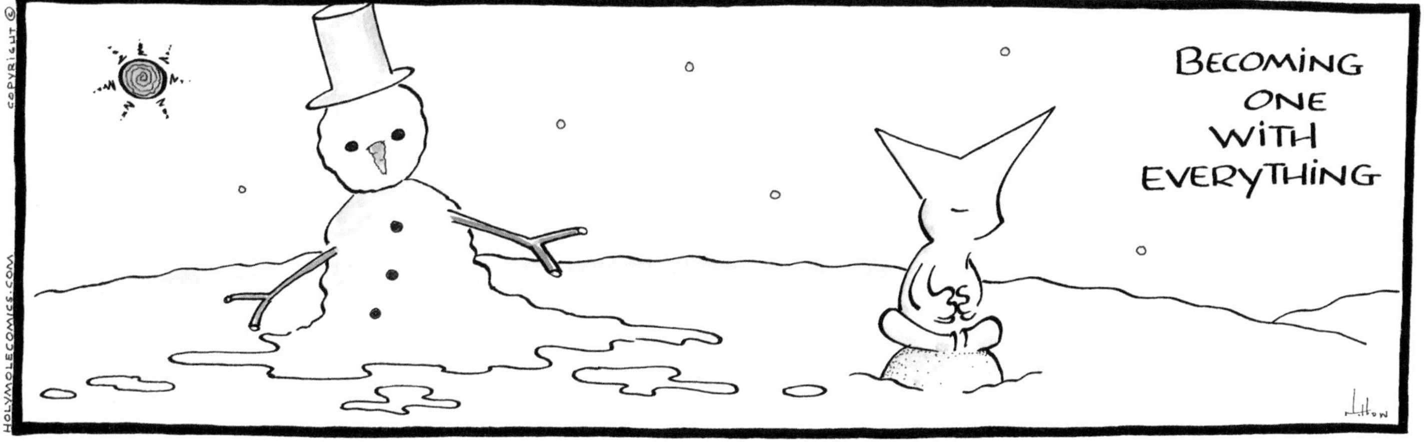
BECOMING ONE WITH EVERYTHING
HOLYMOLECOMICS.COM COPYRIGHT ©

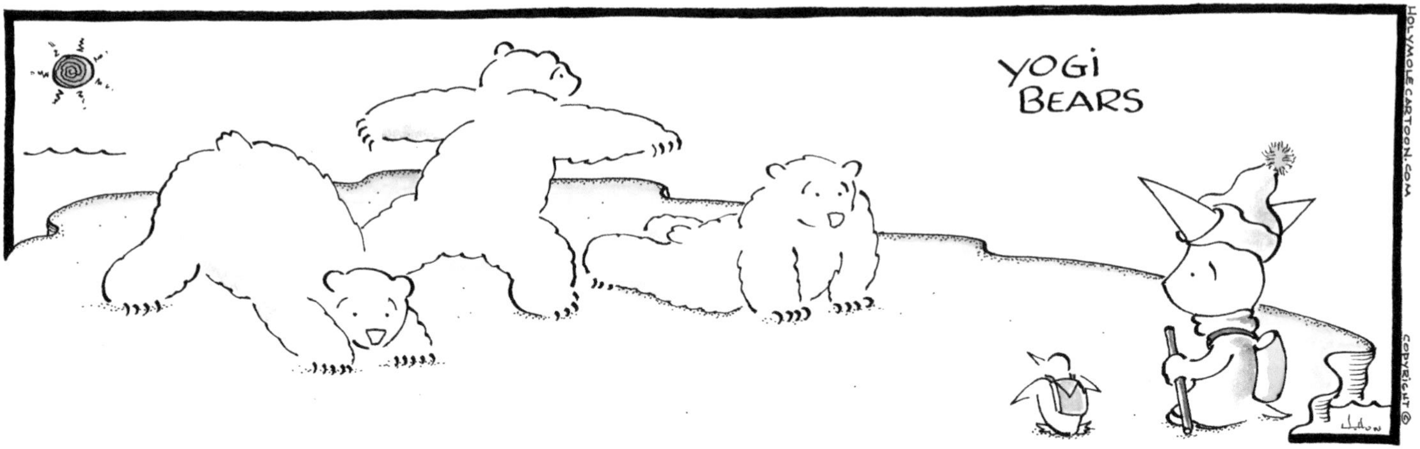
YOGI BEARS
HOLYMOLECARTOON.COM
COPYRIGHT ©

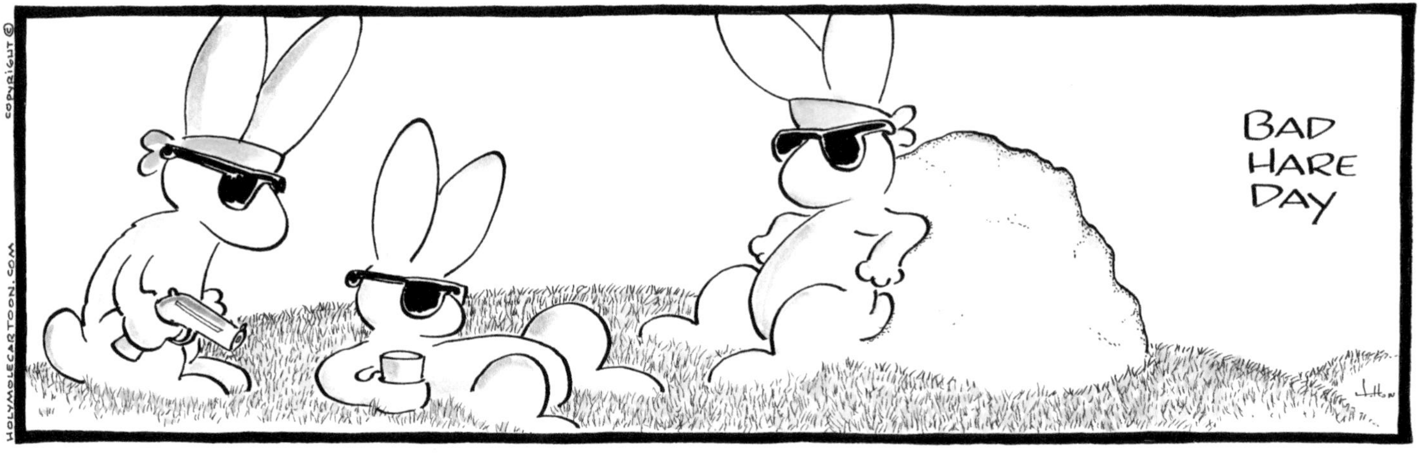
BAD HARE DAY
COPYRIGHT ©
HOLYMOLECARTOON.COM

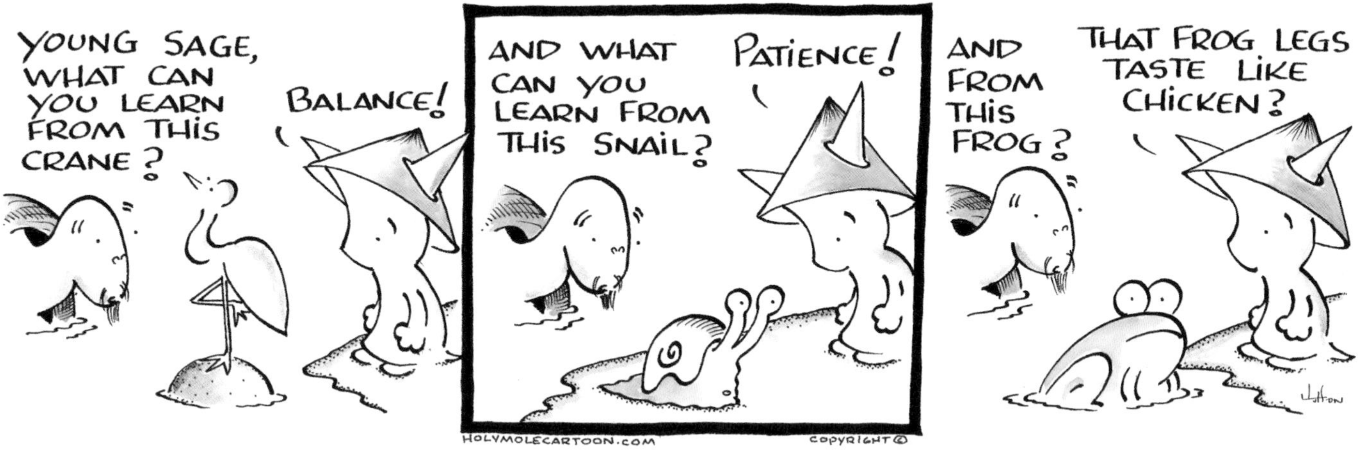
YOUNG SAGE, WHAT CAN YOU LEARN FROM THIS CRANE?
BALANCE!
AND WHAT CAN YOU LEARN FROM THIS SNAIL?
PATIENCE!
AND FROM THIS FROG?
THAT FROG LEGS TASTE LIKE CHICKEN?
HOLYMOLECARTOON.COM
COPYRIGHT ©

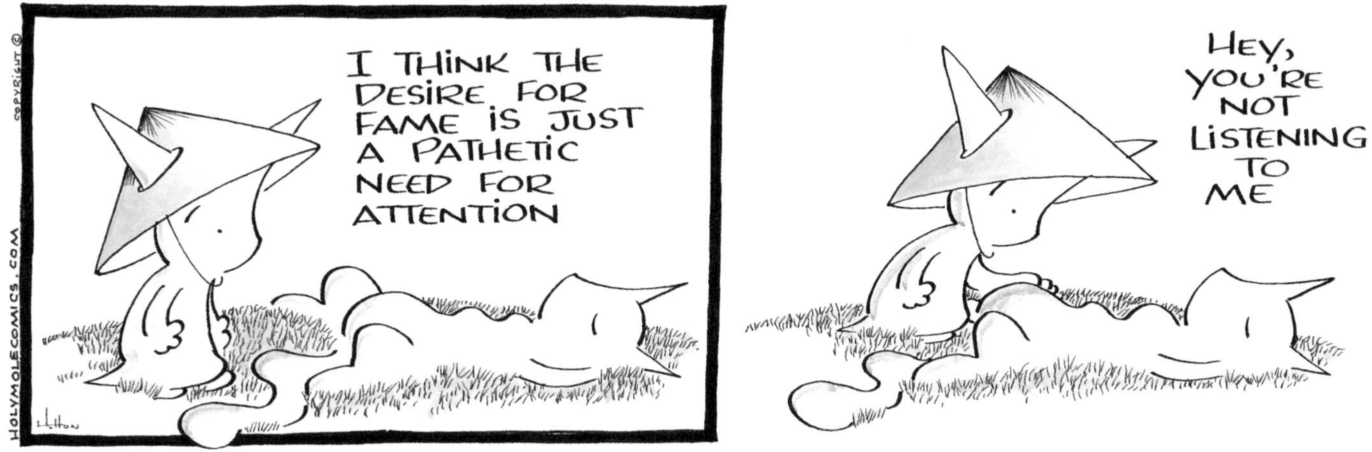
HOLYMOLECOMICS.COM
COPYRIGHT ©
I THINK THE DESIRE FOR FAME IS JUST A PATHETIC NEED FOR ATTENTION
HEY, YOU'RE NOT LISTENING TO ME

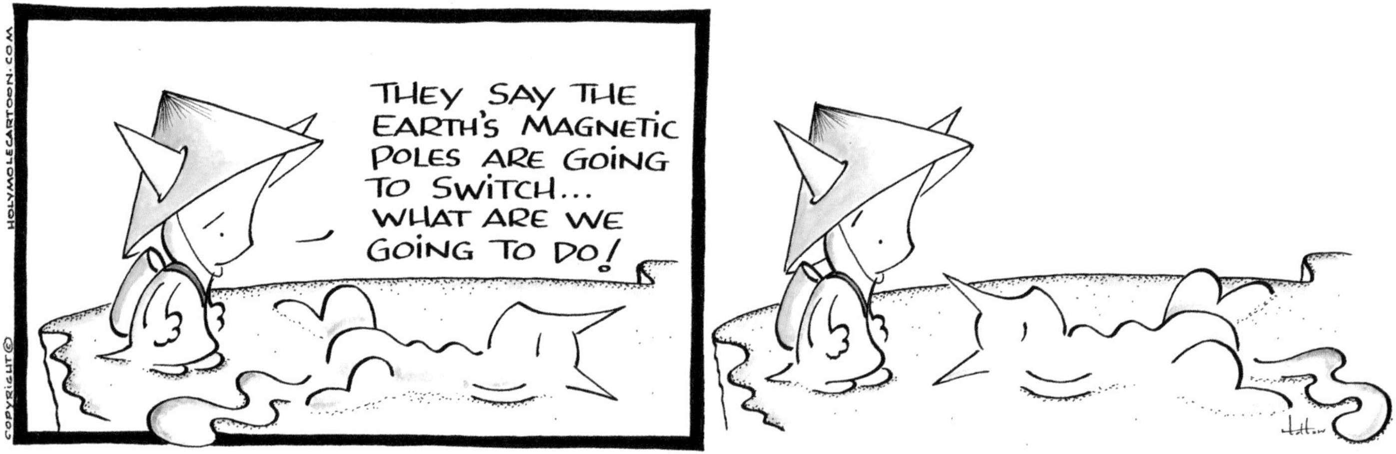
HOLYMOLECARTOON.COM
COPYRIGHT ©
THEY SAY THE EARTH'S MAGNETIC POLES ARE GOING TO SWITCH... WHAT ARE WE GOING TO DO!

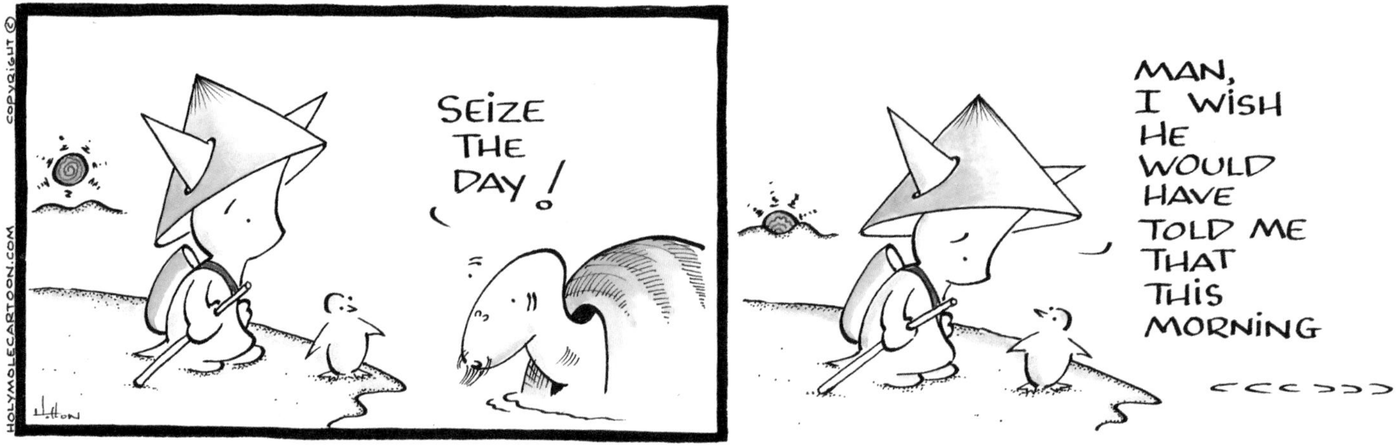
COPYRIGHT ©
HOLYMOLECARTOON.COM
SEIZE THE DAY!
MAN, I WISH HE WOULD HAVE TOLD ME THAT THIS MORNING

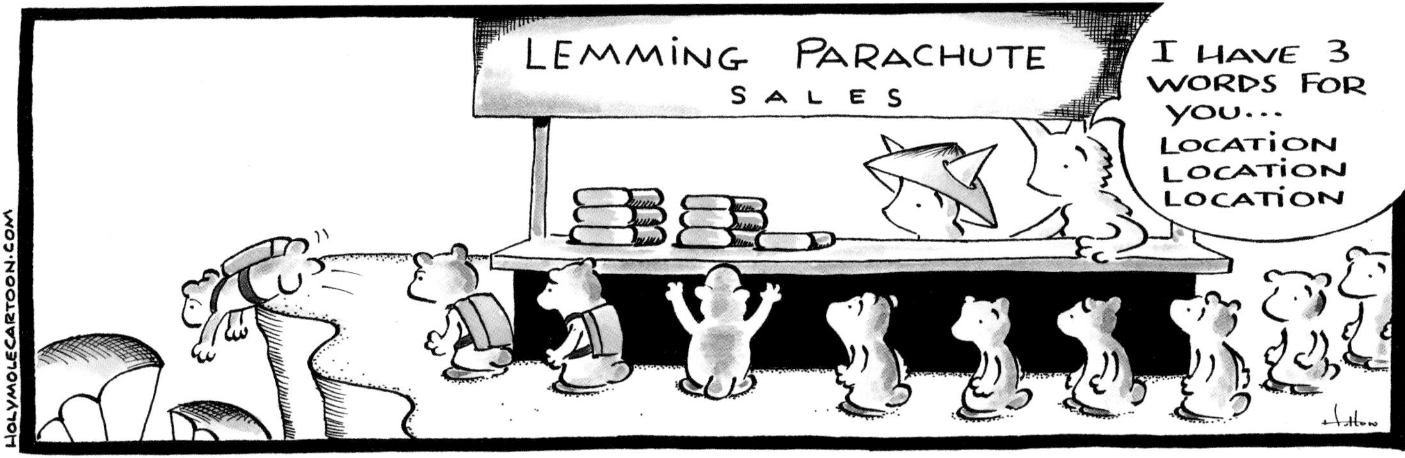
LEMMING PARACHUTE
SALES
I HAVE 3 WORDS FOR YOU... LOCATION LOCATION LOCATION
HOLYMOLECARTOON.COM
COPYRIGHT ©

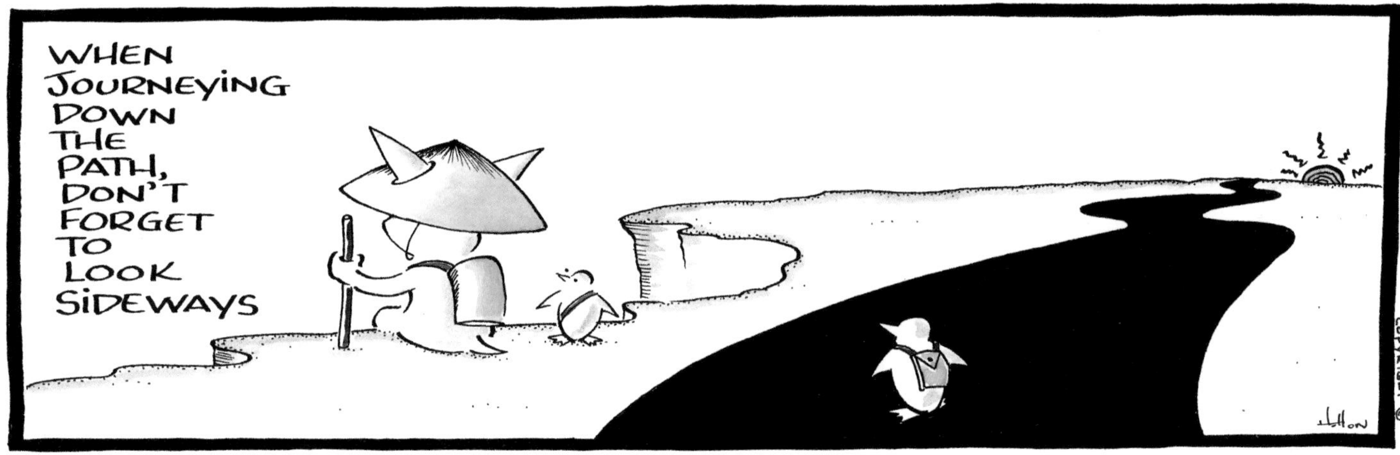
WHEN JOURNEYING DOWN THE PATH, DON'T FORGET TO LOOK SIDEWAYS
HOLYMOLECARTOON.COM
COPYRIGHT ©

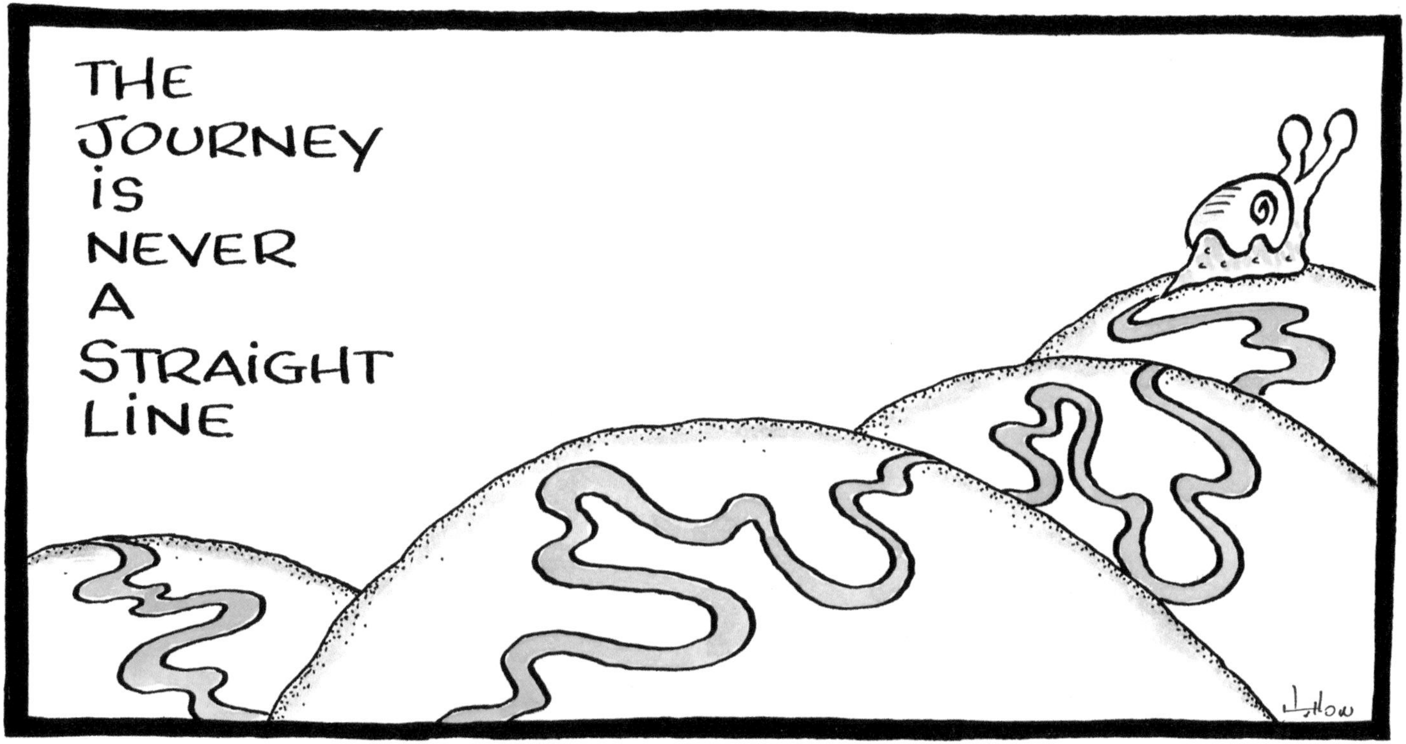
THE JOURNEY IS NEVER A STRAIGHT LINE

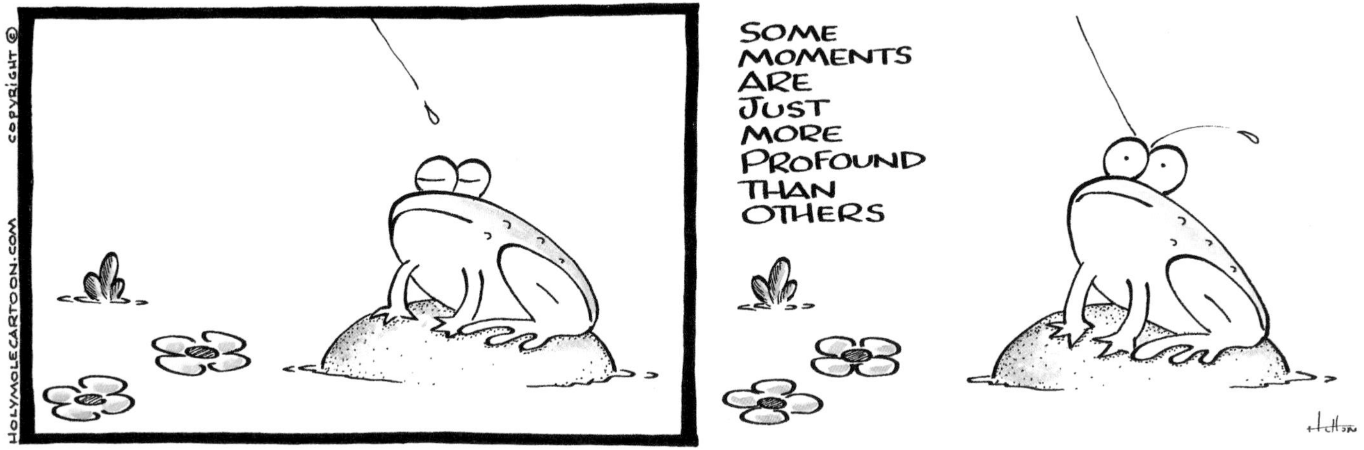
HOLYMOLECARTOON.COM COPYRIGHT ©
SOME MOMENTS ARE JUST MORE PROFOUND THAN OTHERS

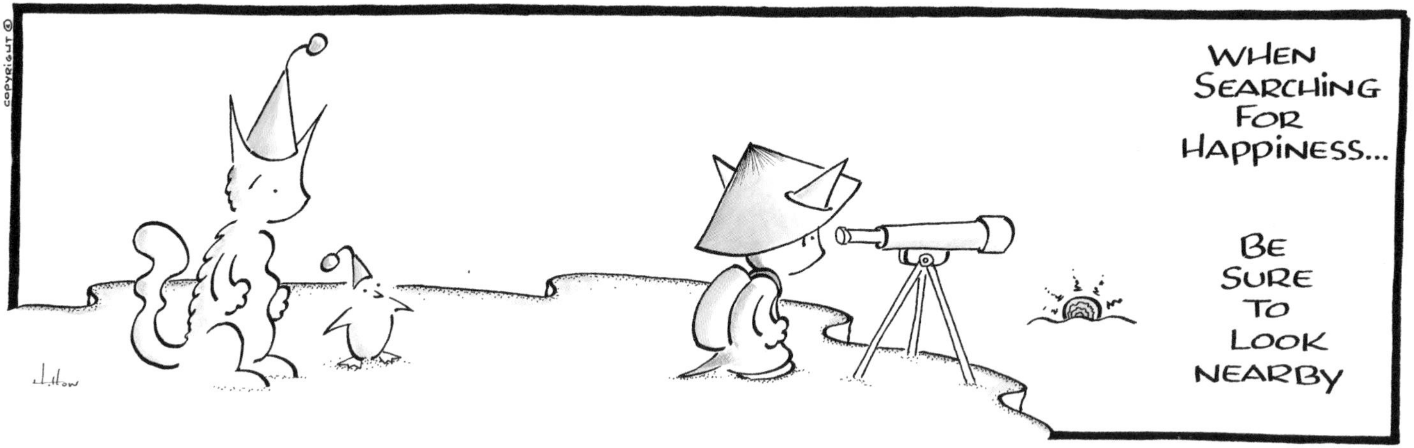
COPYRIGHT ©
WHEN SEARCHING FOR HAPPINESS...
BE SURE TO LOOK NEARBY

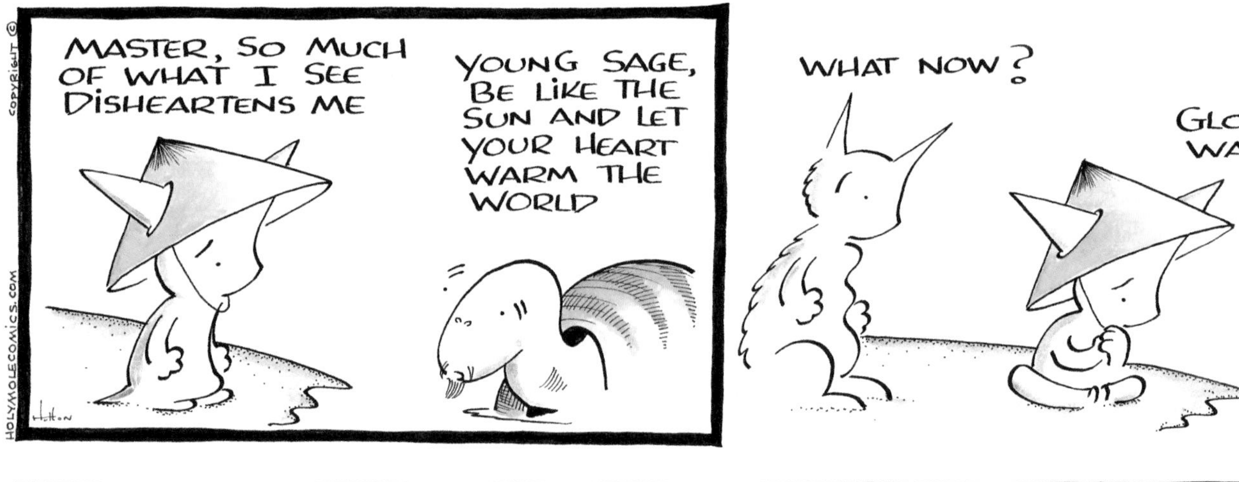
COPYRIGHT ©
HOLYMOLECOMICS.COM
MASTER, SO MUCH OF WHAT I SEE DISHEARTENS ME
YOUNG SAGE, BE LIKE THE SUN AND LET YOUR HEART WARM THE WORLD
WHAT NOW?
GLOBAL WARMING

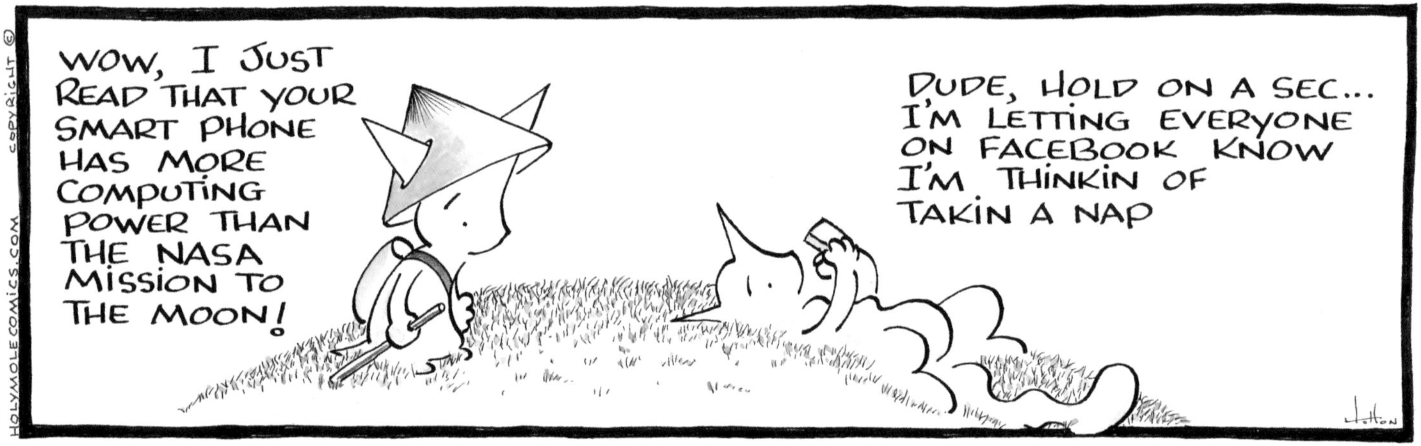
COPYRIGHT ©
HOLYMOLECOMICS.COM
WOW, I JUST READ THAT YOUR SMART PHONE HAS MORE COMPUTING POWER THAN THE NASA MISSION TO THE MOON!
DUDE, HOLD ON A SEC... I'M LETTING EVERYONE ON FACEBOOK KNOW I'M THINKIN OF TAKIN A NAP

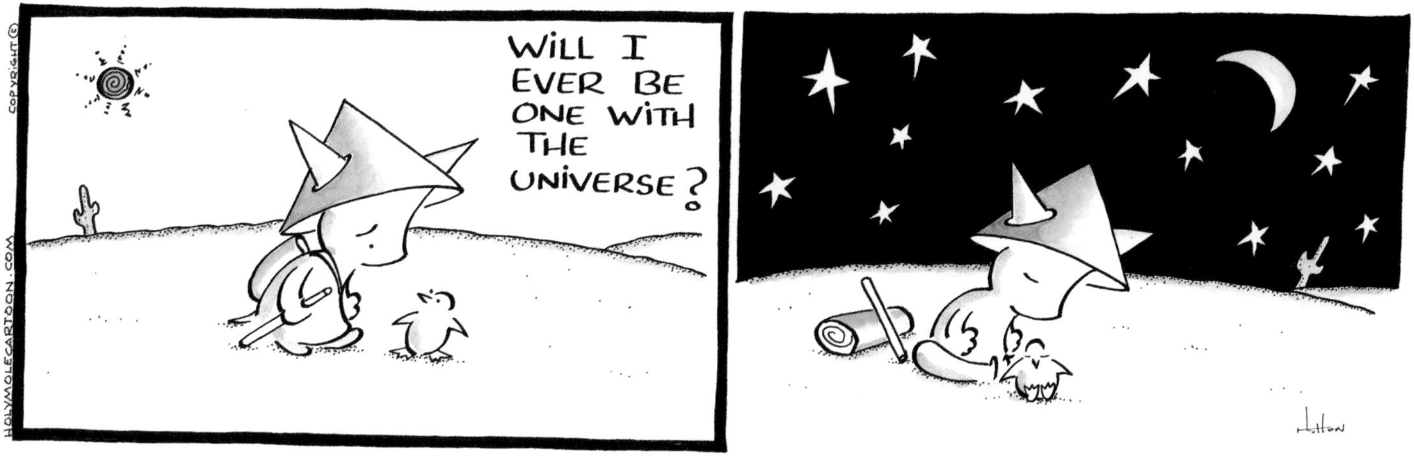
COPYRIGHT ©
HOLYMOLECARTOON.COM
WILL I EVER BE ONE WITH THE UNIVERSE?

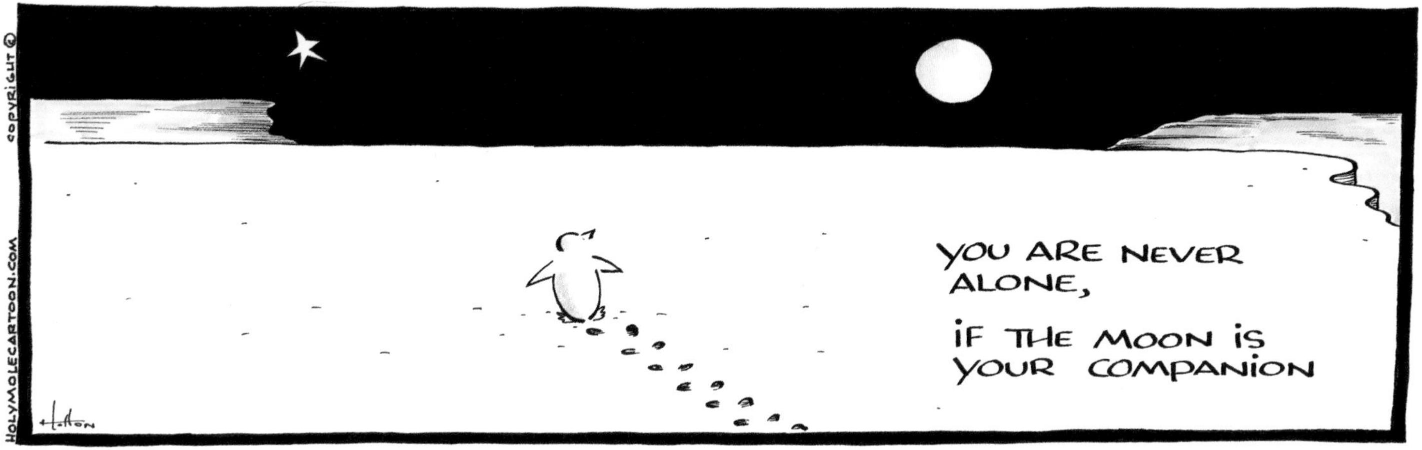
COPYRIGHT ©
HOLYMOLECARTOON.COM
YOU ARE NEVER ALONE,
IF THE MOON IS YOUR COMPANION

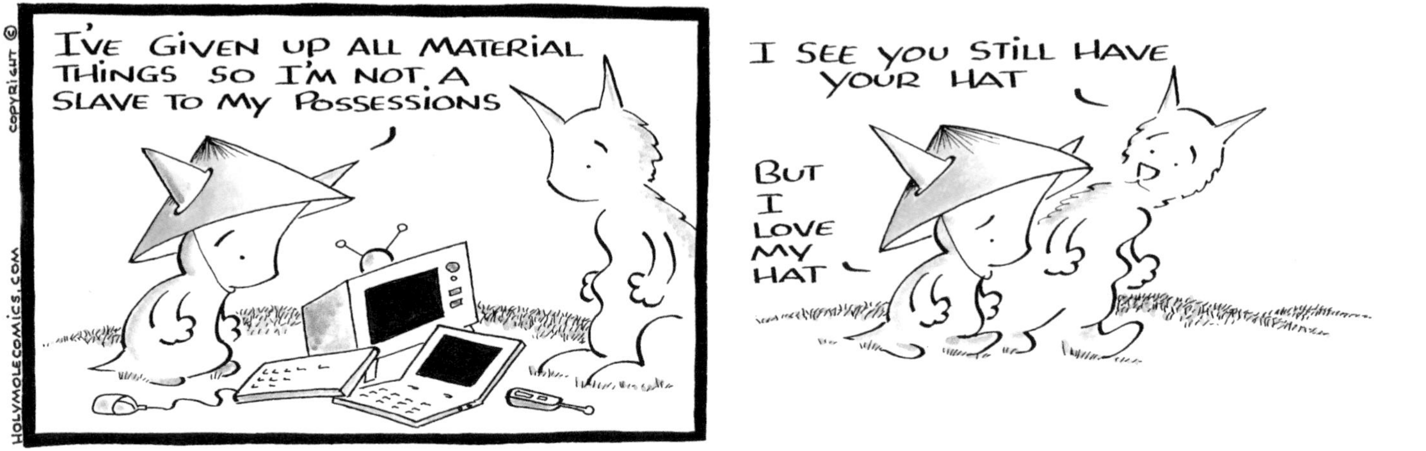
COPYRIGHT ©
HOLYMOLECOMICS.COM
I'VE GIVEN UP ALL MATERIAL THINGS SO I'M NOT A SLAVE TO MY POSSESSIONS
I SEE YOU STILL HAVE YOUR HAT
BUT I LOVE MY HAT

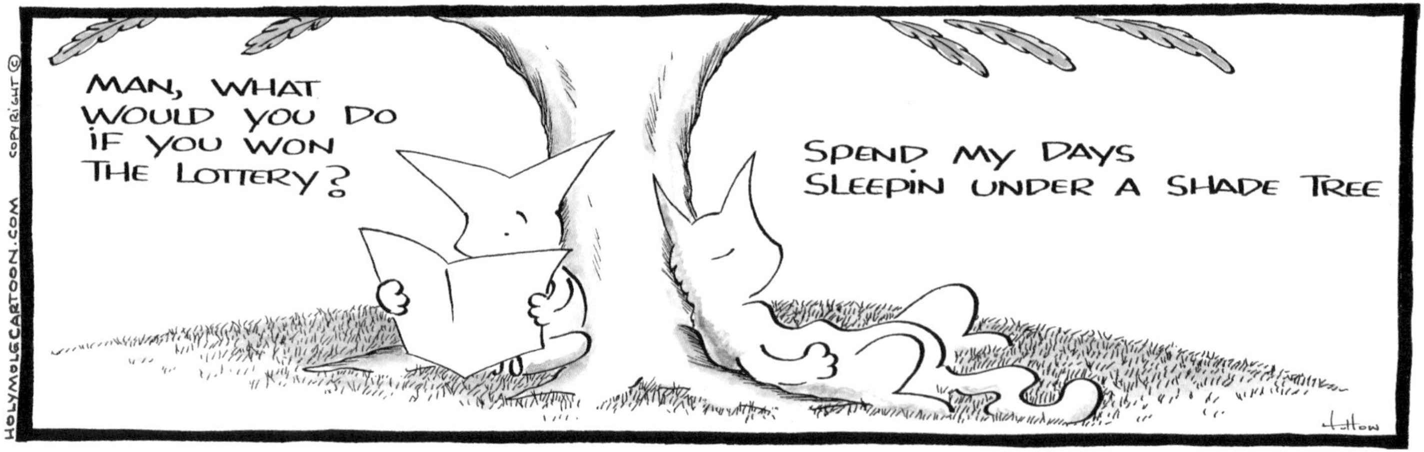
COPYRIGHT ©
HOLYMOLECARTOON.COM
MAN, WHAT WOULD YOU DO IF YOU WON THE LOTTERY?
SPEND MY DAYS SLEEPIN UNDER A SHADE TREE

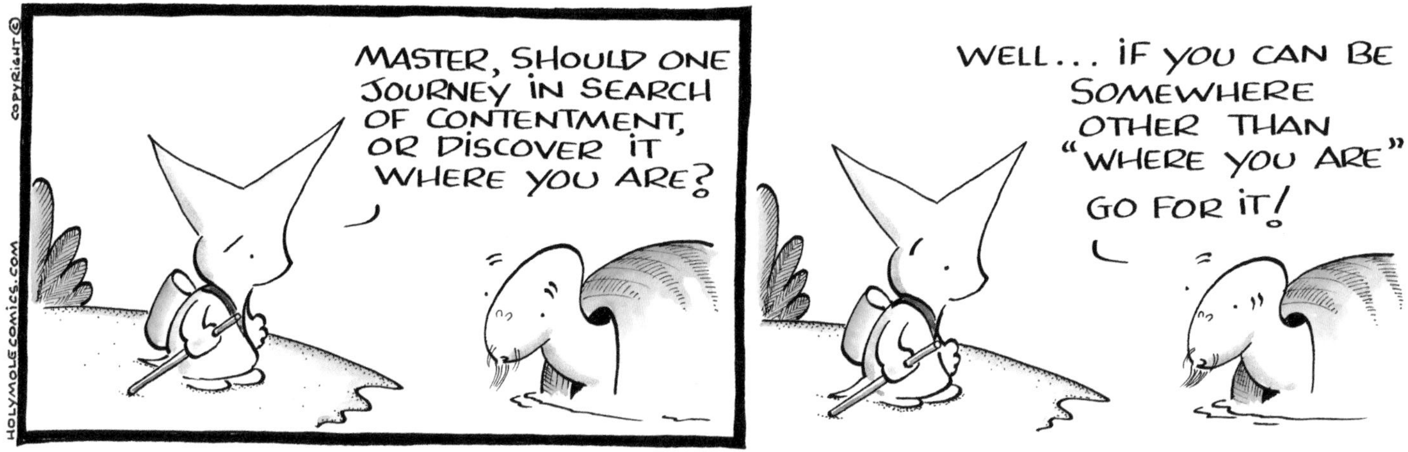
HOLYMOLECOMICS.COM COPYRIGHT ©
MASTER, SHOULD ONE JOURNEY IN SEARCH OF CONTENTMENT, OR DISCOVER IT WHERE YOU ARE?
WELL... IF YOU CAN BE SOMEWHERE OTHER THAN "WHERE YOU ARE" GO FOR IT!

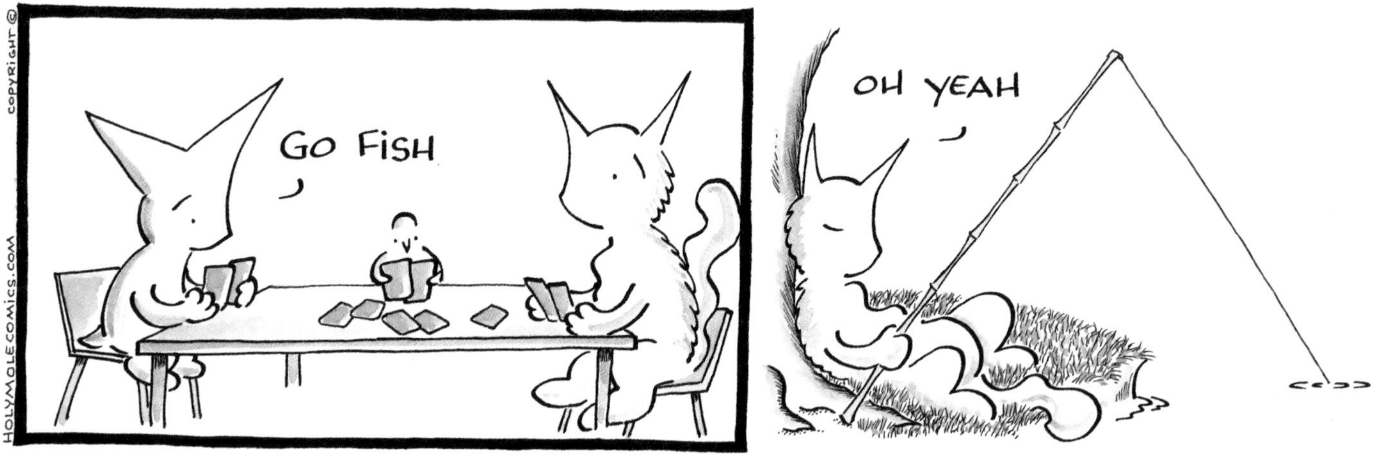
HOLYMOLECOMICS.COM COPYRIGHT ©
GO FISH
OH YEAH

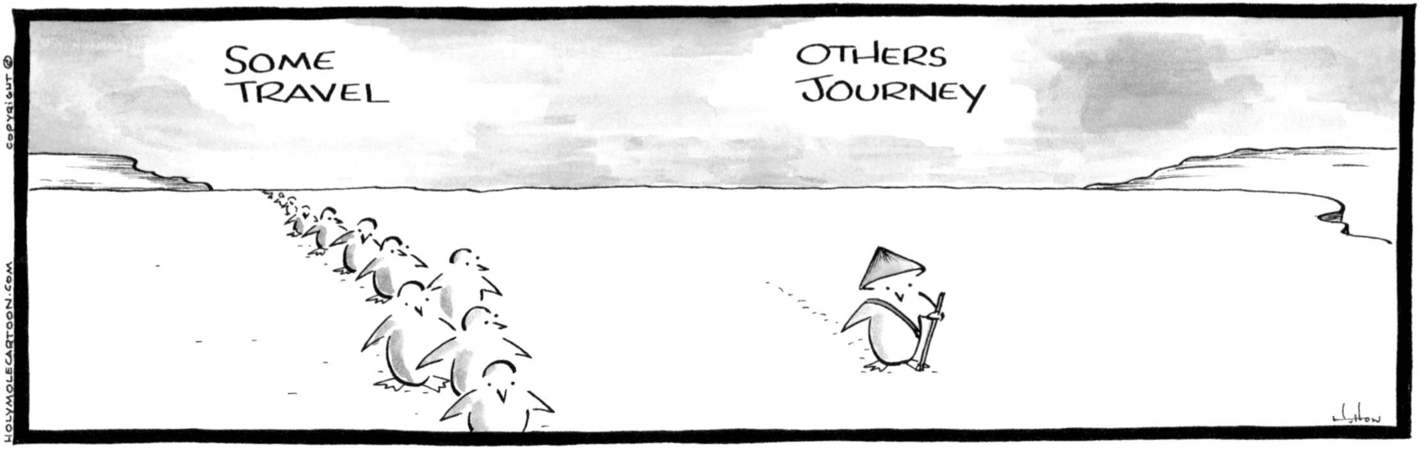
SOME TRAVEL
OTHERS JOURNEY
HOLYMOLECARTOON.COM COPYRIGHT ©

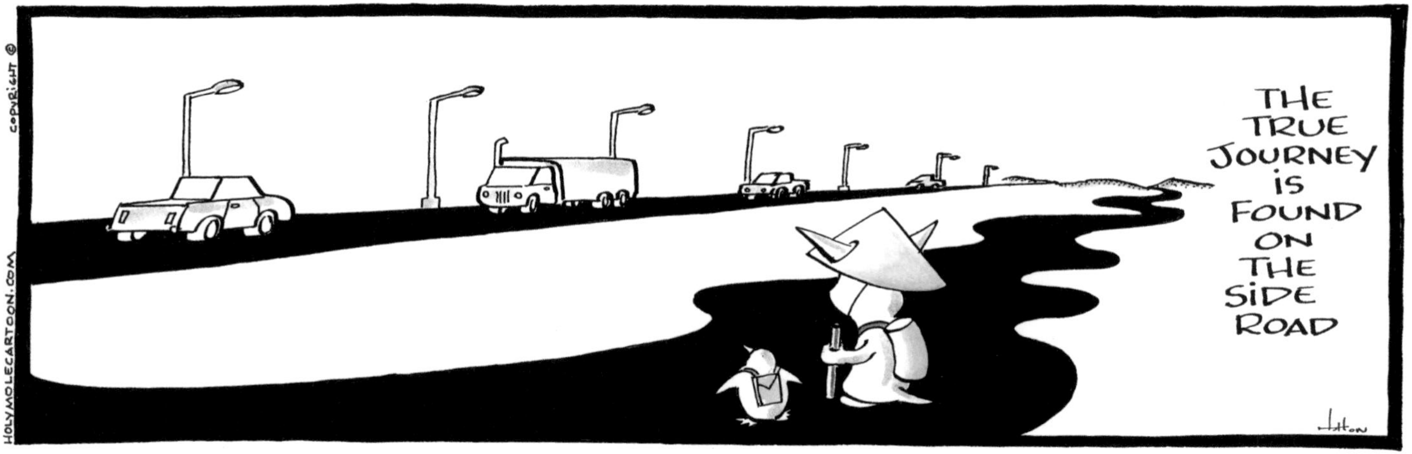
THE TRUE JOURNEY IS FOUND ON THE SIDE ROAD
HOLYMOLECARTOON.COM COPYRIGHT ©

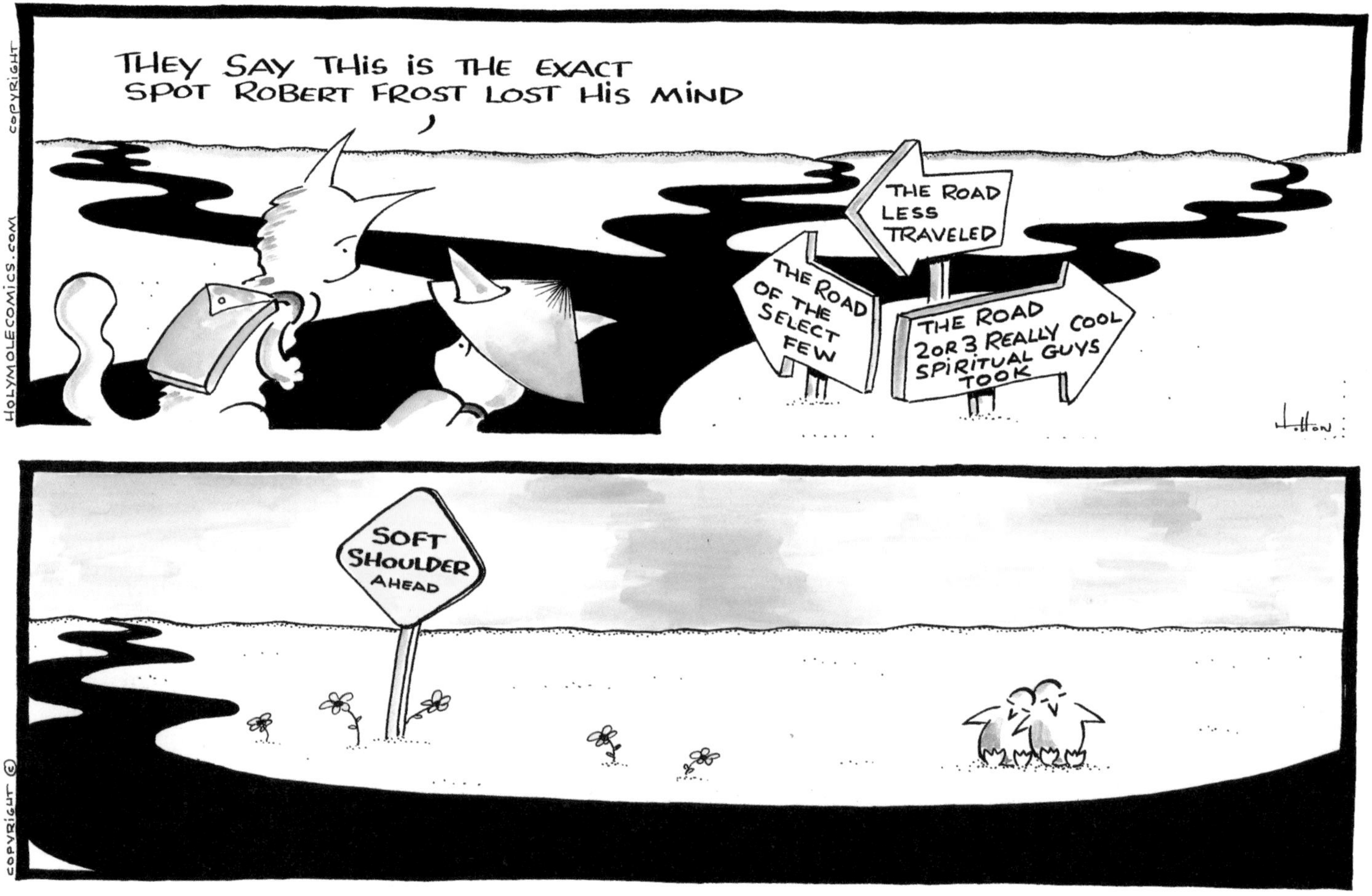
THEY SAY THIS IS THE EXACT SPOT ROBERT FROST LOST HIS MIND
THE ROAD LESS TRAVELED
THE ROAD OF THE SELECT FEW
THE ROAD 2 OR 3 REALLY COOL SPIRITUAL GUYS TOOK
SOFT SHOULDER AHEAD
HOLYMOLECOMICS.COM
COPYRIGHT
COPYRIGHT ©

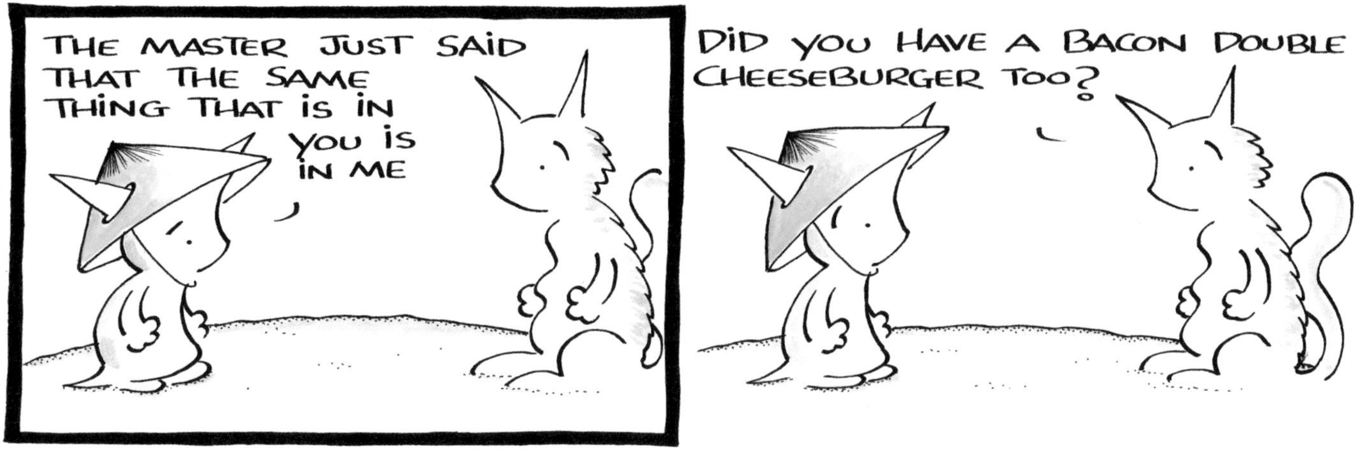
THE MASTER JUST SAID THAT THE SAME THING THAT is IN you is IN ME
DID you HAVE A BACON DOUBLE CHEESEBURGER TOO?

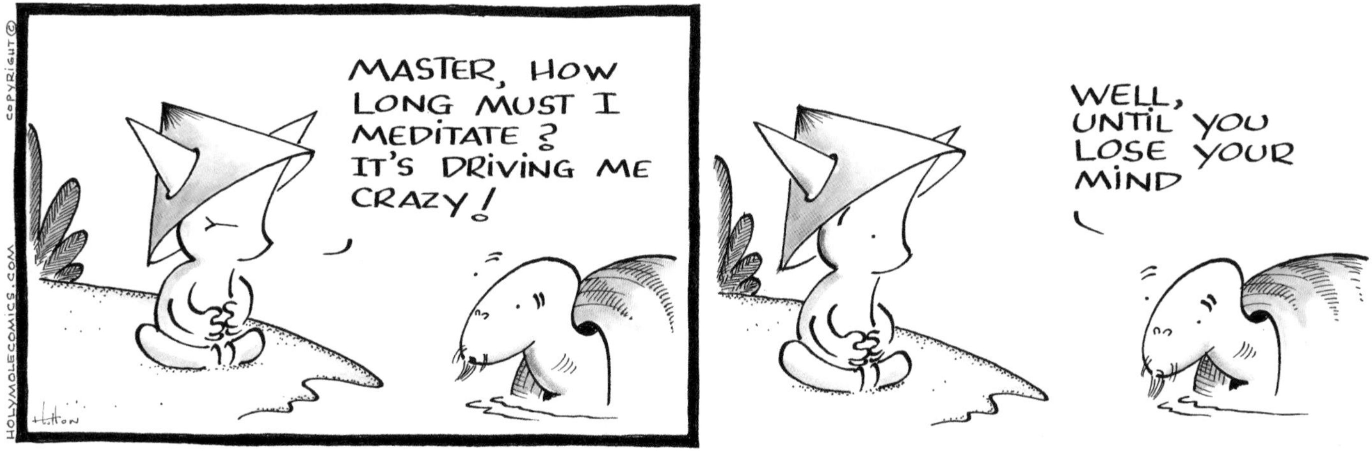
HOLYMOLECOMICS.COM COPYRIGHT ©
MASTER, HOW LONG MUST I MEDITATE? IT'S DRIVING ME CRAZY!
WELL, UNTIL YOU LOSE YOUR MIND

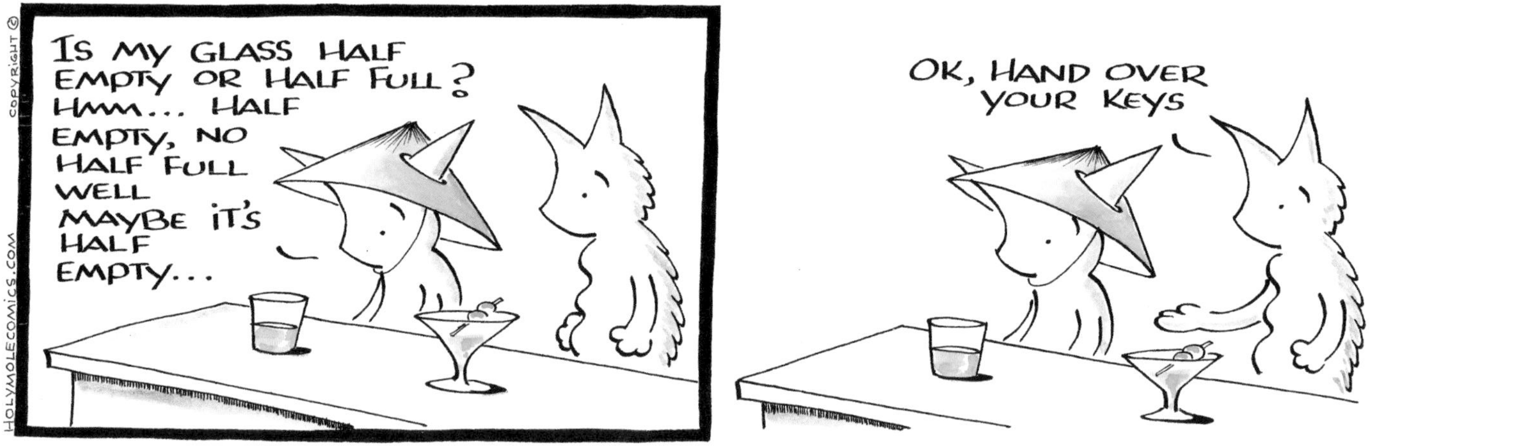
COPYRIGHT ©
HOLYMOLECOMICS.COM
IS MY GLASS HALF EMPTY OR HALF FULL? HMM... HALF EMPTY, NO HALF FULL WELL MAYBE IT'S HALF EMPTY...
OK, HAND OVER YOUR KEYS

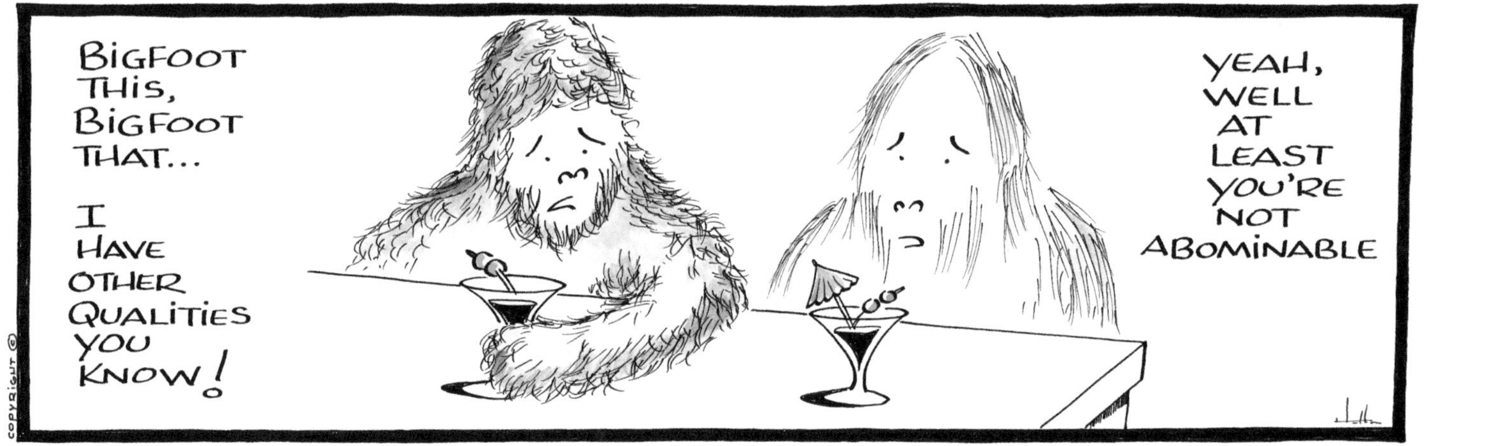
COPYRIGHT ©
BIGFOOT THIS, BIGFOOT THAT... I HAVE OTHER QUALITIES YOU KNOW!
YEAH, WELL AT LEAST YOU'RE NOT ABOMINABLE

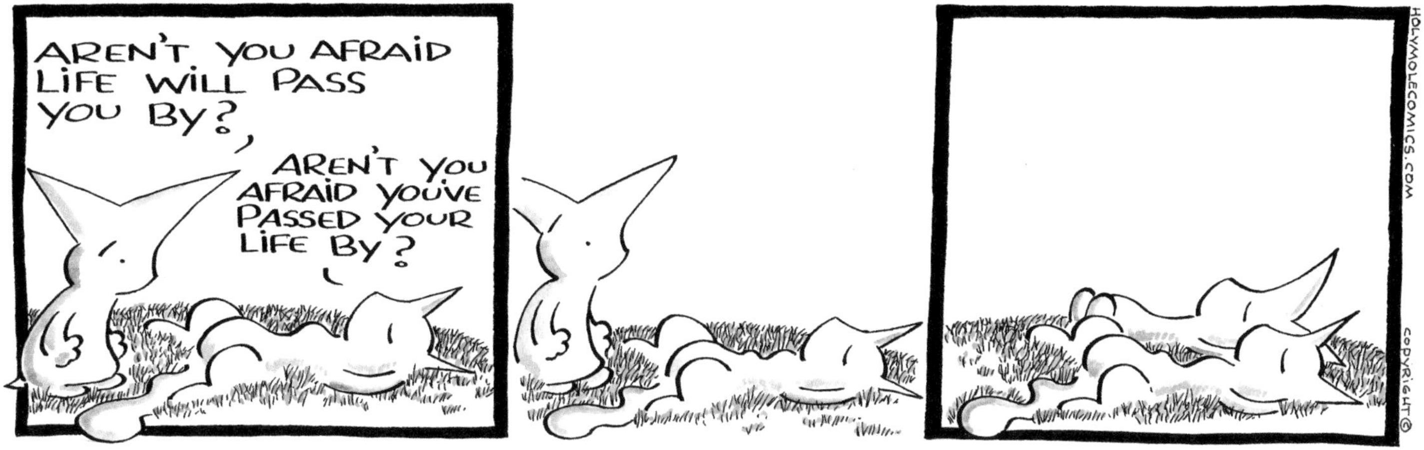
AREN'T YOU AFRAID LIFE WILL PASS YOU BY?
AREN'T YOU AFRAID YOU'VE PASSED YOUR LIFE BY?
HOLYMOLECOMICS.COM
COPYRIGHT ©

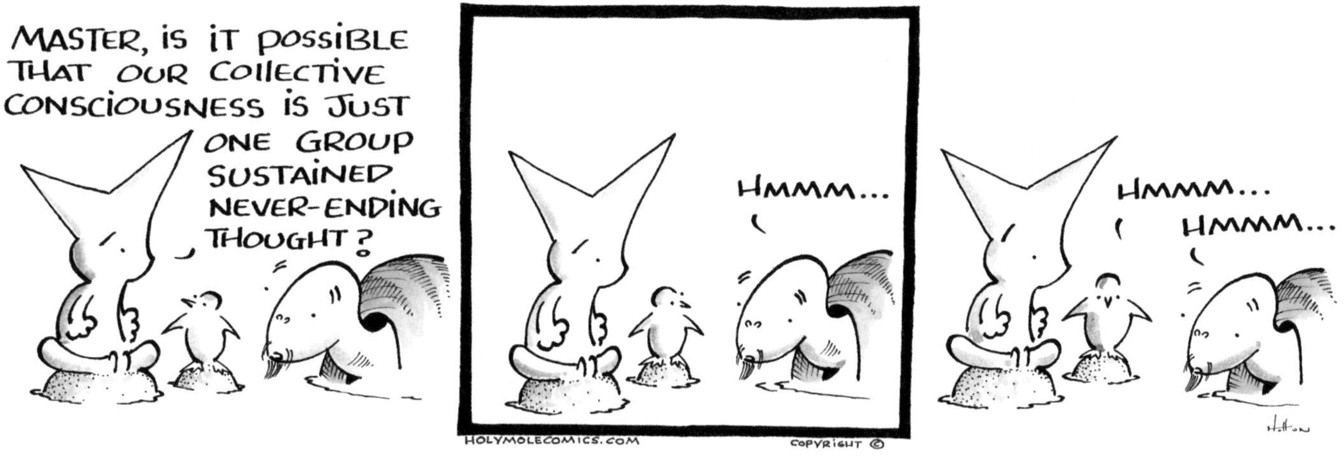
MASTER, IS IT POSSIBLE THAT OUR COLLECTIVE CONSCIOUSNESS IS JUST ONE GROUP SUSTAINED NEVER-ENDING THOUGHT?
HMMM...
HMMM...
HMMM...
HOLYMOLECOMICS.COM
COPYRIGHT ©

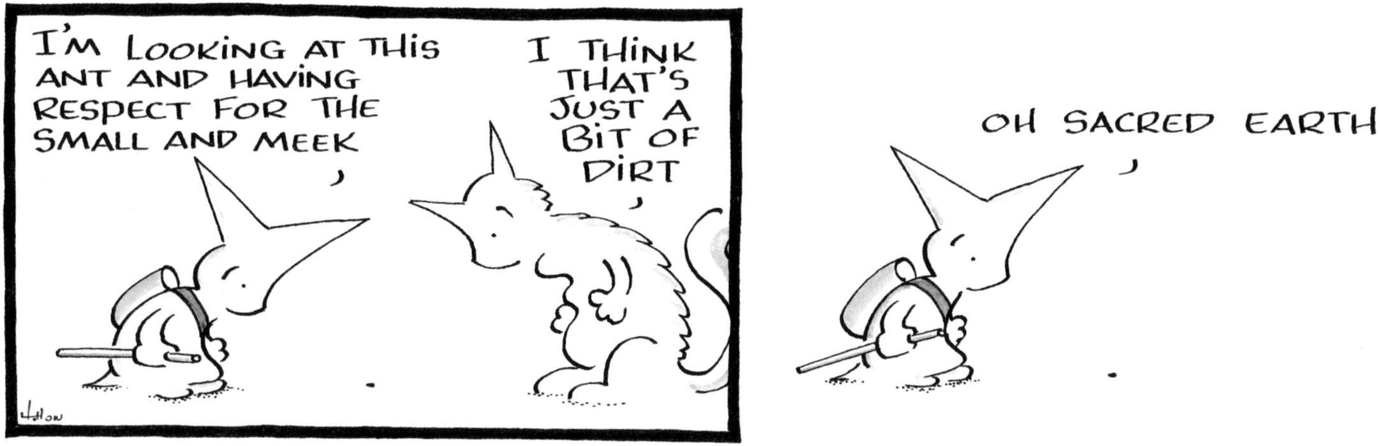
I'M LOOKING AT THIS ANT AND HAVING RESPECT FOR THE SMALL AND MEEK
I THINK THAT'S JUST A BIT OF DIRT
OH SACRED EARTH

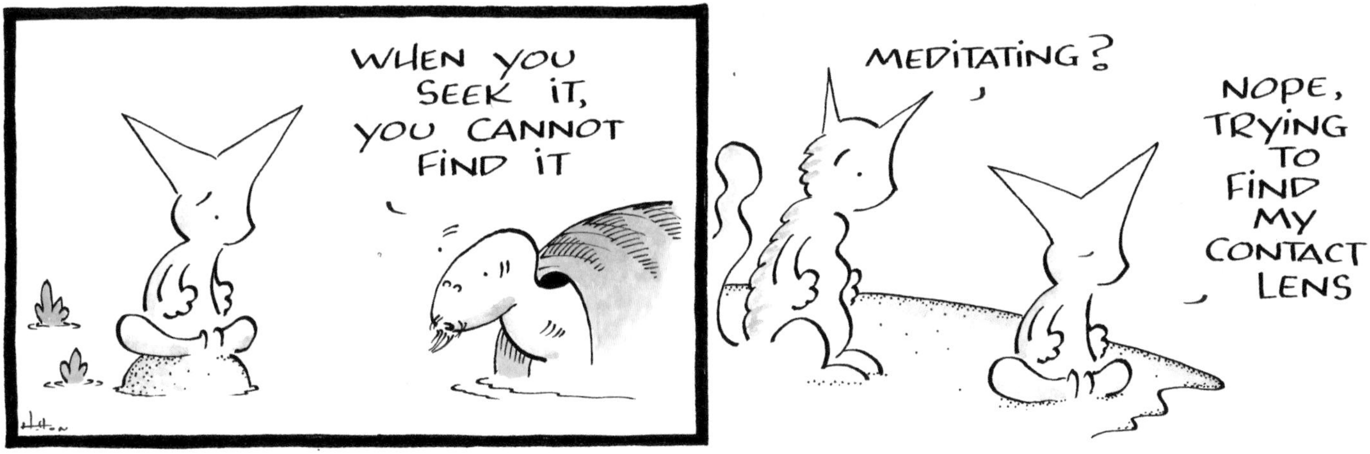
WHEN YOU SEEK IT, YOU CANNOT FIND IT
MEDITATING?
NOPE, TRYING TO FIND MY CONTACT LENS

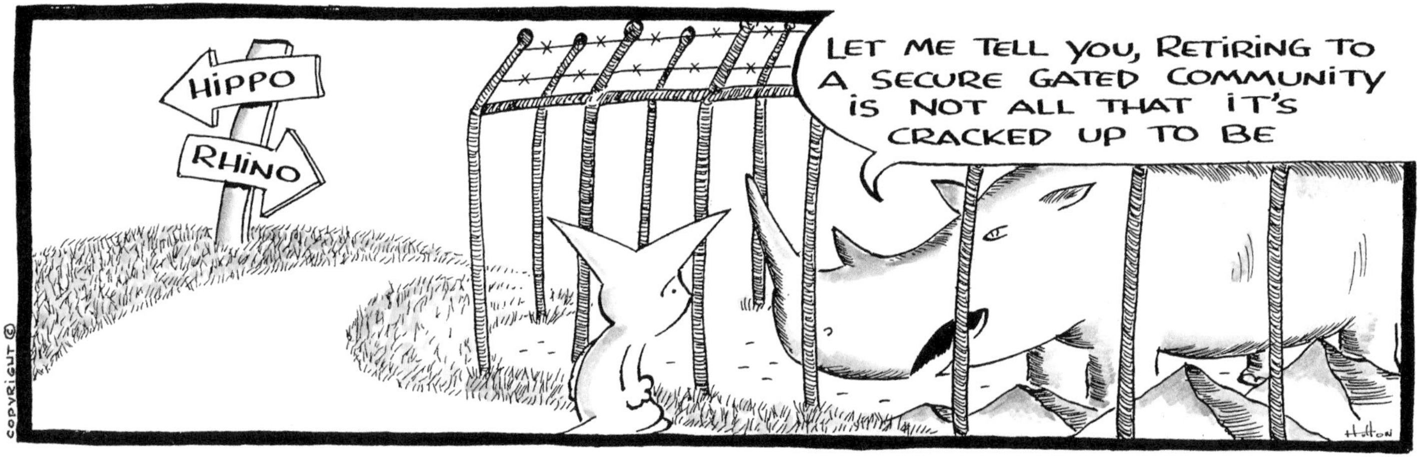
HIPPO
RHINO
LET ME TELL YOU, RETIRING TO A SECURE GATED COMMUNITY IS NOT ALL THAT IT'S CRACKED UP TO BE
COPYRIGHT ©
Hutton

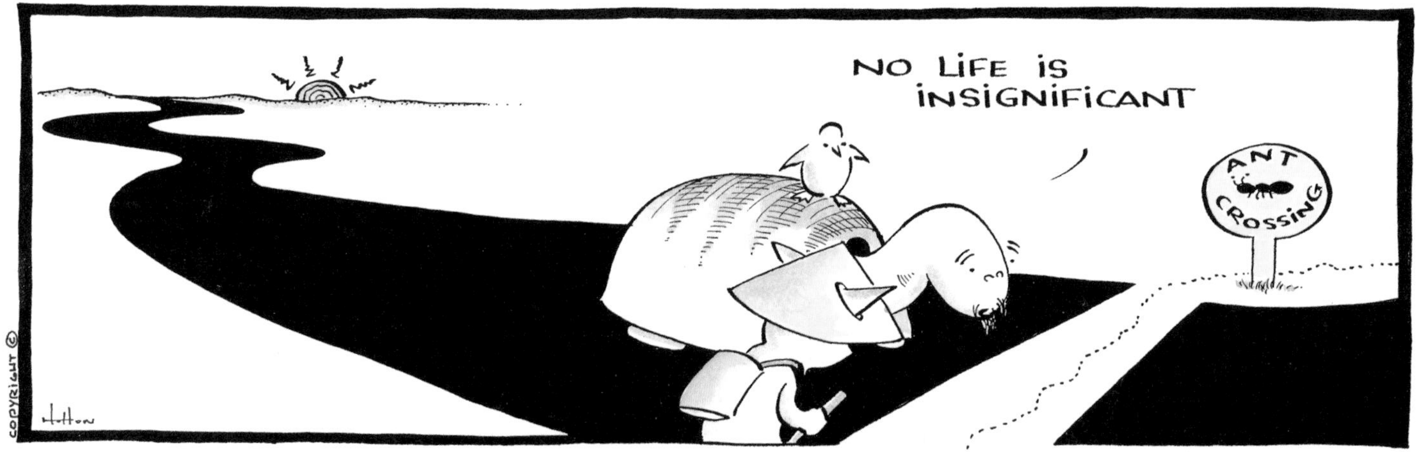
NO LIFE IS INSIGNIFICANT
ANT CROSSING
COPYRIGHT ©
Hutton

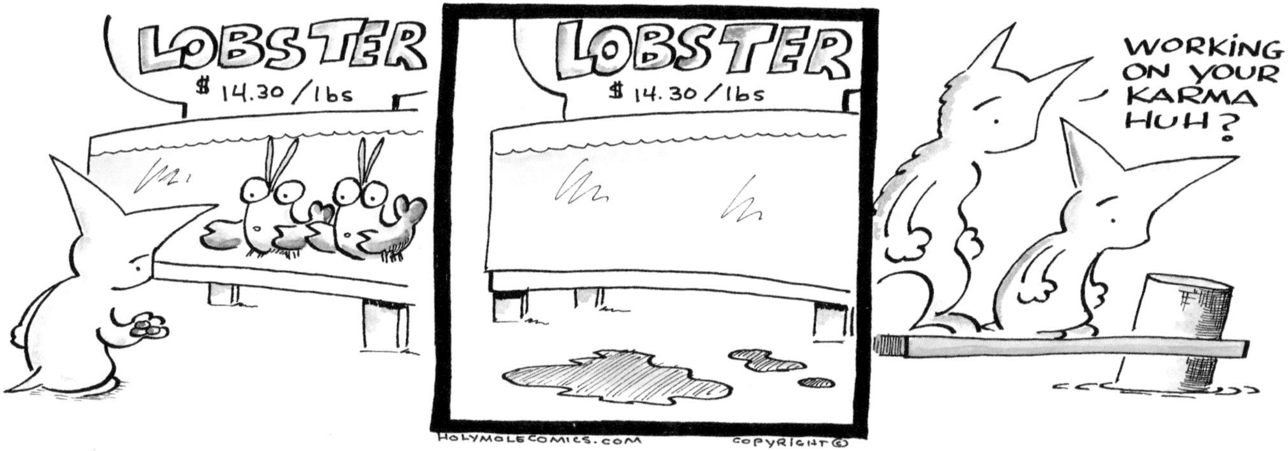
LOBSTER
$ 14.30 / lbs
LOBSTER
$ 14.30 / lbs
WORKING ON YOUR KARMA HUH?
HOLYMOLECOMICS.COM
COPYRIGHT©

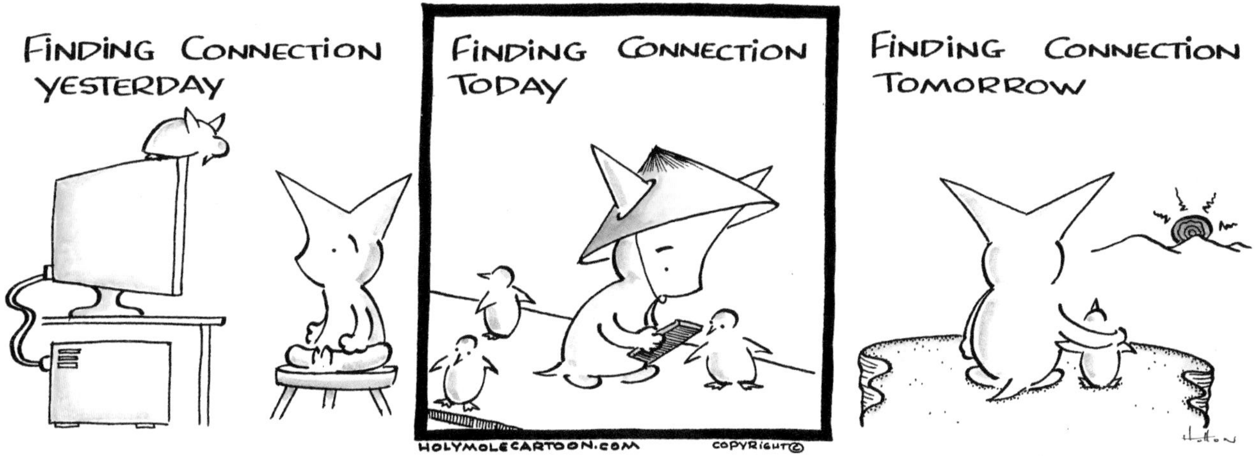
FINDING CONNECTION YESTERDAY
FINDING CONNECTION TODAY
FINDING CONNECTION TOMORROW
HOLYMOLECARTOON.COM
COPYRIGHT©

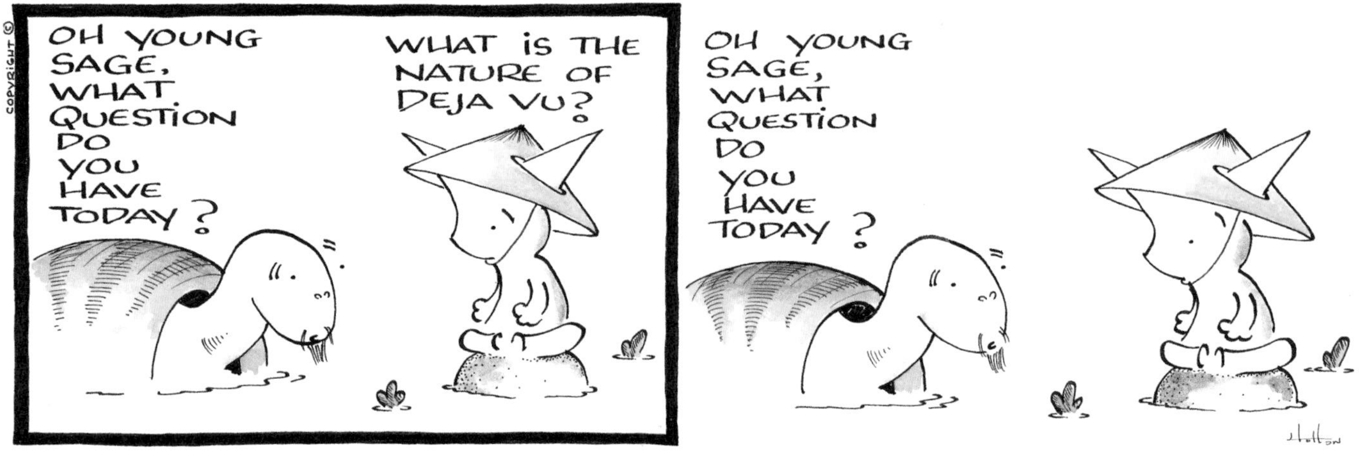
COPYRIGHT ©
OH YOUNG SAGE, WHAT QUESTION DO YOU HAVE TODAY ?
WHAT IS THE NATURE OF DEJA VU?
OH YOUNG SAGE, WHAT QUESTION DO YOU HAVE TODAY ?

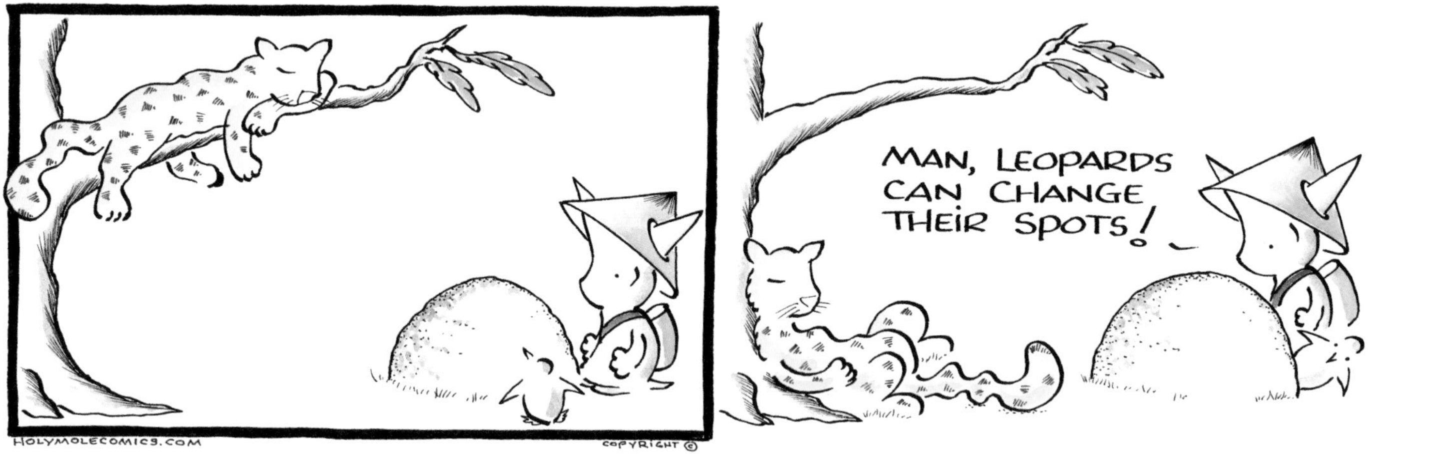
MAN, LEOPARDS CAN CHANGE THEIR SPOTS!
HOLYMOLECOMICS.COM
COPYRIGHT ©

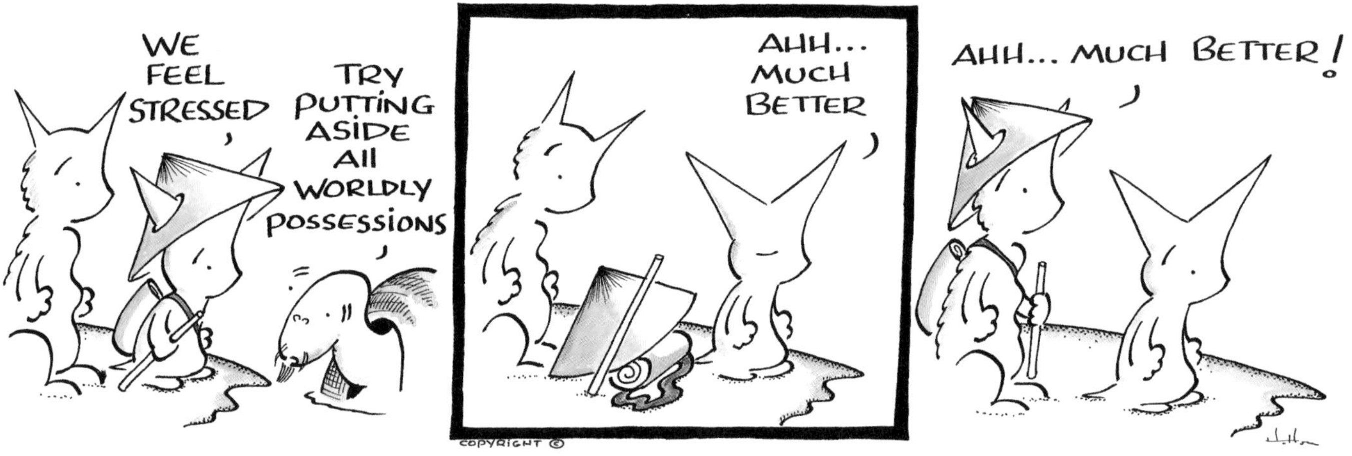
WE FEEL STRESSED
TRY PUTTING ASIDE ALL WORLDLY POSSESSIONS
AHH... MUCH BETTER
AHH... MUCH BETTER!
COPYRIGHT ©

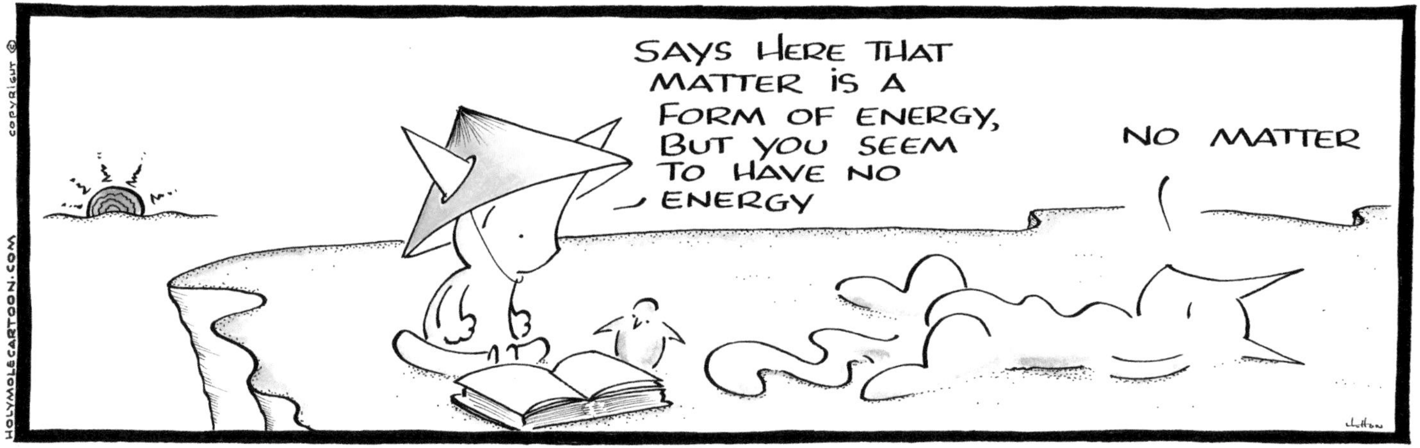
HOLYMOLECARTOON.COM COPYRIGHT ©
SAYS HERE THAT MATTER IS A FORM OF ENERGY, BUT YOU SEEM TO HAVE NO ENERGY
NO MATTER

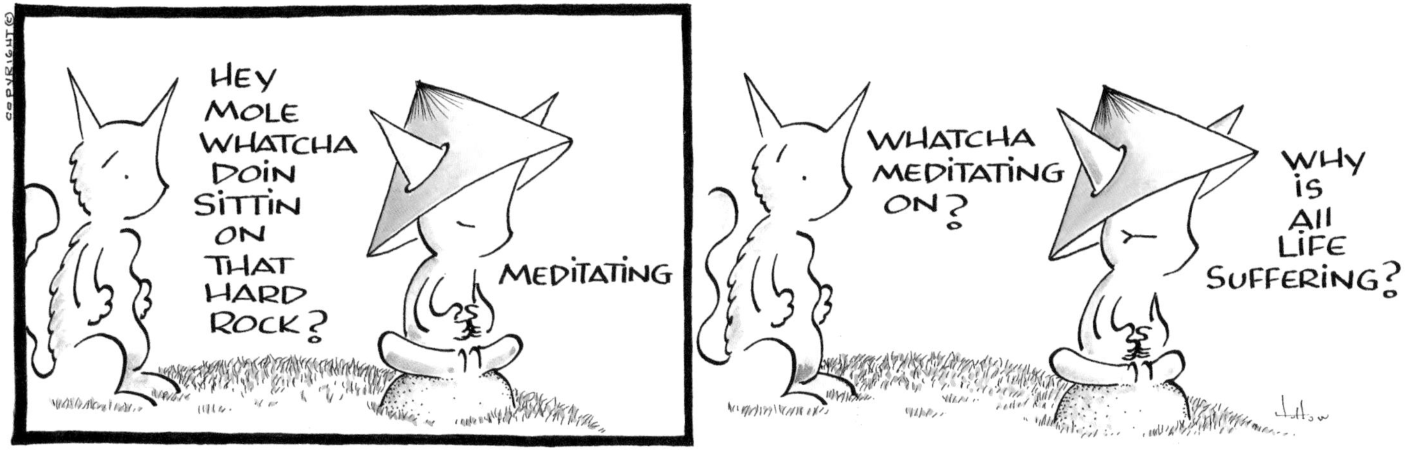
COPYRIGHT ©
HEY MOLE WHATCHA DOIN SITTIN ON THAT HARD ROCK?
MEDITATING
WHATCHA MEDITATING ON?
WHY IS ALL LIFE SUFFERING?

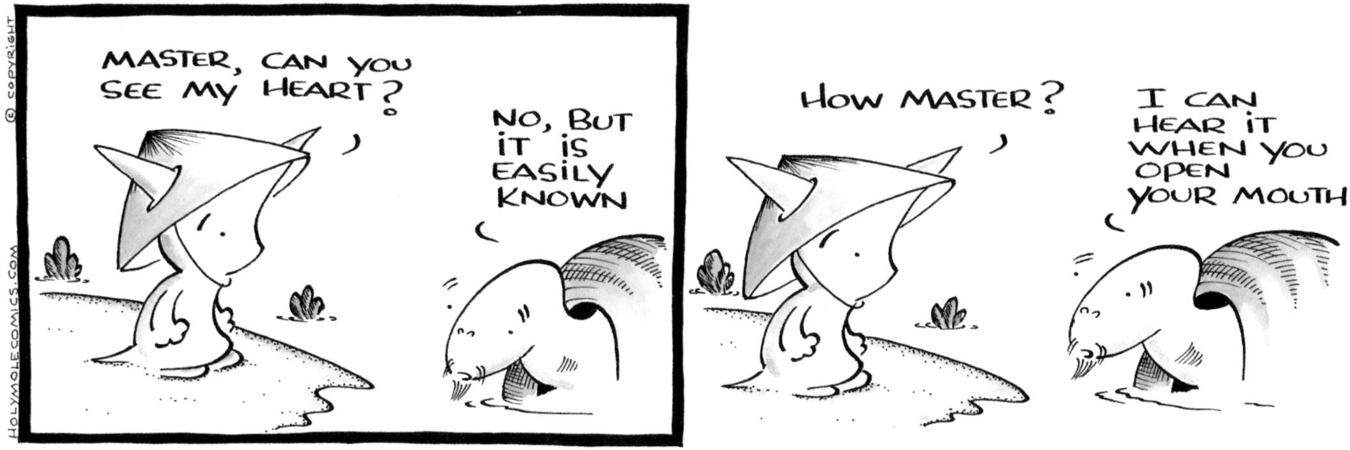
© COPYRIGHT
HOLYMOLECOMICS.COM
MASTER, CAN YOU SEE MY HEART?
NO, BUT IT IS EASILY KNOWN
HOW MASTER?
I CAN HEAR IT WHEN YOU OPEN YOUR MOUTH

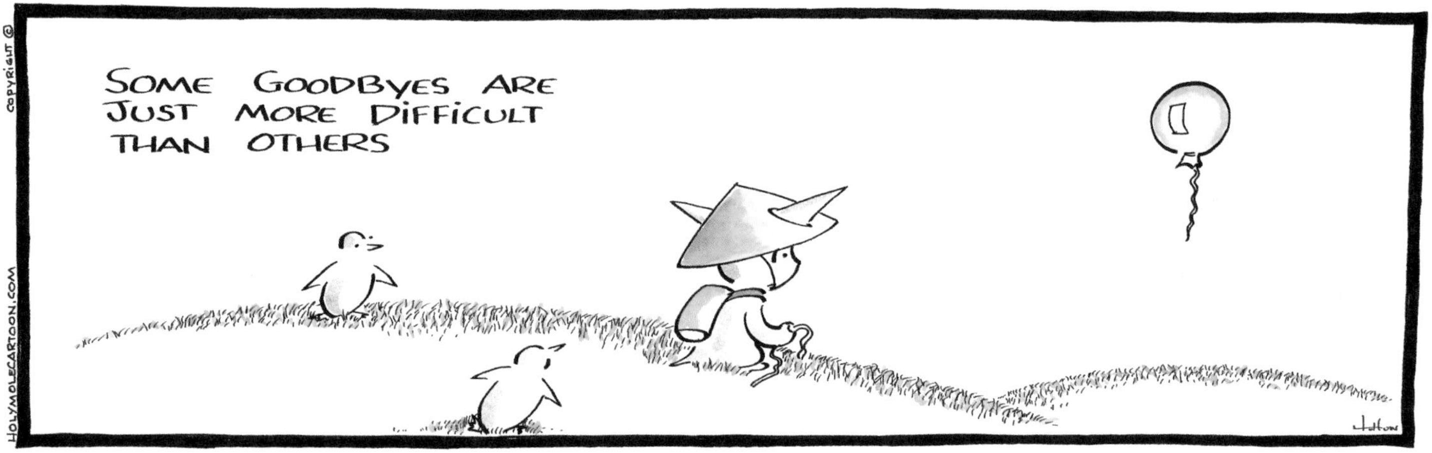
SOME GOODBYES ARE JUST MORE DIFFICULT THAN OTHERS
HOLYMOLECARTOON.COM COPYRIGHT ©

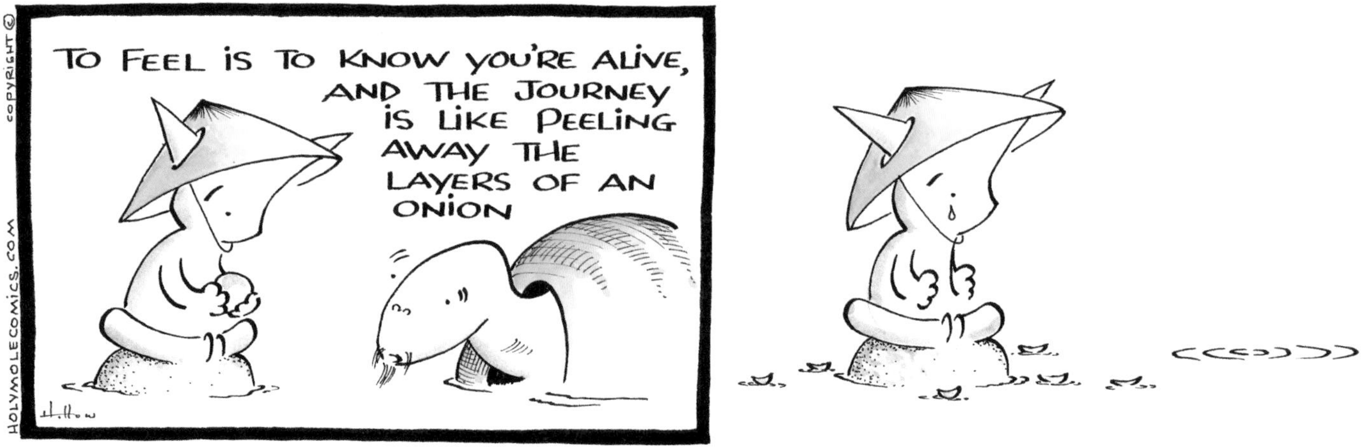
TO FEEL IS TO KNOW YOU'RE ALIVE, AND THE JOURNEY IS LIKE PEELING AWAY THE LAYERS OF AN ONION
HOLYMOLECOMICS.COM COPYRIGHT ©

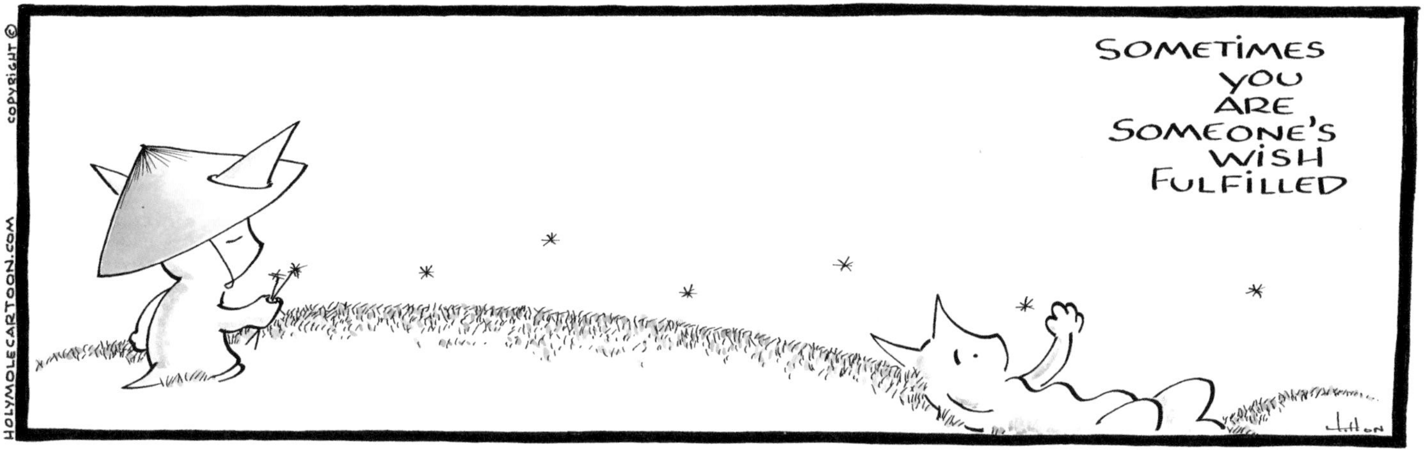
COPYRIGHT ©
HOLYMOLECARTOON.COM
SOMETIMES YOU ARE SOMEONE'S WISH FULFILLED

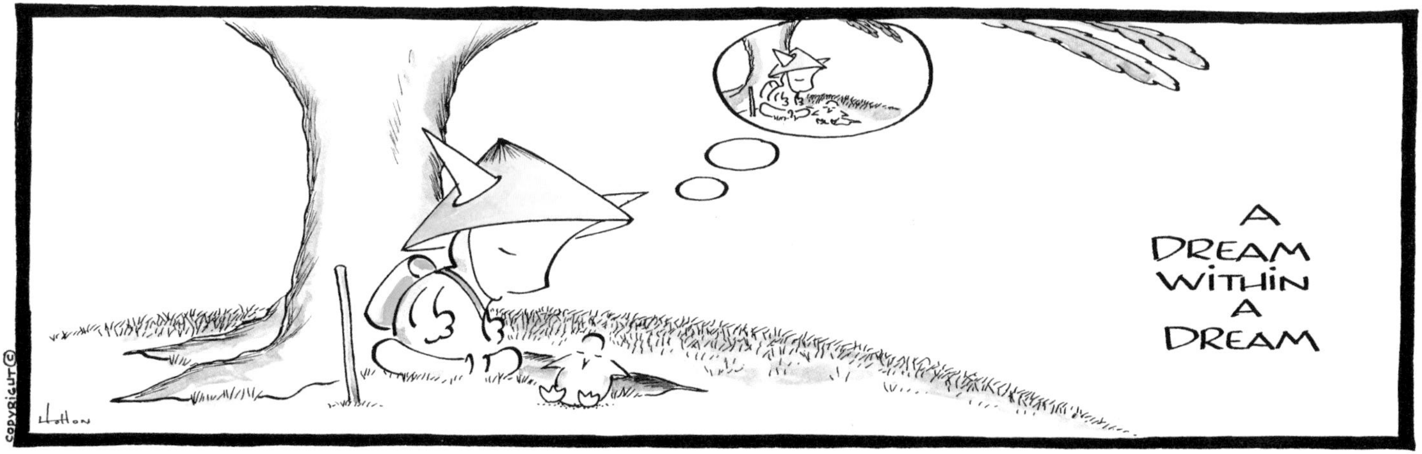
COPYRIGHT ©
A DREAM WITHIN A DREAM

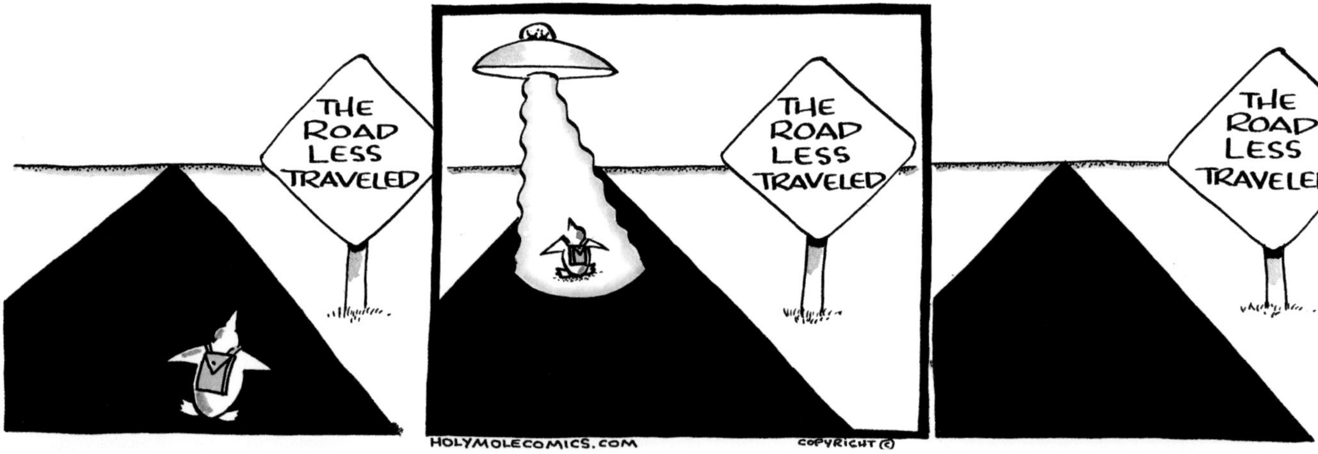
THE ROAD LESS TRAVELED
THE ROAD LESS TRAVELED
THE ROAD LESS TRAVELED
HOLYMOLECOMICS.COM
COPYRIGHT ©

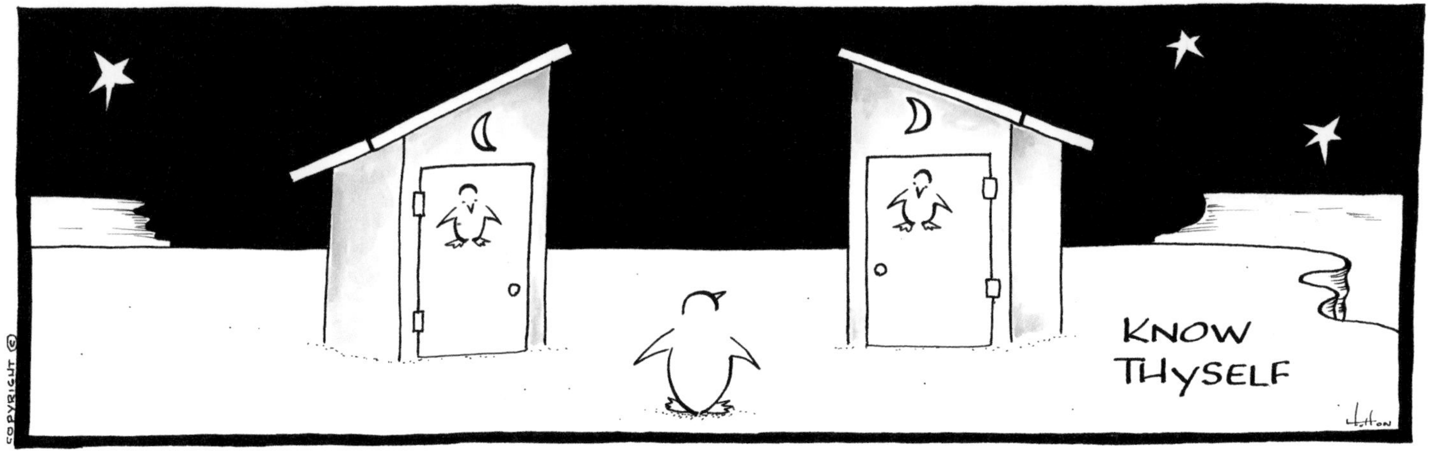
KNOW THYSELF
COPYRIGHT ©

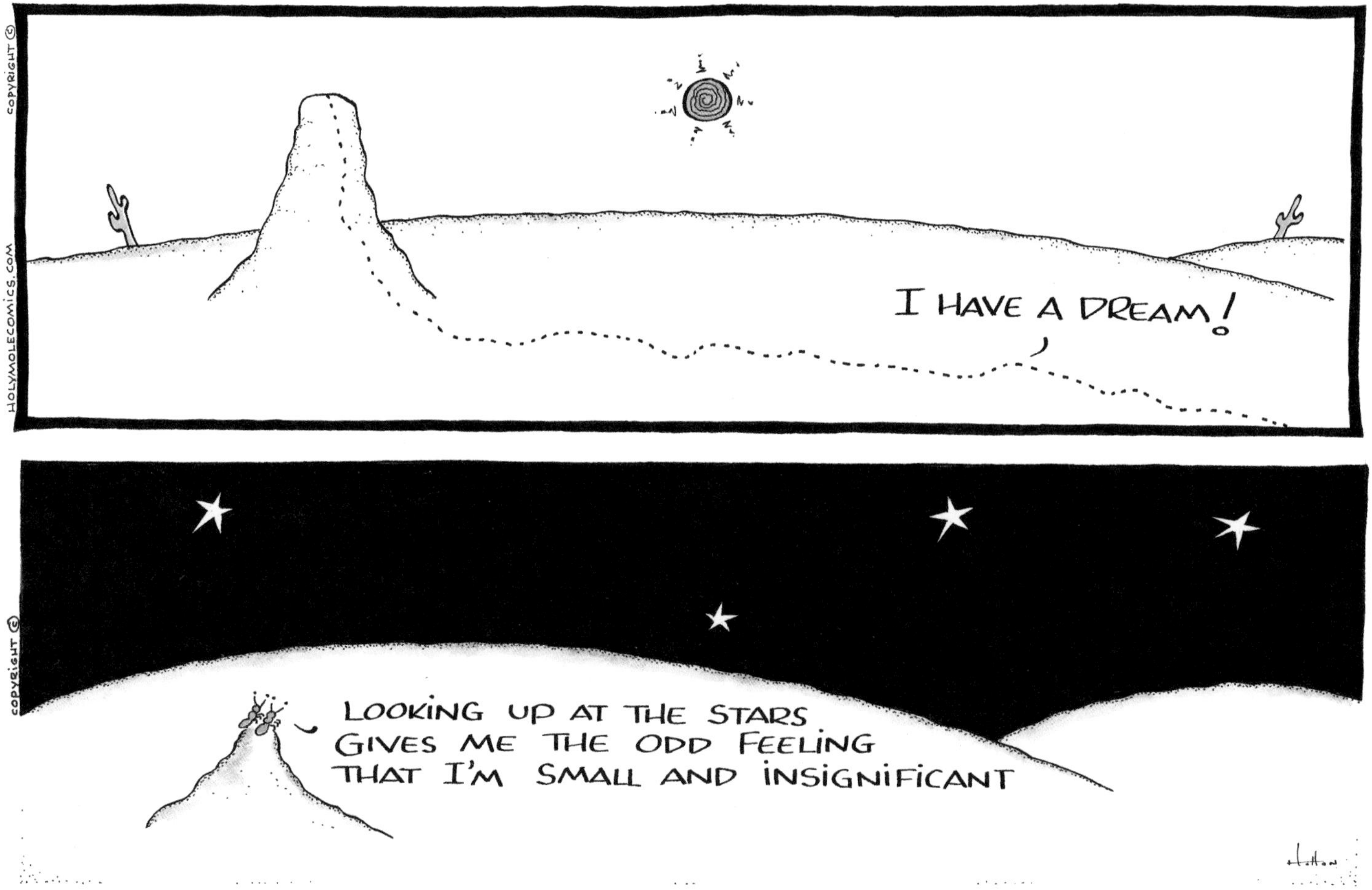
I HAVE A DREAM!
LOOKING UP AT THE STARS GIVES ME THE ODD FEELING THAT I'M SMALL AND INSIGNIFICANT
HOLYMOLECOMICS.COM COPYRIGHT ©
COPYRIGHT ©

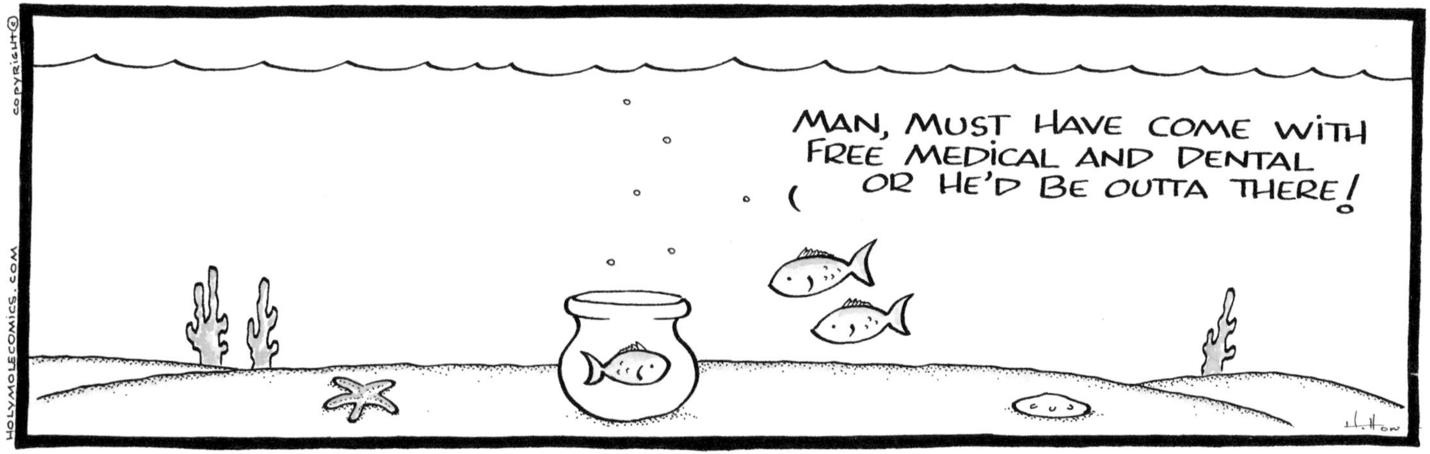
MAN, MUST HAVE COME WITH FREE MEDICAL AND DENTAL OR HE'D BE OUTTA THERE!
HOLYMOLECOMICS.COM
COPYRIGHT ©

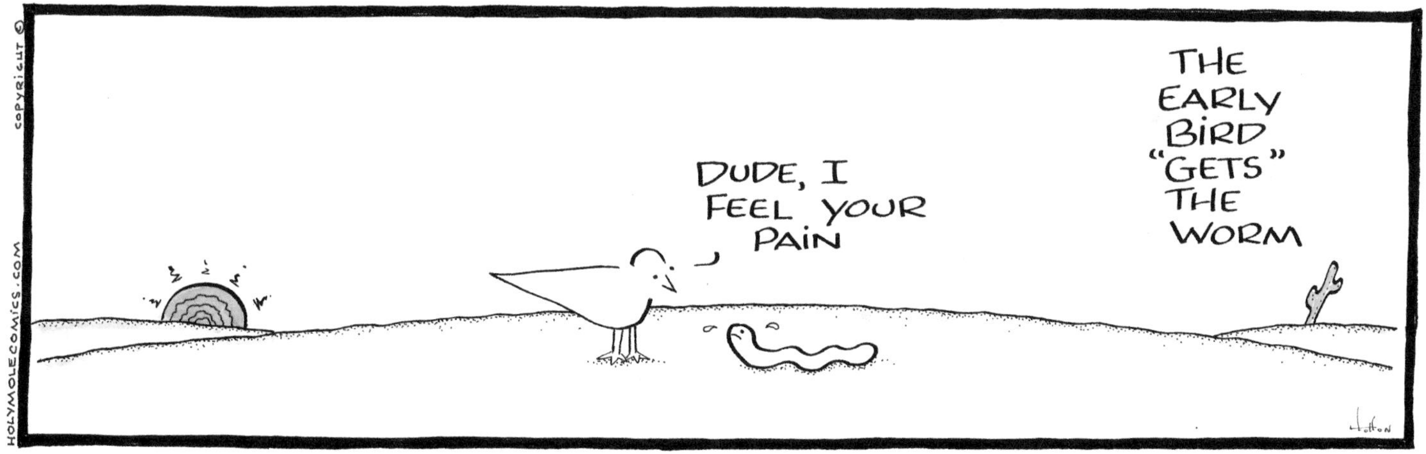
DUDE, I FEEL YOUR PAIN
THE EARLY BIRD "GETS" THE WORM
HOLYMOLECOMICS.COM
COPYRIGHT ©

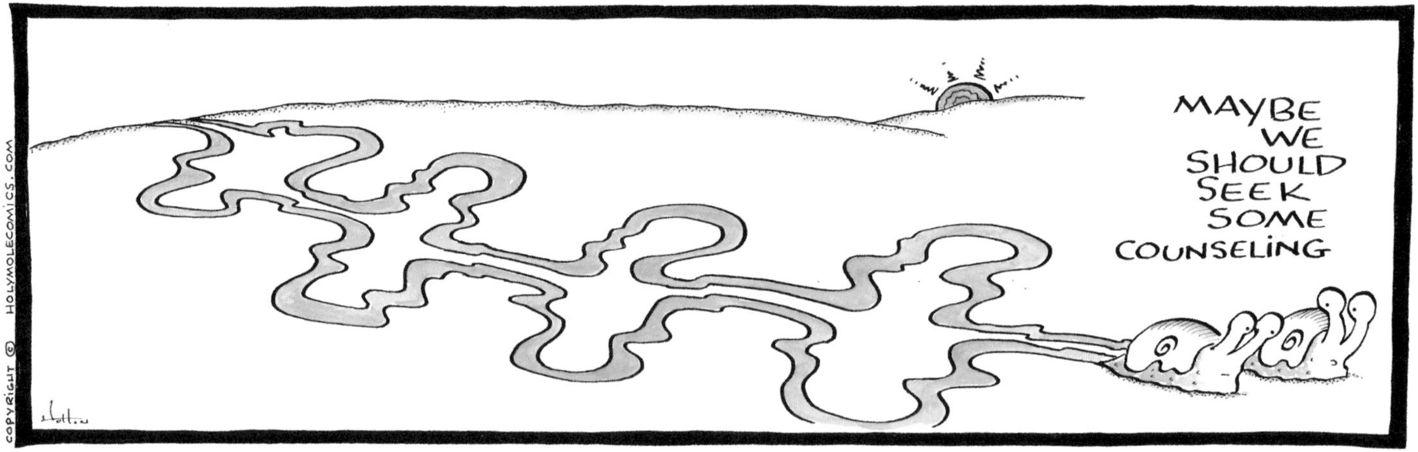
MAYBE WE SHOULD SEEK SOME COUNSELING
COPYRIGHT © HOLYMOLECOMICS.COM

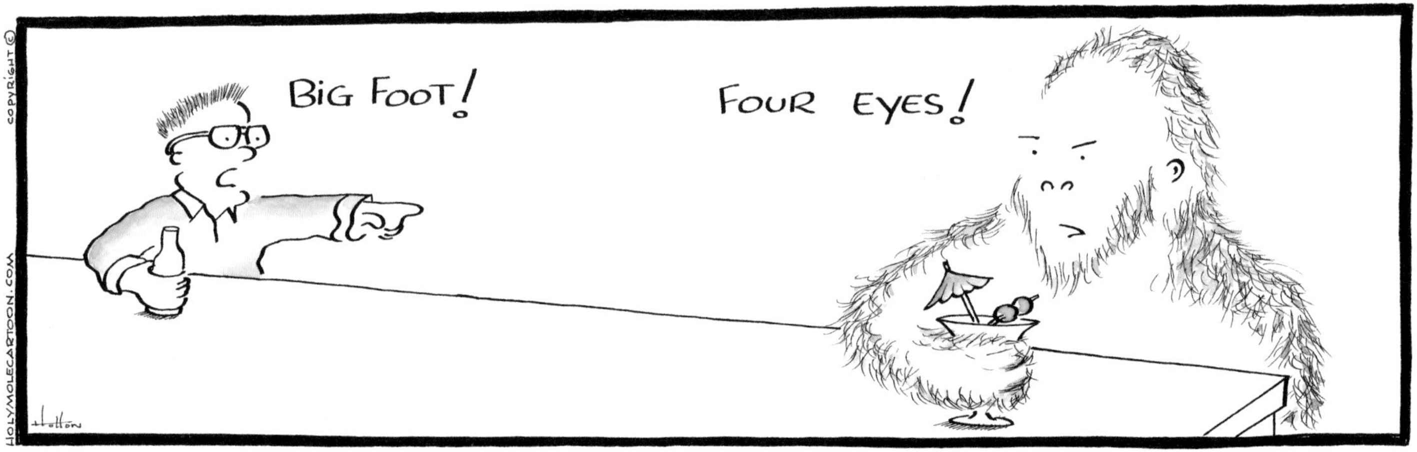
BIG FOOT!
FOUR EYES!
HOLYMOLECARTOON.COM COPYRIGHT ©

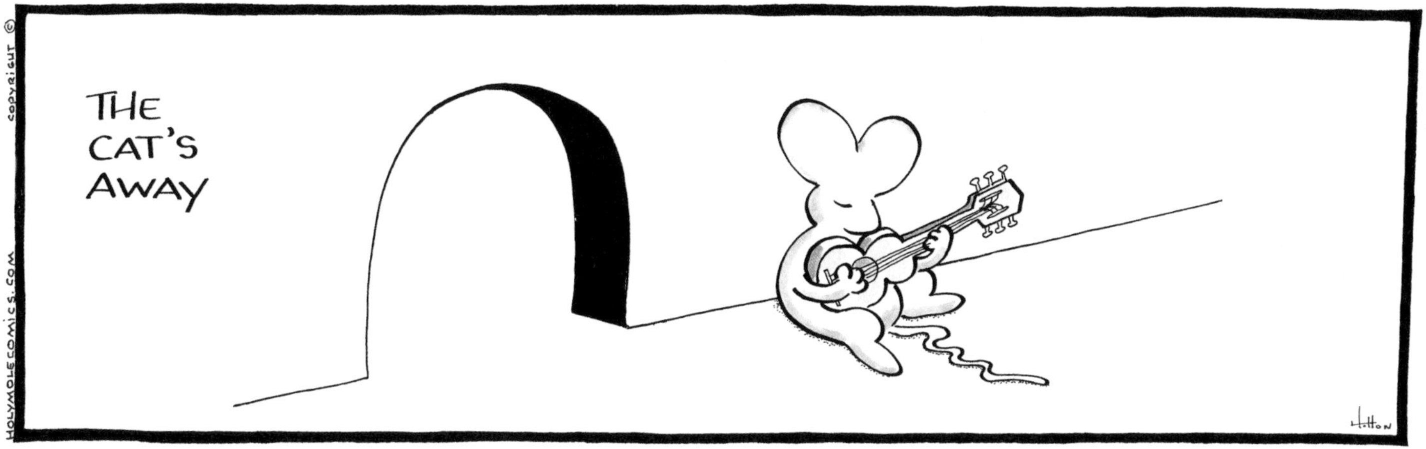
THE CAT'S AWAY
COPYRIGHT ©
HOLYMOLECOMICS.COM

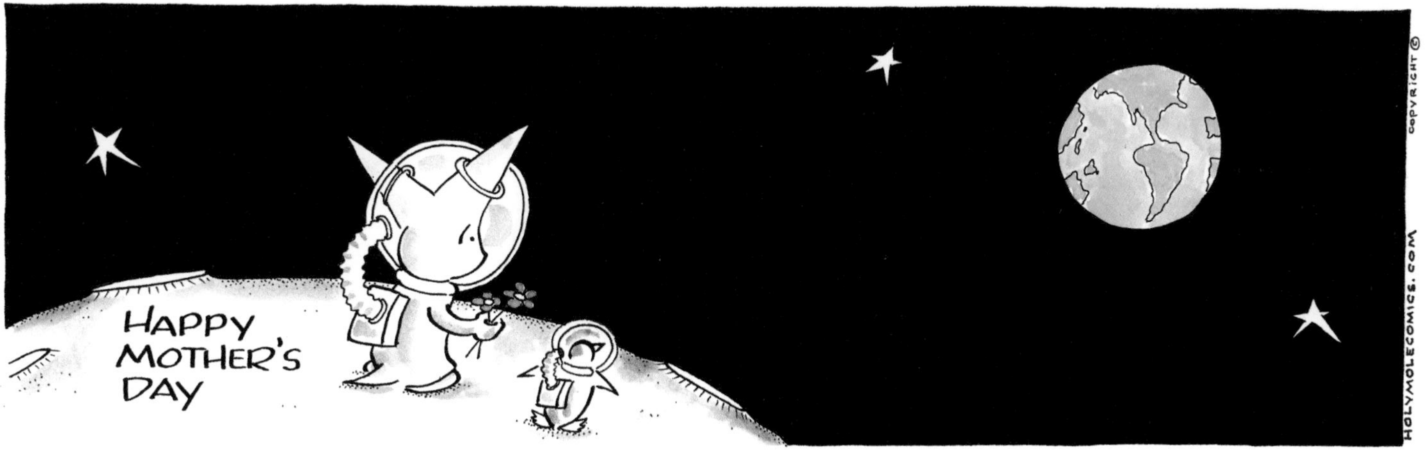
HAPPY MOTHER'S DAY
COPYRIGHT ©
HOLYMOLECOMICS.COM

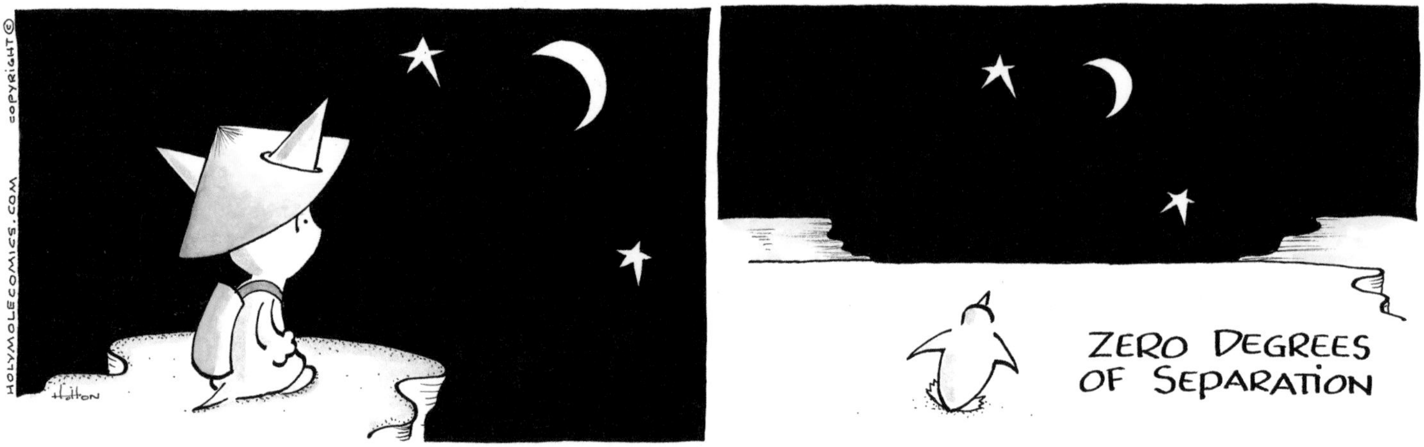
HOLYMOLECOMICS.COM COPYRIGHT ©
Hatton
ZERO DEGREES OF SEPARATION

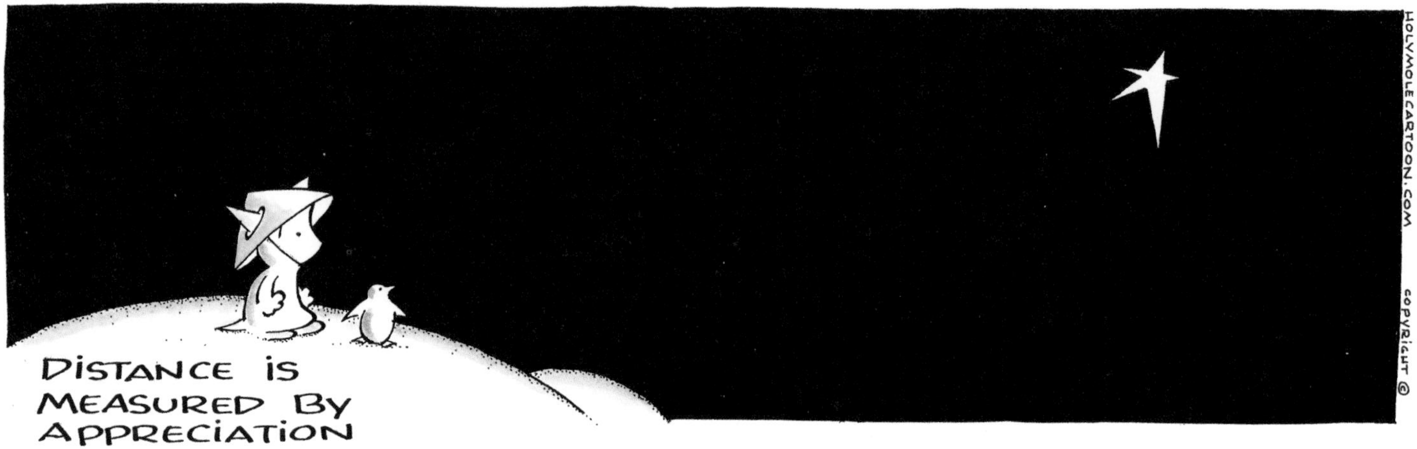
DISTANCE IS MEASURED BY APPRECIATION
HOLYMOLECARTOON.COM COPYRIGHT ©

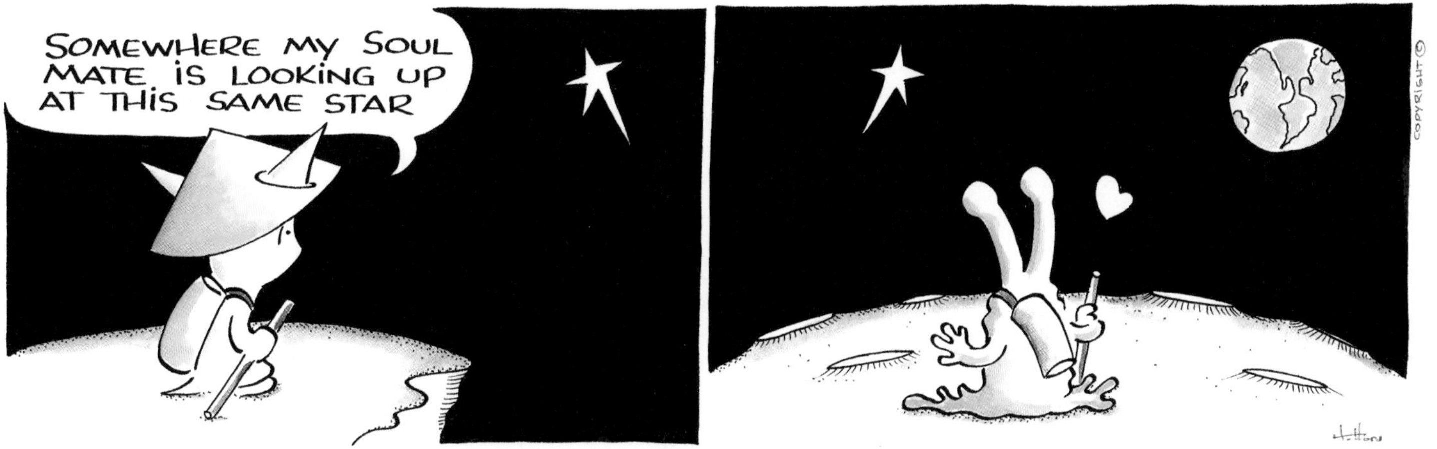
SOMEWHERE MY SOUL MATE IS LOOKING UP AT THIS SAME STAR
COPYRIGHT ©

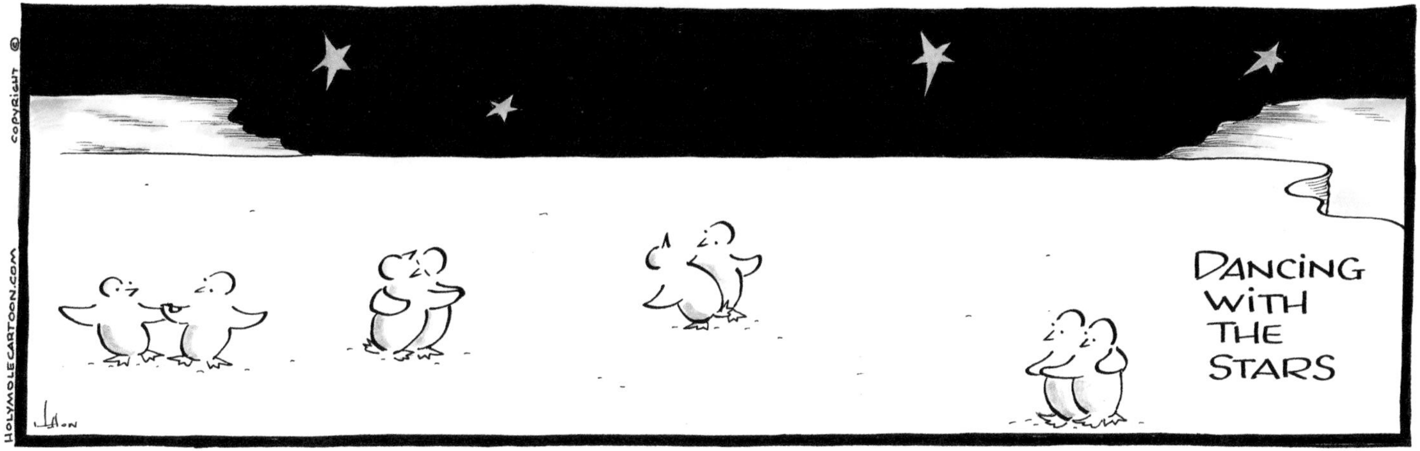
DANCING WITH THE STARS
COPYRIGHT ©
HOLYMOLECARTOON.COM

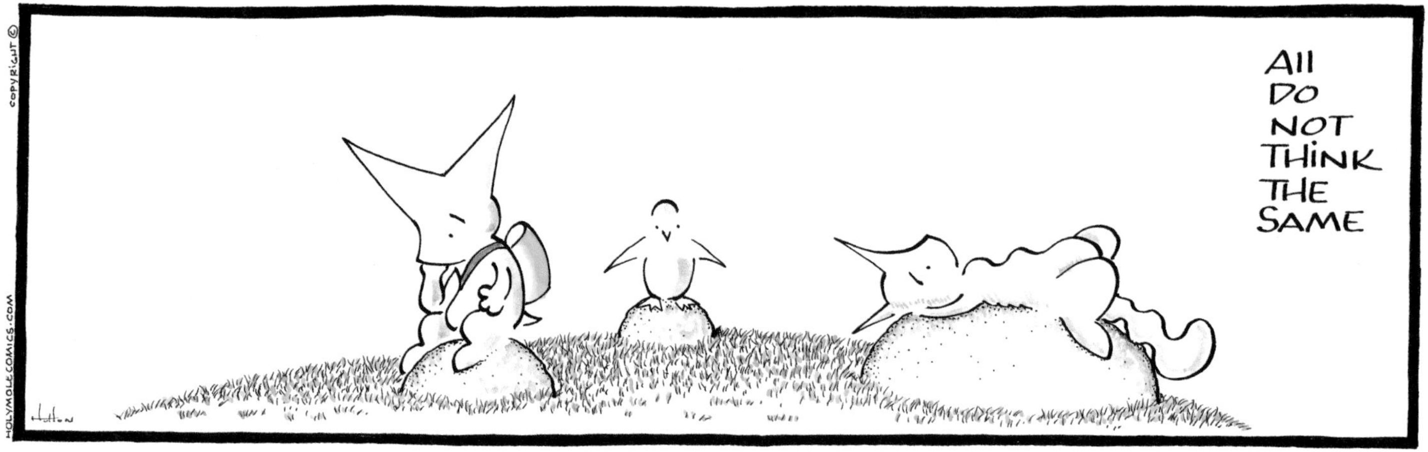
All DO NOT THINK THE SAME
HOLYMOLECOMICS.COM COPYRIGHT ©

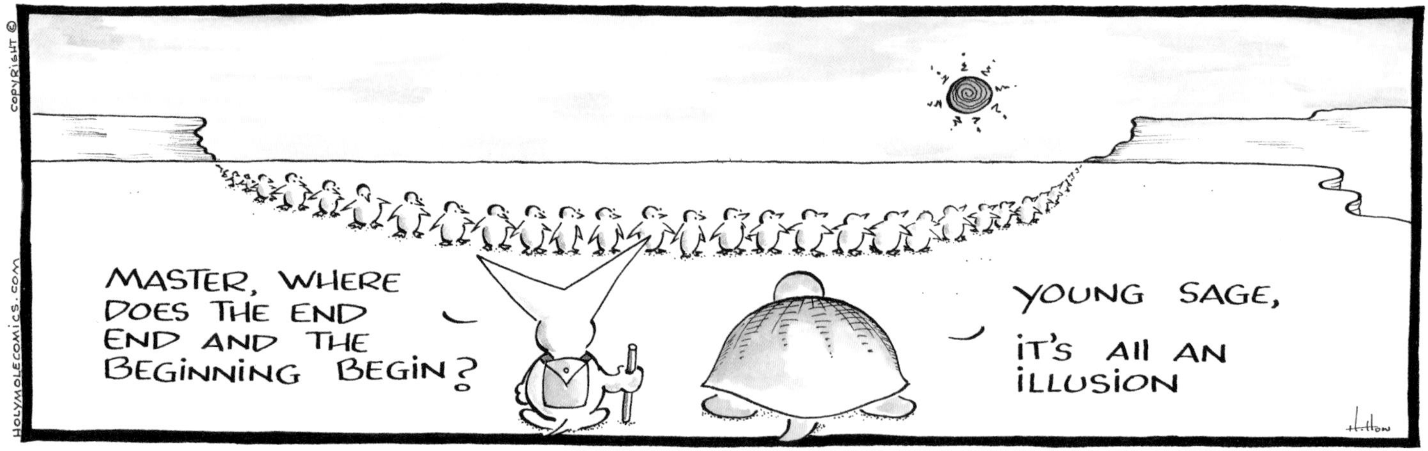
MASTER, WHERE DOES THE END END AND THE BEGINNING BEGIN?
YOUNG SAGE,
IT'S All AN ILLUSION
HOLYMOLECOMICS.COM COPYRIGHT ©

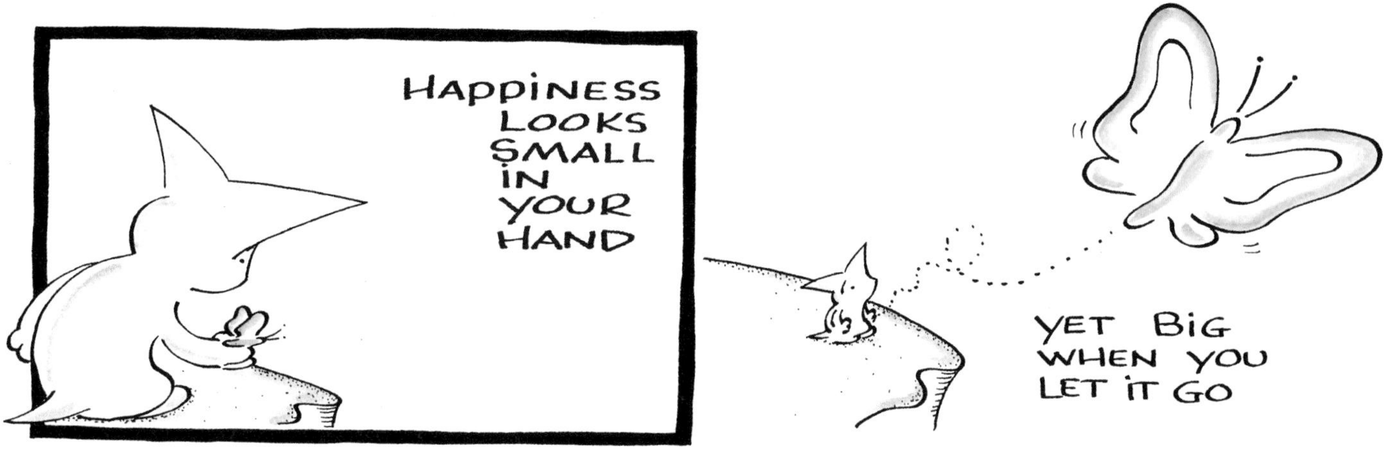
HAPPINESS LOOKS SMALL IN YOUR HAND
YET BIG WHEN YOU LET IT GO

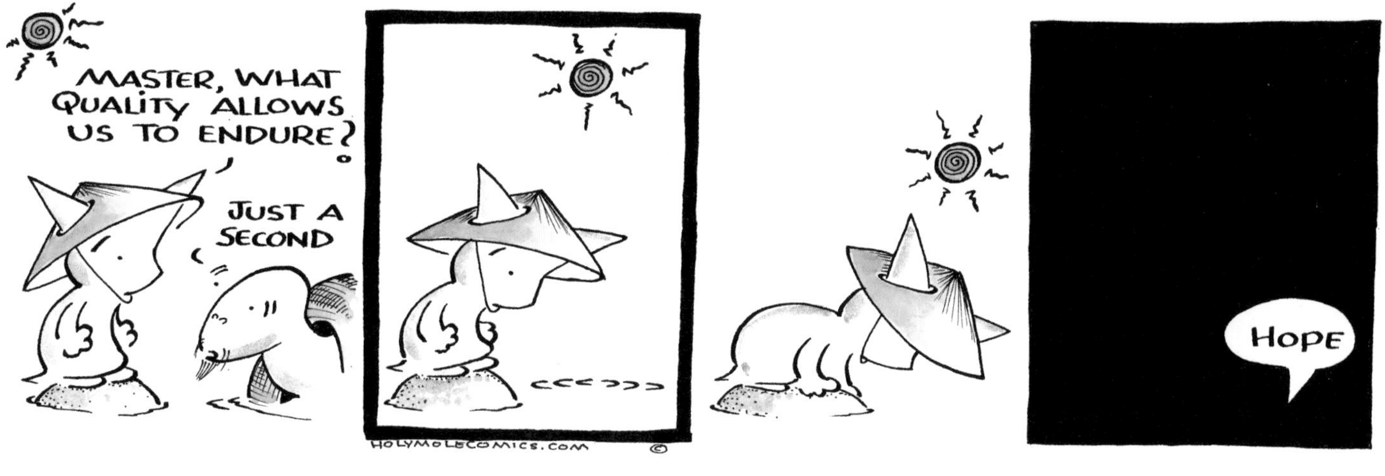
MASTER, WHAT QUALITY ALLOWS US TO ENDURE?
JUST A SECOND
HOPE
HOLYMOLECOMICS.COM ©

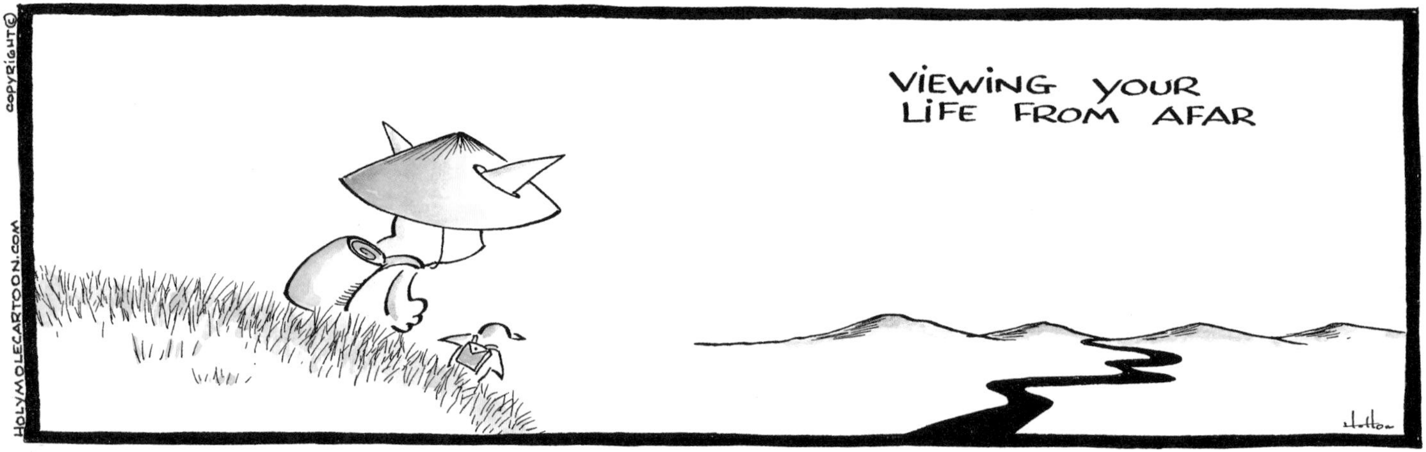
VIEWING YOUR LIFE FROM AFAR
COPYRIGHT ©
HOLYMOLECARTOON.COM

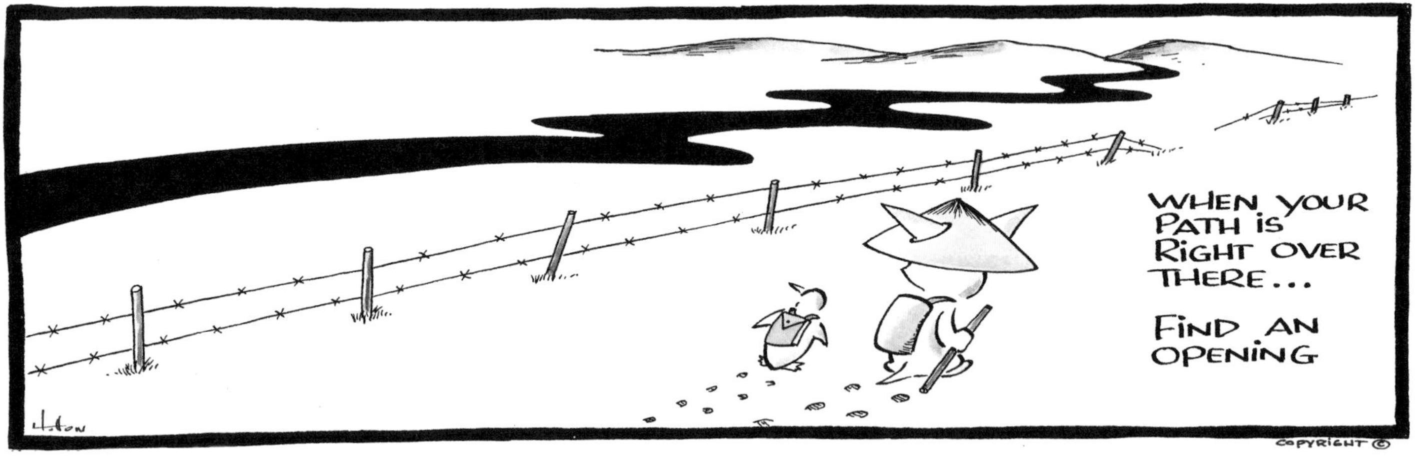
WHEN YOUR PATH IS RIGHT OVER THERE...
FIND AN OPENING
COPYRIGHT ©

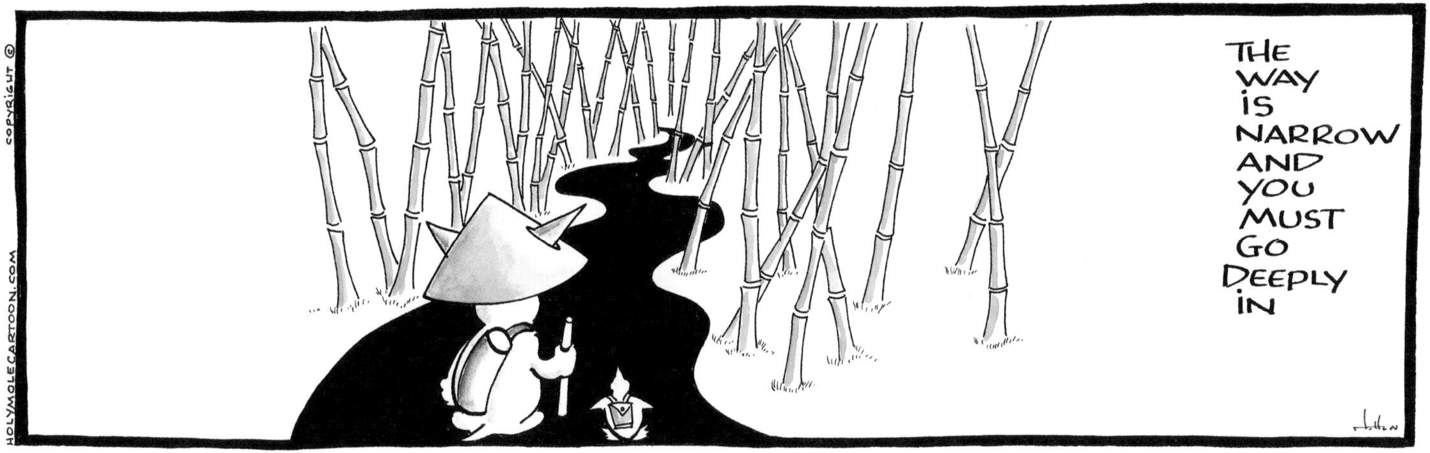
THE WAY IS NARROW AND YOU MUST GO DEEPLY IN
HOLYMOLECARTOON.COM COPYRIGHT ©

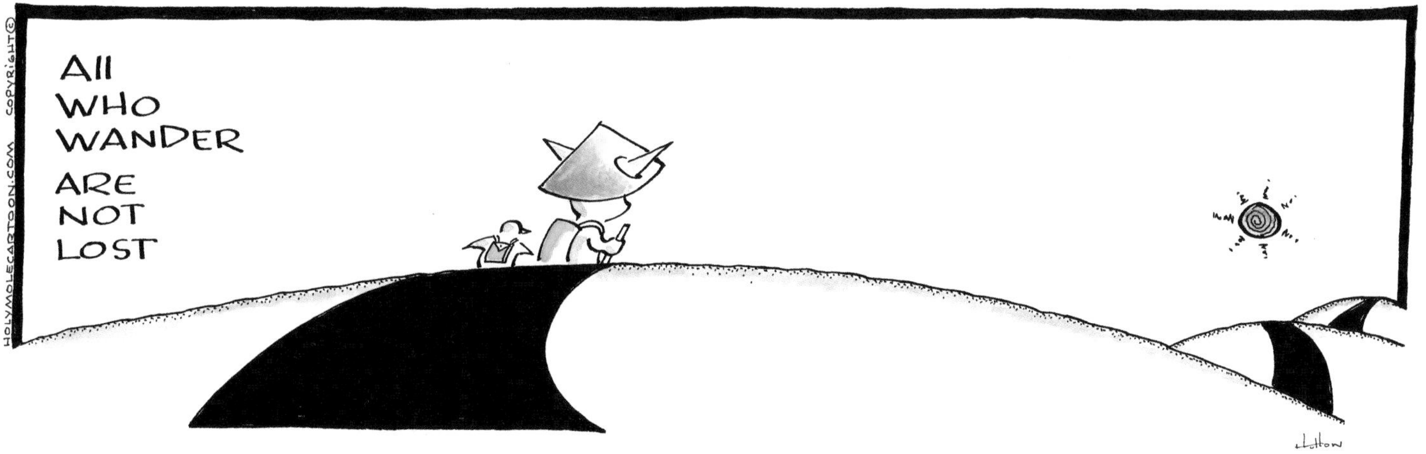
All WHO WANDER ARE NOT LOST
HOLYMOLECARTOON.COM COPYRIGHT ©

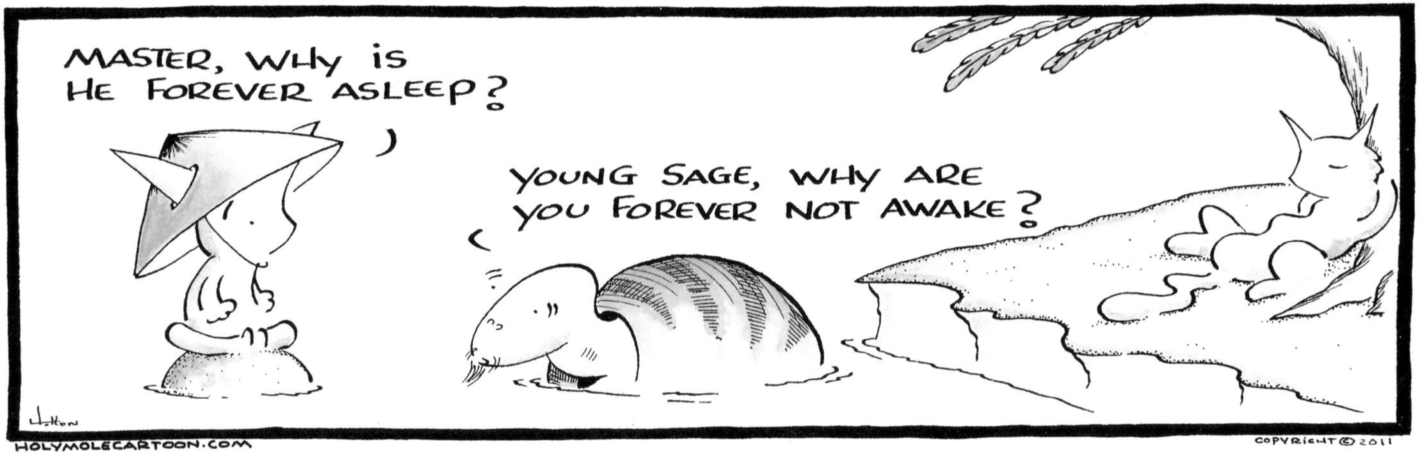
MASTER, WHY IS HE FOREVER ASLEEP?
YOUNG SAGE, WHY ARE YOU FOREVER NOT AWAKE?
HOLYMOLECARTOON.COM
COPYRIGHT © 2011

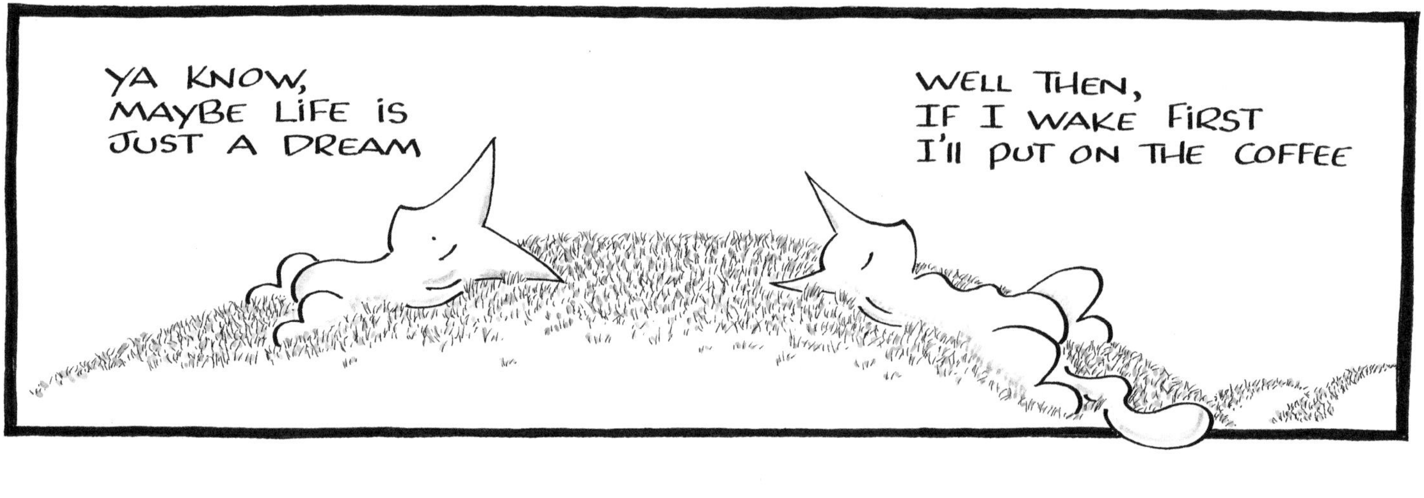
YA KNOW, MAYBE LIFE IS JUST A DREAM
WELL THEN, IF I WAKE FIRST I'LL PUT ON THE COFFEE

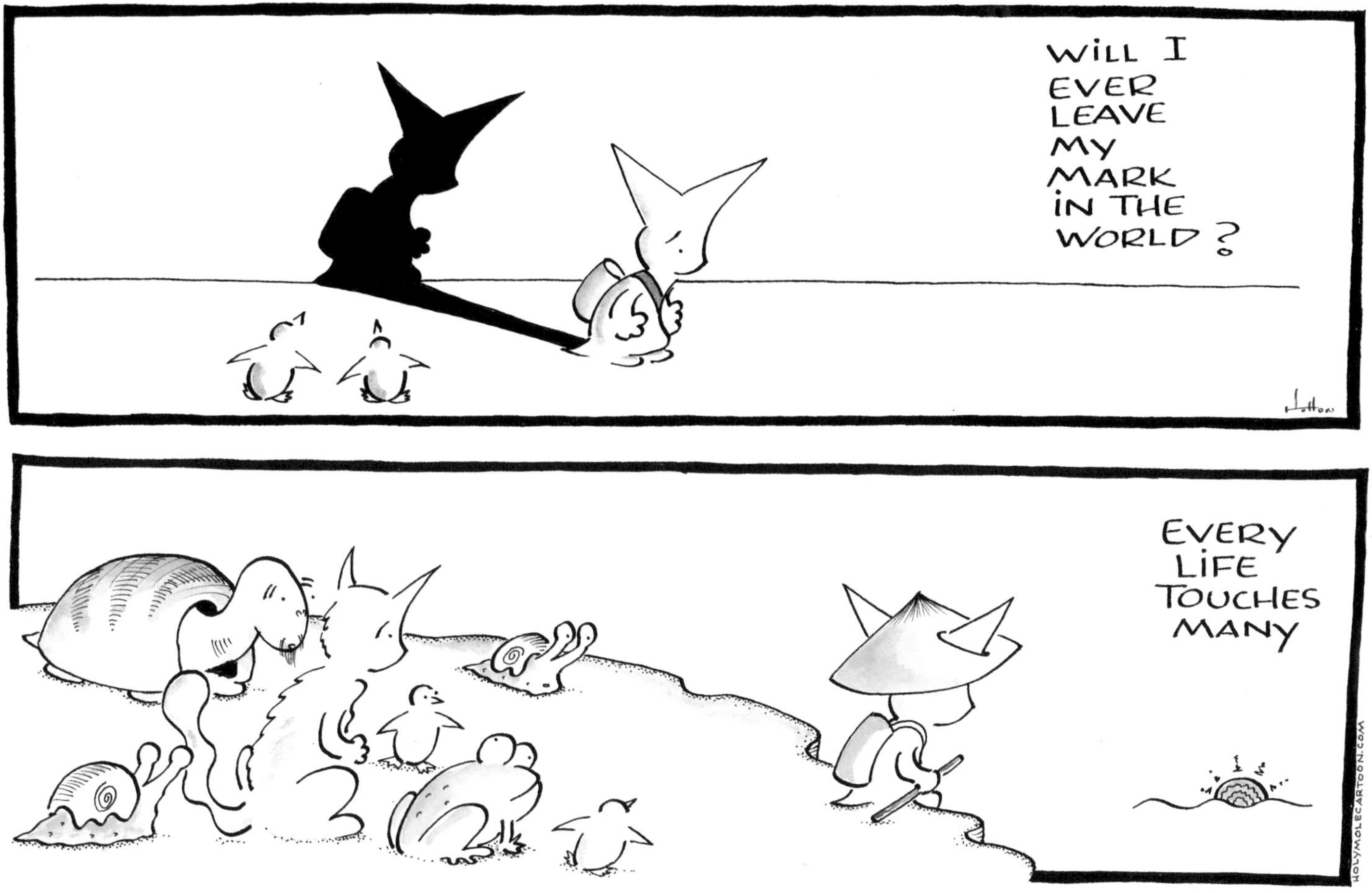
WILL I EVER LEAVE MY MARK IN THE WORLD?
EVERY LIFE TOUCHES MANY
HOLYMOLECARTOON.COM

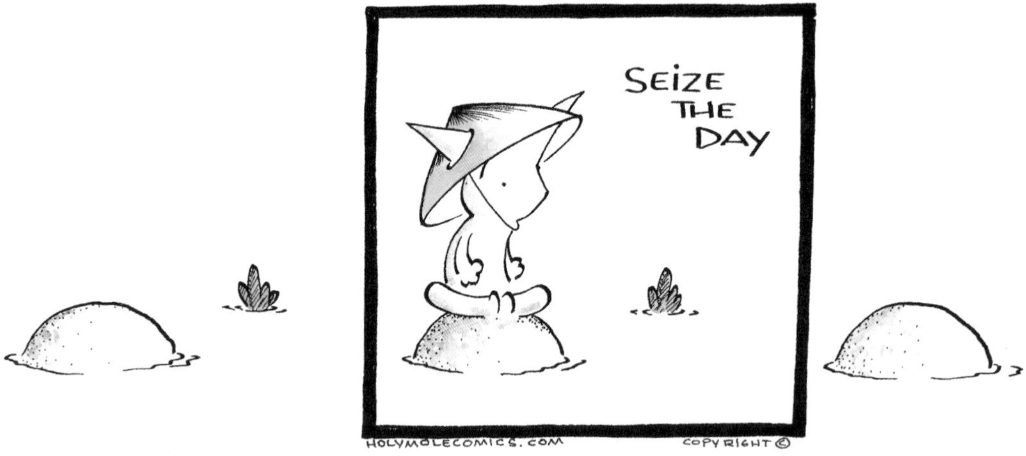
SEIZE THE DAY
HOLYMOLECOMICS.COM
COPYRIGHT ©

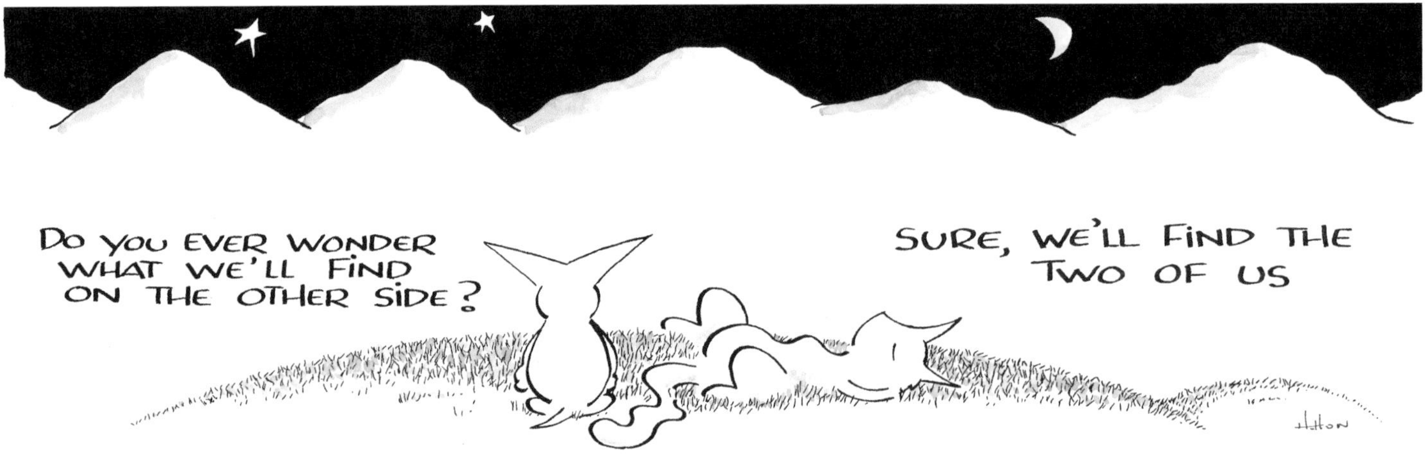
DO YOU EVER WONDER WHAT WE'LL FIND ON THE OTHER SIDE?
SURE, WE'LL FIND THE TWO OF US
Hatton

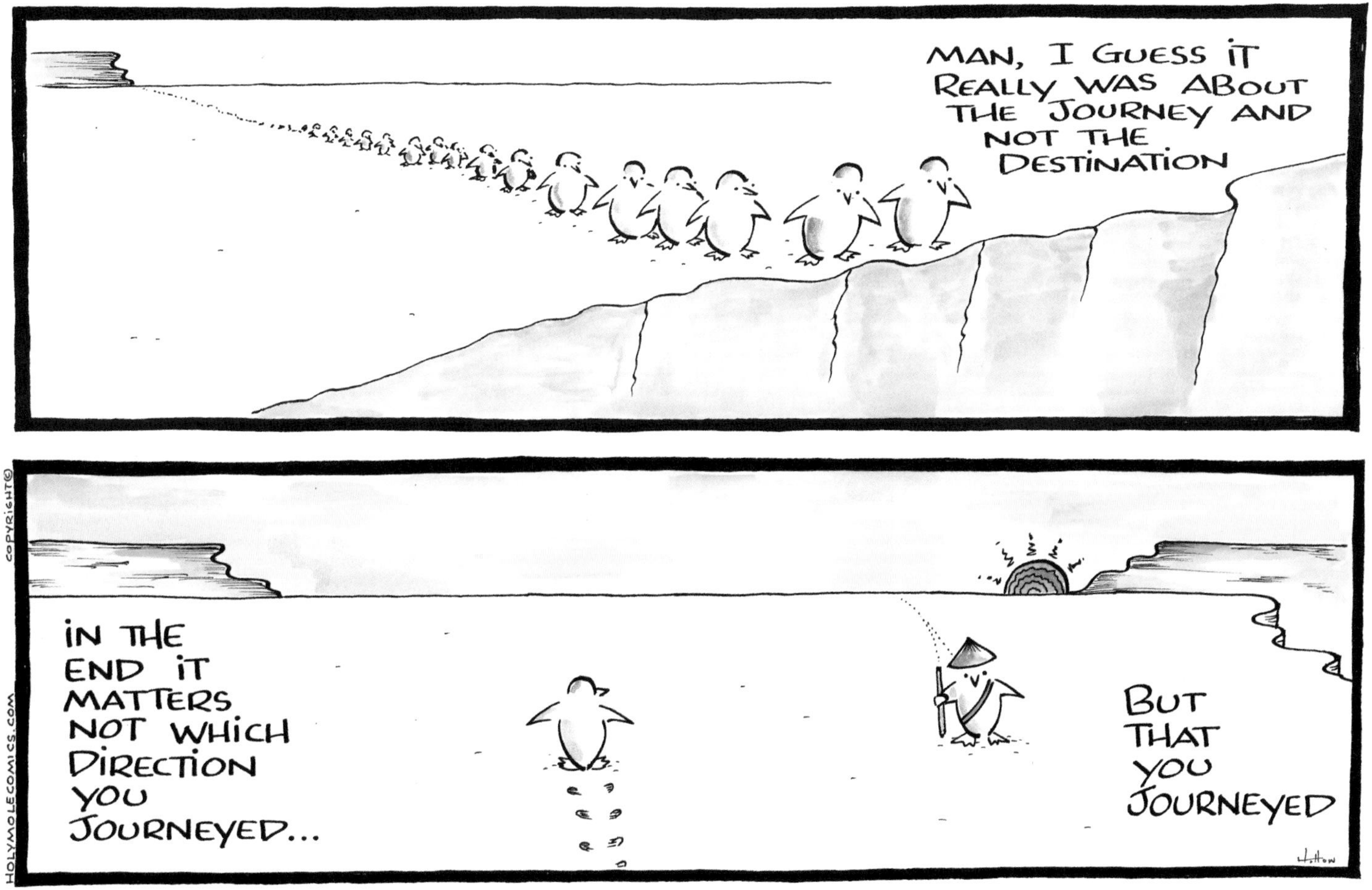
MAN, I GUESS IT REALLY WAS ABOUT THE JOURNEY AND NOT THE DESTINATION
IN THE END IT MATTERS NOT WHICH DIRECTION YOU JOURNEYED...
BUT THAT YOU JOURNEYED
HOLYMOLECOMICS.COM
COPYRIGHT©

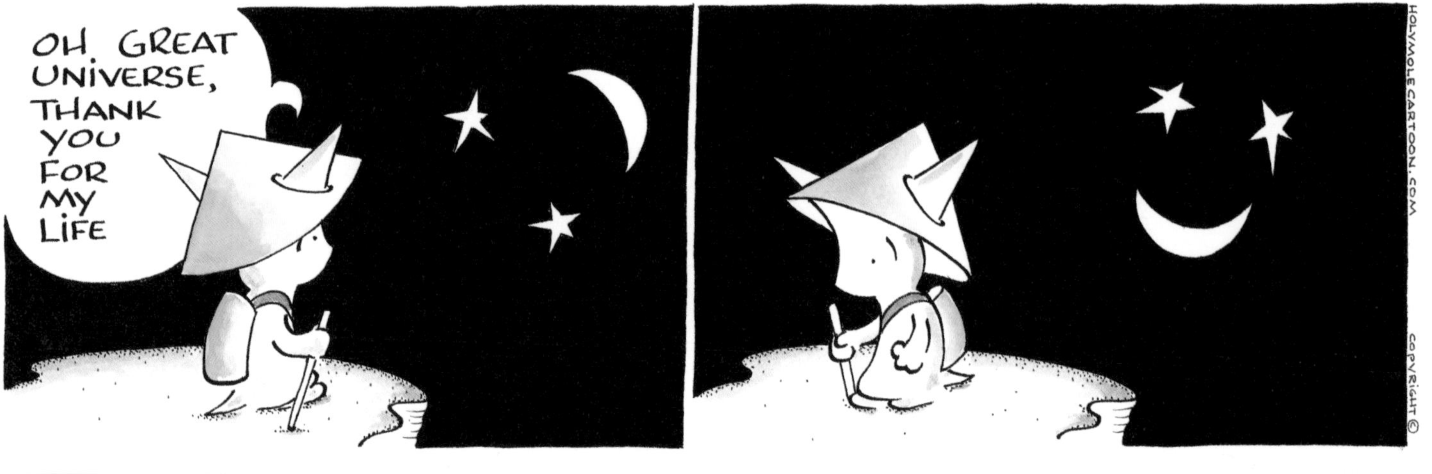
OH, GREAT UNIVERSE, THANK YOU FOR MY LIFE
HOLYMOLECARTOON.COM
COPYRIGHT ©

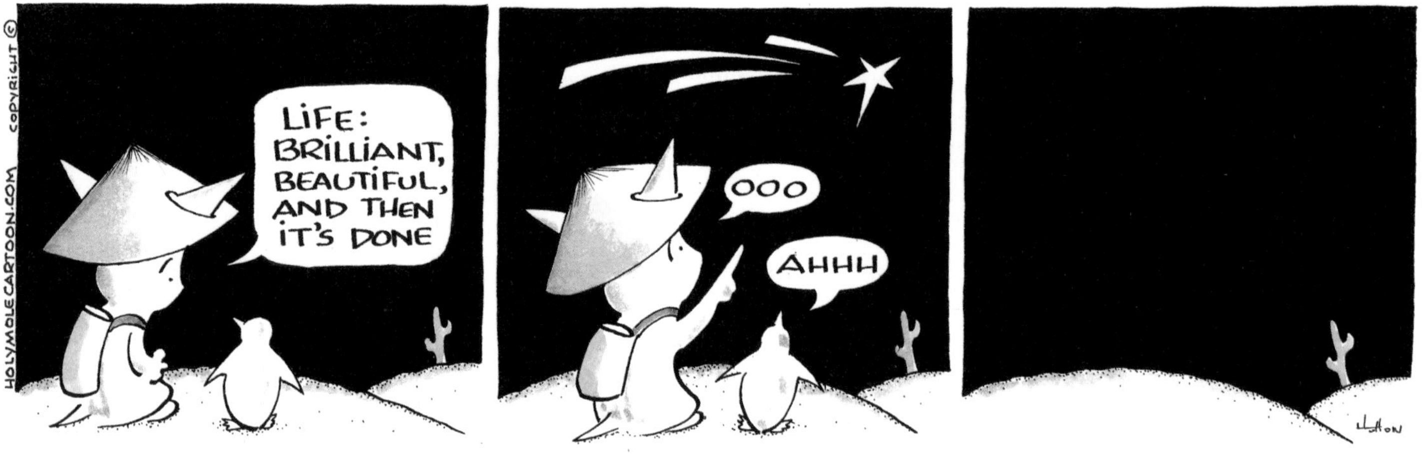
HOLYMOLECARTOON.COM
COPYRIGHT ©
LIFE: BRILLIANT, BEAUTIFUL, AND THEN IT'S DONE
OOO
AHHH

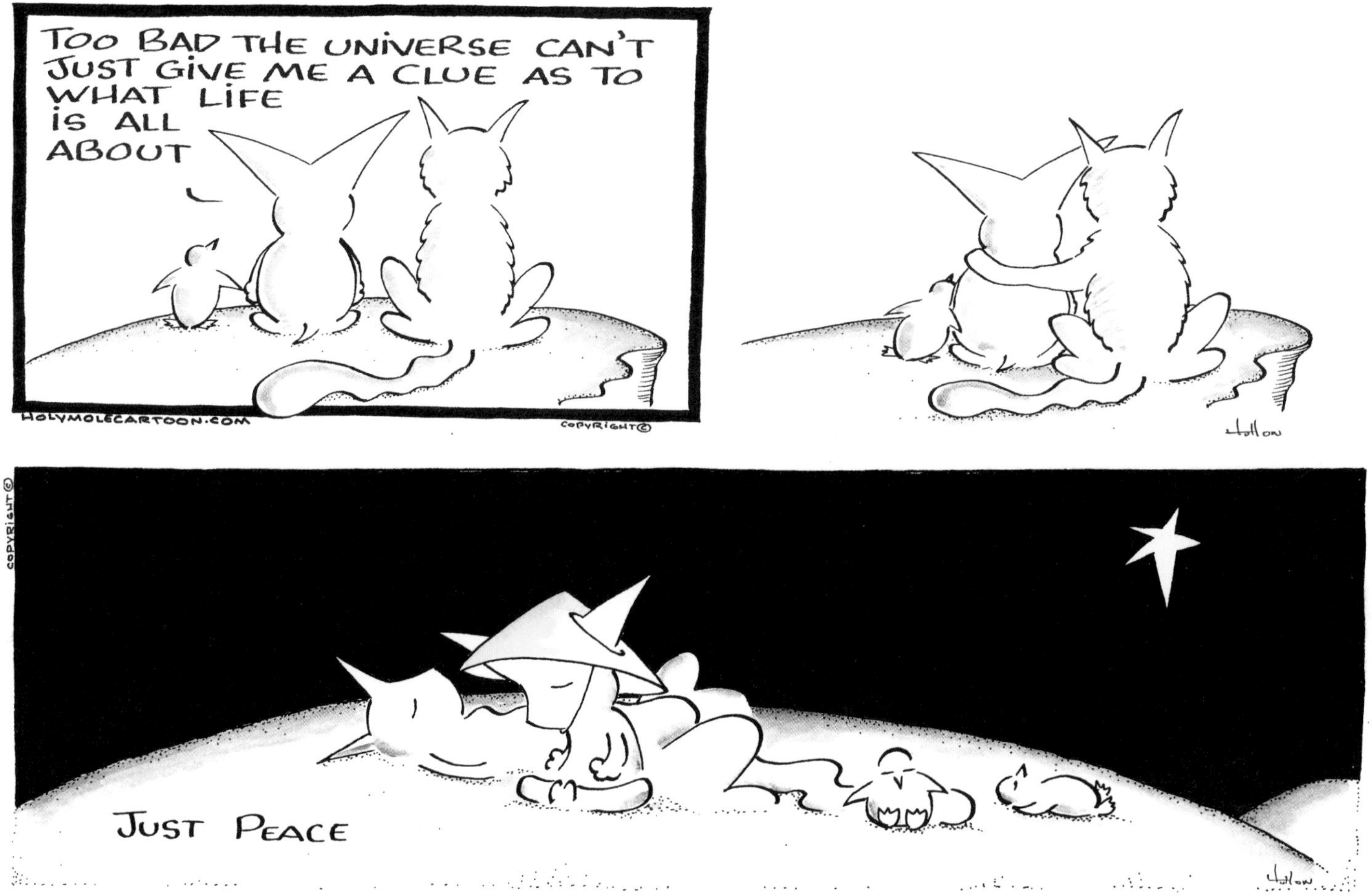
TOO BAD THE UNIVERSE CAN'T JUST GIVE ME A CLUE AS TO WHAT LIFE IS ALL ABOUT
HOLYMOLECARTOON.COM
COPYRIGHT©
COPYRIGHT©
JUST PEACE

About the Author

Rick Hotton is the creator of *Holy Molé*. Born in 1958, he has spent the majority of his adult life as a teacher. he is the owner and chief instructor of West Wind Karate Do, a traditional karate school that he established in Sarasota, Florida in 1976. Much of the wisdom embodied in *Holy Molé* stems from Rick's 40 years of martial arts training.

The *Holy Molé* cartoon began as a cathartic exercise to protest an overly manufactured world where profit margins take precedence over the intrinsic spirit of things

Rick has produced more than 1,200 strips and remains dedicated to the art form and the opportunity to reach new readers.